ARTICULAR INFINITIVES
IN THE GREEK OF THE NEW TESTAMENT

New Testament Monographs, 14

Series Editor
Stanley E. Porter

ARTICULAR INFINITIVES
IN THE GREEK OF THE NEW TESTAMENT

ON THE EXEGETICAL BENEFIT
OF GRAMMATICAL PRECISION

Denny Burk

SHEFFIELD PHOENIX PRESS

2006

Copyright © 2006 Sheffield Phoenix Press

Published by Sheffield Phoenix Press
Department of Biblical Studies, University of Sheffield
Sheffield S10 2TN

www.sheffieldphoenix.com

A CIP catalogue record for this book
is available from the British Library

Typeset by Forthcoming Publications
Printed by Lightning Source

ISBN 1-90504-8416
ISSN 1747-9606

οὐκ ἐπ’ ἄρτῳ μόνῳ ζήσεται ὁ ἄνθρωπος,
ἀλλ’ ἐπὶ παντὶ ῥήματι ἐκπορευομένῳ
διὰ στόματος θεοῦ (Mt. 4.4)

CONTENTS

PREFACE

This book is a revision of my doctoral dissertation, so I owe debt of gratitude not only to those who have helped me in this latest work, but also to all those who had a part in supporting my doctoral studies. I would like to thank first of all Dr Stanley Porter whose critical comments on this manuscript proved immensely helpful. His interaction led to the elimination of some weaknesses in my argument (though any remaining weaknesses are still all my own). I would also like to thank Dr Daniel B. Wallace who mentored me in all things Greek when I was a Master's student and who inspired the thesis of this work. I am extremely thankful for the members of my doctoral supervisory committee who toiled over the minutiae of my work. My gratitude goes to Dr John B. Polhill for his taking time to read some of the early chapters before the final work was done. My thanks also go to Dr Robert L. Plummer for coming onto my committee at a time when I really needed him. Also, my gratitude goes to Buist Fanning, who taught me advanced Greek Grammar when I was a Master's student at Dallas Theological Seminary and who graciously agreed to take time out of his busy schedule to be the outside reader of my dissertation. Of course, I am profoundly grateful to Dr Tom Schreiner for his careful supervision of my work. Reading these chapters on the finer points of the articular infinitive requires a great commitment of time and effort, and Dr Schreiner was involved at every stage of my writing. His interaction has been immensely helpful in driving me to think about the exegetical implications of my thesis.

Reverend James Lipscomb served as an adjunct professor at the state university that I attended for my undergraduate studies. For two years he instructed me in elementary Greek and taught me how to read Greek New Testament. He was a retired Presbyterian minister, and he donated his time to me and to the university. He never charged me or the college one dime. His enthusiasm for the Greek text was infectious and played not small part in inspiring my own love of the Greek New Testament.

Martha and Rodney Pollard are long-time family friends who financially supported me during my time as a Master's student and as a PhD candidate. Their quiet, faithful giving has made all the difference in my having more time to devote to scholarly pursuits and to a timely completion of the dissertation that led to this work. I am so thankful that the Lord brought the Pollards into my family's life so many years ago.

Also, my parents in-law, Carol and David Loudon, have been so supportive during these years that I have been a student and a husband to their daughter. I will always be thankful for their continued encouragement and contributions to our new family. I am so thankful to be a part of their family.

Of course, the greatest period of theological formation in my lifetime happened in the home of my own beloved parents, Sandra and Dennis Burk. They have taught me more about God and His faithfulness than they will ever know. I am so thankful to them not only for the numerous material and non-material ways that they have supported me throughout my seminary years, but also for their loving me enough to teach me the Gospel of Jesus Christ from my very earliest years. Thank you, Mom and Dad.

And, yes, I have saved the very best for last. My dear wife Susan is the greatest blessing that the Lord has ever set upon my life. Her love and support have outdone everyone else's. During my time as a doctoral candidate, she happily worked outside our home while I chipped away at this work. All the while she somehow managed to maintain the warmest home that any man could ever hope for. Susan, you are still lovelier to me than anyone could ever be. I love you.

Soli Deo Gloria!

Dennis Ray Burk, Jr
Dallas, Texas
30 September 2005

ABBREVIATIONS

BDAG	W. Bauer, F.W. Danker, W.F. Arndt, and F.W. Gingrich, *Greek-English Lexicon of the New Testament and Other Early Christian Literature* (Chicago: University of Chicago Press, 3rd edn, 2000).
BDB	F. Brown, S.R. Driver, and C.A. Briggs. *A Hebrew and English Lexicon of the Old Testament* (Oxford: Clarendon Press, 1907)
BDF	F. Blass and A. Debrunner, *A Greek Grammar of the New Testament and Other Early Christian Literature* (trans. and rev. Robert W. Funk; Chicago: University of Chicago Press, 1961)
CBQ	*Catholic Biblical Quarterly*
GTJ	*Grace Theological Journal*
ICC	International Critical Commentary
JETS	*Journal of the Evangelical Theological Society*
JSNT	*Journal for the Study of the New Testament*
JSNTSup	*Journal for the Study of the New Testament*, Supplement Series
JTS	*Journal of Theological Studies*
L&N	Johannes P. Louw and Eugene A. Nida (eds.), *Greek-English Lexicon of the New Testament Based on Semantic Domains* (2 vols.; New York: United Bible Societies, 1988)
LSJ	H.G. Liddell, R. Scott, and H.S. Jones (eds.), *A Greek–English Lexicon with a Revised Supplement* (rev. and aug. Sir Henry Stuart Jones; Oxford: Clarendon Press; New York: Oxford University Press, 9th edn, 1996).
LXX	Septuagint
MM	James Hope Moulton and George Milligan, *The Vocabulary of the Greek Testament Illustrated from the Papyri and Other Non-Literary Sources* (Grand Rapids: Eerdmans, 1930)
MT	Masoretic Text
NA[27]	Eberhard Nestle, Barbara and Kurt Aland, Johannes Karavidopoulos, Carlo M. Martini, and Bruce M. Metzger (eds.), *Novum Testamentum Graece* (Stuttgart: Deutsche Bibelgesellschaft, 27th edn, 1993).
Neot	*Neotestamentica*
NASB	New American Standard Bible
NICNT	New International Commentary on the New Testament
NIDNTT	Colin Brown (ed.), *New International Dictionary of New Testament Theology* (3 vols.; Grand Rapids: Zondervan, 1978)
NIGTC	New International Greek Testament Commentary
NIV	New International Version
NKJV	New King James Version
NovT	*Novum Testamentum*
NRSV	New Revised Standard Version
NTS	*New Testament Studies*
PNTC	Pillar New Testament Commentaries

Robertson	A.T. Robertson, *A Grammar of the Greek New Testament in the Light of Historical Research* (Nashville: Broadman Press, 4th edn, 1934)
RSV	Revised Standard Version
SBG	Studies in Biblical Greek
SBLDS	SBL Dissertation Series
SBLSP	SBL Seminar Papers
Smyth	Herbert Weir Smyth, *Greek Grammar* (rev. Gordon M. Messing; Cambridge, MA: Harvard University Press, rev. edn, 1956)
TynBul	*Tyndale Bulletin*
UBS[4]	Kurt Aland, Matthew Black, Carlo M. Martini, Bruce M. Metzger, and Allen Wikgren (eds.), *The Greek New Testament* (United Bible Societies; Stuttgart: Deutsche Bibelgesellschaft, 4th rev. edn, 1993), GRAMCORD database
WBC	Word Biblical Commentary
Zerwick	Maximilian Zerwick, *Biblical Greek: Illustrated by Examples* (trans. and adapted Joseph Smith; Rome: Scripta Pontificii Instituti Biblici, 1963)

LIST OF TABLES AND FIGURES

1

AN INTRODUCTION TO A LINGUISTIC ANALYSIS
OF THE ARTICULAR INFINITIVE
IN NEW TESTAMENT GREEK

1. *Introduction*

Ten years ago, J.J. Janse van Rensburg observed that many New Testament scholars still operate under the mistaken notion that all of the problems of New Testament Greek Grammar were worked out in the nineteenth century.[1] This false assumption arises from an ignorance of developments in the field of modern linguistics. Max Turner explains,

> Despite the alarm sounded by James Barr's *The Semantics of Biblical Language* —modern linguistics has had relatively little influence on New Testament exegesis. New Testament study remains largely dominated by the prescientific 'linguistics' encapsulated in the standard (but now dated) grammars, lexicons, and theological 'dictionaries' and mediated to each new generation of theological students by commentaries and New Testament Greek primers.[2]

For this reason, Turner, van Rensburg, and a growing number of other voices have been pointing out 'that there is an urgent need for a new reference grammar which utilizes the results of recent research in the fields of linguistics and semantics'.[3] While this book certainly does not propose to generate

---

1. J.J. Janse van Rensburg, 'A New Reference Grammar for the Greek New Testament: Exploratory Remarks on a Methodology', *Neotestamentica* 27 (1993), pp. 133-52 (133); cf. Lars Rydbeck, 'What Happened to New Testament Greek Grammar after Albert Debrunner?', *NTS* 21 (1975), pp. 424-27; Richard A. Young, *Intermediate New Testament Greek: A Linguistic and Exegetical Approach* (Nashville: Broadman & Holman, 1994), x.

2. Max Turner, 'Modern Linguistics and the New Testament', in Joel B. Green (ed.), *Hearing the New Testament: Strategies for Interpretation* (Grand Rapids: Eerdmans; Carlisle: Paternoster, 1995), pp. 146-74 (147).

3. Van Rensburg, 'A New Reference Grammar', p. 133. Note also the comments by Michael Palmer: 'Are the grammatical categories assumed in the major grammars of New Testament Greek adequate for a full description of the language of New Testament

that new reference grammar, it does propose a linguistic analysis of one important aspect of that grammar—the articular infinitive.

2. *Thesis*

In this book I seek to ask and answer the following question: What is the semantic and/or syntactic value of the articular infinitive in New Testament Greek? Another way of posing the question would be as follows: What does the article contribute to the *meaning* of the infinitive in New Testament Greek? I conceive of this task as a 'linguistic' investigation. By that I mean that I will pursue this study utilizing some of the results and methods of modern linguistic analysis, an approach that can be distinguished from traditional grammar.[4] Before my preliminary hypothesis and answer to the above question can be set forth, some linguistic groundwork must be laid.

In trying to define meaning, modern linguistics makes a distinction between *lexical* meaning and *structural* meaning.[5] Lexical meaning has to do with the separate meanings of individual words or morphemes.[6] It has to

texts? I argue that they are not' (Michael W. Palmer, *Levels of Constituent Structure in New Testament Greek* [ed. D.A. Carson; SBG; New York: Peter Lang, 1995], p. 1).

4. Stanley Porter provides a nice summary of the differences between a modern linguistic approach and a more traditional study of Greek Grammar: (1) 'In traditional grammar priority is given to written over spoken language', (2) 'The literary remains of a language are often not representative of the range of use of the language, often preserving a particular kind of text on account of various political, economic or social reasons', (3) 'Languages studied according to traditional categories are usually regularized forms of the language found only in grammar books... This kind of approach rarely takes into account regional or dialectal differences, and gives virtually no attention to shifts in register or style', (4) 'Descriptions of Greek and Hebrew are often made in terms of the language of the students and teachers', (5) 'Traditional grammar often imposes standards of logic which are foreign to natural languages', (6) 'The concerns of traditional grammarians have often been dictated in terms of the interests of other, related subjects, such as theology, history, philosophy, rhetoric, literature, etc.', (7) 'Traditional language study has often analyzed language atomistically' (Stanley E. Porter, 'Studying Ancient Languages from a Modern Linguistic Perspective: Essential Terms and Terminology', *Filologia Neotestamentaria* 2 [1989], pp. 147-72 [163-66]; cf. David Crystal, *Linguistics* [Harmondsworth: Penguin, 1971], pp. 56-76).

5. David Alan Black, *Linguistics for Students of New Testament Greek: A Survey of Basic Concepts and Applications* (Grand Rapids: Baker Book House, 2nd edn, 1995), pp. 8, 97-98; Eugene Van Ness Goetchius, *The Language of the New Testament* (New York: Charles Scribner's Sons, 1965), pp. 21-22.

6. The two most basic elements of language that linguists study are the *phoneme* and *morpheme* (H.A. Gleason, *An Introduction to Descriptive Linguistics* [New York: Henry Holt, 1955], pp. 9-11). Although linguists sometimes have difficulty defining *morpheme* (e.g. Gleason, *Introduction*, p. 52), Goetchius provides a nice starting-point for this discussion: 'The simplest grammatical form, the smallest element of language which has

do with the meaning that one might find in the dictionary of a language. Structural meaning refers to the meaning associated with the combination of morphemes or words. Perhaps the best way to demonstrate the difference between *structural* and *lexical* meaning is by way of illustration.[7] Observe the following two sentences:

1. broke man stick the
2. The sponkish fids finningly harpled the smallyparps.

In the first sentence, while we can discern the conventional meanings associated with these common English words (e.g. man = male human), we cannot perceive any grammatical relation between the individual terms. In the second sentence, while we can see the grammatical relations between the individual words (e.g. sponkish [adj.], harpled [verb], smallyparps [direct object], finningly [adv.]), we cannot discern what the individual words mean. They are in fact nonsense words. On the one hand, sentence number 1 contains lexical meaning, but no structural meaning. On the other hand, sentence number 2 has structural meaning but no lexical meaning.

Modern linguistics is concerned with ascertaining both *structural* and *lexical* meaning in order to set forth what is known as *total linguistic meaning*: 'The *total linguistic meaning* of an utterance consists of the lexical meanings of the separate words it contains plus the structural meanings of the grammatical devices connecting them'.[8] So when we ask the question, 'What is the linguistic explanation for the article appearing with the infinitive in New Testament Greek?' we are trying to ascertain the semantic and syntactic value of each of its constituent parts and how each of these contributes to the total linguistic meaning of the articular infinitive.

Associated with the distinction between structural meaning and lexical meaning is the distinction between *content* words and *function* words.[9]

---

meaning, is called a *morpheme*. Morphemes may be words or parts of words' (Goetchius, *The Language of the New Testament*, p. 15 [emphasis in original]).

7. Black provides a similar illustration (*Linguistics*, pp. 97-98).

8. Black, *Linguistics*, 97; cf. Goetchius, *The Language of the New Testament*, p. 22 (emphasis in original).

9. The technical terms are actually *functors* and *contentives*. Charles F. Hockett writes, '"Function words" and "content words" will not do, because the forms which belong to the two classes are not always whole words' (*A Course in Modern Linguistics* [New York: Macmillan, 1958], p. 264; cf. Robert A. Hall, Jr, *Introductory Linguistics* [Philadelphia: Chilton, 1964], p. 15). For now, we will retain the above terminology with the understanding that individual words more or less combine lexical and structural features though one or the other feature may be more prominent. Robert Funk adopts the same rationale that I am advocating: 'It must not be supposed that structure signals are confined to words. Some structure signals are less than words…some are greater than a single word… Only in the case of function words is the structure signal coextensive with the word, and even then there are composite function words and there is often correlation

Content words are those items which possess little structural meaning but great lexical meaning. *Function* words are those items which have little lexical meaning but great structural meaning. Goetchius writes that 'The most important function words are prepositions (*to, for, with, by*, etc.), conjunctions (*and, or, but, because*, etc.), and the articles (*a, an, the*)'.[10] One way to think about the difference between *function* words and *content* words is by analogy. If structure words make up the mortar of a language, then content words are the bricks that provide the substance of a language.[11]

Having outlined some terminology, we can now set forth a preliminary hypothesis and answer to the question, 'What is the linguistic explanation for the article appearing with the infinitive in New Testament Greek?' The article primarily serves as a function word when used with the infinitive. That is, when the article appears in conjunction with the infinitive, it *marks*[12] a grammatical–structural relation that may not otherwise be apparent.[13] The article bears great structural meaning, but little, if any, lexical meaning.[14] The article does not effect a remarkable semantic difference to the meaning of the infinitive.[15] Unlike uses of the article with other parts of speech, the articular infinitive reveals no semantic difference from the anarthrous infinitive in terms of *definiteness*, though the articular infinitive does reveal syntactic differences from the anarthrous infinitive. Therefore, it is not correct to say (as many do) that the article can have the same significance with the verbal noun as it does with any other noun (e.g. anaphora, marker of definiteness, substantivizer, etc.). Nor is it correct to say that the article adds no meaning at all to the infinitive. On the contrary, the *structural* significance of the article is prominent when the articular infinitive appears in the New Testament.

with some other signal' (*A Beginning–Intermediate Grammar of Hellenistic Greek* [Sources for Biblical Study; 3 vols.; Missoula, MT: Society of Biblical Literature, 2nd edn, 1973], I, p. 2).

    10. Goetchius, *The Language of the New Testament*, p. 25.

    11. Black, *Linguistics*, p. 98.

    12. I will have more to say on the phenomenon of *markedness* in the introduction to Chapter 3.

    13. Michael W. Palmer writes that the article 'disambiguates' (*Levels*, p. 41) the '*structural ambiguity*' (p. 40) of some Greek phrases.

    14. In this respect it is interesting to note the remarks concerning the Greek article in Bauer's lexicon, 'The treatment of the inclusion and omission of the art. belongs to the field of grammar' (BDAG, *s.v.* ὁ, ἡ, τό, p. 686).

    15. David Sansone observes that the presence or absence of the article likely does not affect the lexical meaning of other types of abstract nouns in Greek; see his 'Towards a New Doctrine of the Article in Greek: Some Observations on the Definite Article in Plato', *Classical Philology* 88 (1993), pp. 191-205; cf. Smyth, §1126.

3. *History of Research*

While I maintain that the article is employed primarily as a *function* marker, other grammarians have proposed different answers. Generally speaking, New Testament scholars have attributed more semantic value to the articular infinitive than is warranted. These scholars go beyond what I maintain to be a strict structural significance for the article. However there are those who have at times underestimated the significance of the article. These interpreters fall short of seeing the article's value as a *function* marker. In this survey of previous research, we will look at the various ways in which scholars have either over-interpreted or under-interpreted the articular infinitive. To this end, we will first survey the debate among scholars of the classical dialects. Then, we will turn to the state of research among New Testament grammarians.

a. *The Debate among Scholars of Classical Dialects*
Because a sizable portion of the specialized work on the articular infinitive has been done by scholars of the classical dialects, a brief survey of the state of their discussion is in order.[16] Not least among these contributions is

16.   Whereas a comprehensive account of the literature on New Testament Greek is in order, I do not intend to account for everything written by classicists on the infinitive. They tend to cover a wide swath of literature that is beyond the scope of what I intend mainly to be a synchronic analysis of Hellenistic usage found in the New Testament. Though some of these classical analyses are fairly recent, others are quite dated: see Panagiotis Dimitropoulos, *Untersuchungen zum finalen Genetiv des substantivierten Infinitivs bei Thukydides* (Commentationes humanarum litterarum, 114; Helsinki: Societas scientiarum fennica, 1999); Aurelio J. Fernández García, *El infinitivo en el Dafnis y Cloe de Longo: estudio funcional* (ed. G. Giangrande and H. White; Classical and Byzantine Monographs; Amsterdam: Adolf M. Hakkert, 1997); Giulio Giannecchini, *Il controllo infinitivo in greco antico* (Università degli Studi di Perugia; Napoli: Edizioni scientifiche italiane, 1995); L. Grünenwald, *Der freie formelhafte Infinitiv der Limitation im Griechischen* (Beiträge zur historischen Syntax der griechischen Sprache; Würzburg: A. Stuber, 1888); Maximilian Hebold, *De infinitivi syntaxi Euripidea* (Halle: Fr. Lintz, 1881); Adolphus Hoehne, *De infinitivi apud graecos classicae aetatis poetas usu qui fertur pro imperativo* (Bratislava: Typis Grassi, Barthii et Soc. [W. Friedrich], 1867); Ture Kalén, *Selbständige Finalsätze und imperativische Infinitive im Griechischen* (Skrifter utgivna av K. Humanistiska Vetenskaps-Samfundet I Uppsala, 34.2; Uppsala: Almqvist & Wiksell, 1941); Helena Kurzová, *Zur syntaktischen Struktur des griechischen Infinitiv und Nebensatz* (Tschechoslowakische Akademie der Wissenschaften; Amsterdam: Adolf M. Hakkert; Prague: Academia, 1968); Carl Mutzbauer, *Das Wesen des griechischen Infinitivs und die Entwicklung seines Gebrauchs bei Homer: Ein Beitrag zur historischen Syntax der griechischen Sprache* (Bonn: F. Cohen, 1916); Charles Jones Ogden, *De infinitivi finalis vel consecutivi constructione apud priscos poetas graecos* (New York: Columbia University Press, 1909); Richard Wagner, *Der Gebrauch des*

Stephen Brooks Heiny's dissertation on 'The Articular Infinitive in Thucydides'.[17] Heiny observes that classical scholars have more or less accounted for the articular infinitive in one of two ways. On the one hand, some scholars contend that the article contributes a semantic value to the infinitive so that one observes a semantic difference between the articular infinitive and the anarthrous infinitive (an over-interpretation of the article). On the other hand, some scholars argue the article appears purely as a grammatical marker. Heiny writes, 'This debate is significant because scholars are generally divided on just these lines as to the reasons for the use of the articular infinitive'.[18]

(1) *The article as a signal of semantic modification.* Some classicists[19] understand the article to effect a semantic change in the infinitive to which it is connected. In this respect, these scholars see the article as a substantivizer—that is, they think the article came into use in order to make the infinitive into a noun. In 1888, Franz Birklein spoke of 'the infinitive, which is nominalized by the article'.[20] He describes the articular infinitive in a way

imperativischen Infinitivs im Griechischen (Wissenschaftliche Beilage zum Programm des grossherzoglichen Gymnasium Fridericianum zu Schwerin I. M. für des Schuljahr 1890/91; Leipzig: Hesse & Becker, 1891).

17. Stephen Brooks Heiny, 'The Articular Infinitive in Thucydides' (PhD Dissertation, Indiana University, 1973). I am especially indebted to Heiny for his summary of research among classicists (pp. 1-39). I follow his presentation very closely here, though I emphasize those aspects which are most relevant for my thesis.

18. Heiny, 'Articular Infinitive', p. 25.

19. Some of these writers (e.g. Pentti Aalto, *Studien zur Geschichte des Infinitivs im Griechischen* [Helsinki: Suomalaisen Tiedeakatemian Toimituksia, 1953]) extend their treatment into the New Testament era. However, since they do not maintain a strict synchronic focus on first-century Hellenistic Greek, they are included with the authors whose focus is on the Classical dialects.

20. Franz Birklein, *Entwicklungsgeschichte des substantivierten Infinitivs* (Beiträge zur historischen Syntax der griechischen Sprache; Würzburg: A. Stuber's Verlagshandlung, 1888), p. 92. Birklein also states: 'Die Substantivierung des Infinitivs durch den Artikel' (p. 1). Birklein traced the development of the articular infinitive through the classical period. I have attached an adaptation of his statistics in Table 15 of the Appendix, 'How the Articular Infinitive Grew in Use in the Classical Period'. Antonius N. Jannaris uses Birklein's statistics to divide the gradual development of the articular infinitive among the classical authors into three groups: Group 1—Homer 1; Hesiod 2; Hymns–; Pind. 9; Lyrics 9; Group 2—Aesch. 51; Soph. 97; Eur. 93; Ar. 65; Hdt. 49; Group 3—Th. 298; Antiph. 26 (including the spurious writings 36); Andoc. 18; Lys. 36 (44); Isocr. 271 (306); Isae. 36; Lyc. 26; Dem. 784 (1130); Aeschin. 61; Din. 33; Hyp. 42; Pl. 1680 (2032); Xen. 1306 (1310). Jannaris states: 'In group I the infinitive occurs only in the nominative (τό). In group II, it occurs chiefly in the nominative and accusative, but also in the genitive and dative preceded or not by a preposition (τό, τοῦ, τῷ). In group III, it is equally frequent through all the cases with or without a preposition' (*An*

that would become characteristic of later studies. Birklein alleges that the article actually makes the infinitive into a substantive.[21] Relying on Birklein's work, Antonius N. Jannaris elaborates an identical point of view in his grammar of Attic dialects, saying that the articular infinitive is 'substantivized by means of the article'.[22] Jannaris clearly states that without the article, the infinitive partakes more of the characteristics of a verb than of a noun.[23] In his 1911 grammar, Basil Gildersleeve agrees, 'The article... enables the infinitive to assume all the constructions of the substantive that are not inconsistent with its verbal nature'.[24] Even though Herbert Smyth's watershed 1920 *Greek Grammar* eliminates the notion of the article as a substantivizer,[25] more recent studies reprise versions of Birklein's, Jannaris's,

Historical Greek Grammar Chiefly of the Attic Dialect as Written and Spoken from Classical Antiquity Down to the Present Time, Founded upon the Ancient Texts, Inscriptions, Papyri and Present Popular Greek [London/New York: Macmillan, 1897; repr., Hildesheim: Georg Olms, 1987], p. 576 n. 1).

For a recent study on the origin of the Greek infinitive from its Indo-European roots, see Sylvie Vanséveren, *Prodige à voir: recherches comparatives sur l'origine casuelle de l'infinitif en grec ancien* (Bibliothèque des Cahiers de l'Institut de linguistique de Louvain; Louvain-la-Neuve: Peeters, 2000).

21. The term *substantive* can be somewhat slippery. I use it here and throughout the rest of this book in the way that Stanley Porter defines it. A *substantive* is 'a term given to any word which may be used like a noun. For example, in Greek, participles, infinitives, and especially adjectives, besides nouns, are often used as substantives' (*Idioms of the Greek New Testament* [Biblical Languages: Greek, 2; Sheffield: JSOT Press, 1992], p. 313; cf. Henry R. Moeller and Arnold Kramer, 'An Overlooked Structural Pattern in New Testament Greek', *NovT* 5 [1962], pp. 25-35 [25 n.1]).

22. Jannaris, *An Historical Greek Grammar*, p. 576.

23. It is this semantic distinction that governs Jannaris's analysis of the infinitive. Whereas many grammarians divide their analysis of the infinitive along formal lines (i.e. anarthrous vs. articular), Jannaris strenuously objects to such a procedure, 'It is a distinction which appeals, it is true, to the eye, but does not satisfy the mind' (Jannaris, *An Historical Greek Grammar*, p. 568; cf. pp. 480-89).

24. Basil Lanneau Gildersleeve, *Syntax of Classical Greek from Homer to Demosthenes* (2 vols.; New York: American Book Company, 1911), II, p. 268.

25. The earlier studies seem to reason that the article substantivizes the infinitive in much the same way that it does the participle. At times they seem to indicate that the infinitive is not as much of a noun without the article than with the article. In his section on the articular infinitive, Smyth offers a more measured judgment, pointing out that the infinitive with or without the article partakes of the characteristics of both noun and verb. As such, it is always a noun and always a verb (Smyth, pp. 437-38). However, in his section on the 'Substantive-Making Power of the Article' (pp. 292-93), he lists the infinitive as one of the kinds of words that are substantivized by the article. Yet the text that he cites as an example does not reveal a substantival use of the article, καλοῦσί γε ἀκολασίαν τὸ ὑπὸ τῶν ἡδονῶν ἄρχεσθαι ('they call being ruled by one's pleasures intemperance', P. Ph. 68 e; Smyth, p. 293). In this instance, the neuter article appears not to substantivize the infinitive, but to distinguish the accusative object from the accusative

and Gildersleeve's ideas. For instance, Pentti Aalto argues in her 1953 monograph that the use of the article with the infinitive was originally employed as a device to form new abstract substantives.[26]

(2) *The article as a signal of structural meaning.* Though some classicists regard the article as a substantivizer, others observe that the article appears with the infinitive merely as a syntactical marker, not as effecting a semantic change in the meaning of the infinitive. Herbert Weir Smyth writes, 'The article is regularly used when the connection uniting the infinitive to another word has to be expressed by the genitive, the dative, or a preposition'.[27] In other words, Smyth notices that the case of the article is needed in certain instances in order to clarify the syntactical function of the infinitive. A. Ernout expresses agreement with this observation and takes it a step further, claiming that the *primary* reason for the article is clearly to identify the function of the infinitive. He writes,

> Given the multiple meanings which the infinitive in the sentence could have, the vagueness of this indeclinable form was not without involving some obscurity. This use, which spreads after Homer, to treat the infinitive like a neuter name, accompanied by the article, made it possible to cure this disadvantage. In order to achieve a greater clarity of expression, little by little Greek adopted the practice of attaching to the infinitive the article which is put into the case corresponding to the syntactic role which it played.[28]

Likewise, Paul Burgière argues that since the infinitive is indeclinable, the use of the article becomes absolutely critical in certain contexts. The use of τό helped Greek writers to refine their style of writing by giving a more precise indication of how the infinitive functioned within its clause, 'when the relationship between infinitive and its context did not appear rather

---

complement. The article is syntactically required in this text to mark the function of the infinitive phrase, thereby clarifying which accusative is the object and which is the complement.

26. Aalto, *Studien zur Geschichte des Infinitivs im Griechischen*, p. 71: 'Der ursprüngliche Zweck der Verwendung des Artikels neben dem Infinitiv war es anfänglich, neue, leicht brauchbare Abstrakta zu gewinnen, wie oben schon mehrmals angedeutet worden ist' (cf. pp. 28, 38).

27. Smyth, p. 451.

28. A. Ernout, 'Infinitif grec et gérondif latin', *Revue de philologie, de littérature et d'histoire anciennes* 19 (1945), pp. 93-115 (99): 'Etant donné les multiples valeurs que pouvait avoir l'infinitif dans la phrase, l'indétermination de la forme indéclinable n'était pas sans entraîner quelque obscurité. L'usage qui se répand après Homère de traiter l'infinitif comme un nom neutre, accompagné de l'article, permit de remédier à cet inconvénient. Pour plus de clarté dans l'expression, le grec prit peu à peu l'habitude d'accompagner l'infinitif de l'article mis au cas correspondent au rôle syntaxique qu'il jouait.'

clearly'.[29] Stephen Brooks Heiny agrees that the article was not employed to effect a semantic change in the meaning of the infinitive,[30] but that 'the article serves to indicate the grammatical relationship between the infinitive and its context... It can be used to bracket extensive phrases as well as to show by its case, the correct grammatical function.'[31] The variety of opinions expressed by scholars of the classical dialects serves as a helpful introduction to the conversation among scholars of the Hellenistic Greek of the New Testament.

b. *The Debate among Scholars of New Testament Greek*
(1) *Overestimating the article's significance.* Like some of the classicists, some New Testament scholars understand the article to be a substantivizer. This misunderstanding about the articular infinitive grows out of the assumption that the article carries the same significance with the infinitive that it has with other nouns. BDF sets forth the conventional wisdom on this point: 'The article with the infinitive, strictly speaking, has the same (anaphoric) significance as it has with nouns'.[32] Likewise, A.T. Robertson says, 'When the article does occur with the inf., it should have its real force [that it has with other nouns]'.[33] This presupposition underlies much of the over-interpreting of the Greek articular infinitive. In the area of lexical semantics, James Barr warns against *illegitimate totality transfer*—that is, reading a

29. Paul Burguière, *Histoire de l'infinitif en grec* (Etudes et commentaires, 33; Paris: C. Klincksieck, 1960), p. 113: 'Un pareil faisceau de remarques semble légitimer l'interprétation de τό qui a été avancée plus haut : signe matériel d'une relation, τό aurait été employé *en tant que tel et non pas en considération de son origine casuelle,* lorsque les rapports entre l'infinitif et son contexte n'apparaissaient pas assez nettement, en raison du caractère immédiat de cette "construction", peu adaptée aux besoins de précision d'une langue écrite toujours plus intellectualisée. Il apparaît donc d'ores et déjà qu'à titre de perfectionnement stylistique l'emploi de τό avec l'infinitif a été d'abord le fait d'une langue soignée, sinon recherchée, d'une forme d'expression soucieuse de marquer fortement l'articulation de ses moyens.'
30. Heiny, 'Articular Infinitive', p. 15: 'There seems to be no clear and uniform semantic difference between the plain infinitive and the articular infinitive'. His remarks here do not agree with the alleged use of the 'generic' and 'particular' article, which would imply that the article makes the infinitive definite (p. 20). If the article makes the infinitive definite, then this would comprise a semantic change. Heiny appears inconsistent on this point.
31. Heiny, 'Articular Infinitive', p. 26: 'And it is on just this level that we can speak of style'. This is the main concern of Heiny's dissertation.
32. BDF, p. 205; cf. James Hope Moulton, *A Grammar of New Testament Greek*. III. *Syntax,* by Nigel Turner (Edinburgh: T. & T. Clark, 1963) (hereafter Turner, *Syntax*). Both of these, however, offer a caveat that is not often heeded in studies of the articular infinitive.
33. Robertson, p. 1065.

word's entire lexical range into a given use of that word in context.[34] Grammarians make a similar mistake in the area of syntax when they take the entire range of grammatical functions possible with the article and attribute them to the articular infinitive, as if the article always bears an equivalent significance regardless of the class of word that it is appended to.

Too many grammarians have assumed that because the article is a substantivizer with other kinds of words (e.g. adjectives, participles), it must also function in the same way with the articular infinitive. We can detect early traces of this misconception in Georg Benedict Winer's grammar of New Testament Greek. He writes, 'The infinitive has more weight in the sentence when made substantival by the article'.[35] This comment is unfortunate in two regards. First, it appears to confuse the categories of *substantival/verbal* with the categories *concrete/abstract*. It is not at all clear what 'weight' is added to the infinitive by the article. The infinitive is a *verbal* substantive and in that regard is perhaps more abstract. But the presence of the article hardly makes it more concrete. Second (and related to the first point), Winer's remark fails to apprehend that an infinitive is substantival with or without the article.

It is this second reason that causes A.T. Robertson to take issue with Winer's treatment of the articular infinitive,

> It is not true that the article makes the inf. a substantive as Winer has it. It is not just a substantive, nor just a verb, but both at the same time. One naturally feels that the articular inf. is more substantival than the anarthrous…but that is not correct. The addition of the article made no essential change in the inf. It was already both substantive and verb.[36]

Robertson merely points out the obvious here. The anarthrous infinitive functions as a noun throughout the New Testament and Hellenistic Greek. To point out just one example, the use of the infinitive as the subject of impersonal verbs such as δεῖ is always anarthrous (e.g. Mt. 16.21; 17.10).[37] The idea that the articular infinitive is more of a substantive than the anarthrous simply does not square with such evidence. Therefore, the article does not 'help' the infinitive to be more of a noun than it already is. Nevertheless, numerous grammarians since Winer have more or less stated or implied that

---

34. James Barr, *The Semantics of Biblical Language* (Oxford: Oxford University Press, 1961; repr., Philadelphia: Trinity Press International, 1991), p. 218.

35. G.B. Winer, *A Treatise of the Grammar of New Testament Greek, Regarded as a Sure Basis for New Testament Exegesis* (trans. W.F. Moulton; Edinburgh: T. & T. Clark, 3rd edn, 9th Eng. edn, 1882), p. 403 n. 1; cf. pp. 402-403, 406, 407.

36. Robertson, pp. 1057, 1058, 1063; cf. H.E. Dana and Julius R. Mantey, *A Manual Grammar of the Greek New Testament* (New York: Macmillan, 1927), p. 212.

37. BDF, §393 (my emphasis).

the article is a *substantivizer*.[38] Even BDF manifests this wrong-headed approach in the heading of its section on the nominative and accusative infinitive, 'The nominative and accusative of the *substantivized* infinitive'.[39] This book will show that this line of thinking overestimates the significance of the article with the infinitive.

The assumption that the article has the same significance with the infinitive that it has with other nouns has led some grammarians to liken the articular infinitive to the demonstrative pronoun. These scholars argue that the article with the infinitive can bear the same demonstrative notion that it has with other kinds of substantives. This observation arises in part out of an observation about the history of the article and the demonstrative pronoun.[40] As Herbert Smyth notes, 'The article ὁ, ἡ, τό, was originally a demonstrative pronoun, and as such supplied the place of the personal pronoun of the third person. By gradual weakening it became the definite article'.[41] Likewise, Robert W. Funk writes, 'In contradistinction to Sanskrit and Latin, Greek developed an article from the demonstrative. It often exhibits obvious affinities with its original function.'[42]

With other kinds of nouns, the *specifying* force of this once demonstrative form is clear throughout the New Testament. For instance, Daniel Wallace labels this the *individualizing* use of the article and divides this usage into seven categories: *anaphoric, kataphoric, deictic, par excellence, monadic, well-known*, and *abstract*.[43] Dana and Mantey extend this usage to the infinitive: 'The articular infinitive singles out the act as a particular occurrence'.[44] In commenting on Phil. 1.21, Robertson says similarly, 'Here the article τό has just the effect that the Greek article has with any abstract

38. Hamilton Ford Allen, *The Infinitive in Polybius Compared with the Infinitive in Biblical Greek* (Chicago: University of Chicago Press, 1907), pp. 29, 45; I.T. Beckwith, 'The Articular Infinitive with εἰς', *JBL* 15 (1896), pp. 155-67 (157); L. Cignelli and G.C. Bottini, 'L'articolo nel greco biblico', *Studii biblici franciscani liber annus* 41 (1991), pp. 159-99 (166); Ernest De Witt Burton, *Syntax of the Moods and Tenses in New Testament Greek* (Grand Rapids: Kregel Publications, 3rd edn, 1900), p. 155; Dana and Mantey, *Manual Grammar*, p. 211; C.F.D. Moule, *An Idiom Book of New Testament Greek* (Cambridge: Cambridge University Press, 2nd edn, 1959), p. 126; Porter, *Idioms*, p. 194.

39. BDF, §398, 205.

40. Porter, *Idioms*, p. 106.

41. Smyth, p. 284.

42. Robert W. Funk, 'The Syntax of the Greek Article: Its Importance for Critical Pauline Problems' (PhD Dissertation, Vanderbilt University, 1953), p. 31.

43. See his grammar for numerous examples: Daniel B. Wallace, *Greek Grammar beyond the Basics: An Exegetical Syntax of the New Testament* (Grand Rapids: Zondervan, 1996), pp. 216-27.

44. Dana and Mantey, *Manual Grammar*, p. 138.

substantive, that of distinction or contrast'.[45] Robertson provides no explanation as to why the article bears this *individualizing/specifying* idea when used with the infinitive. The only thing close to an explanation occurs when he says that the article carries with it a force that it has with nouns from other word-classes.

The relevant question is whether or not the article carries this significance when it is connected to the infinitive. In a general way, some grammarians say that it does. Grammarians commonly associate the *anaphoric* use of the article with the *demonstrative* notion that is supposedly inherent in it. Robertson writes, 'There is little doubt that the first use of τό with the inf. was demonstrative as it was with everything. In Mk 9.10, τί ἐστιν τὸ ἐκ νεκρῶν ἀναστῆναι, the article is almost demonstrative, certainly anaphoric.'[46] BDF also picks up this line in its discussion on the nominative and accusative articular infinitive: 'In general the anaphoric significance of the article, i.e., its reference to something previously mentioned or otherwise well known, is more or less evident. Without this anaphoric reference, an infinitive as subject or object is usually anarthrous.'[47] But even here, BDF recognizes that anaphora is not always clear and divides its treatment between those instances which are clear and those which are 'less clearly anaphoric'.[48]

All of these analyses attribute too much significance to the article in the articular infinitive. However, it is important to note that I am certainly not the first to say that the article occurs with the infinitive as a function word and/or case-identifier. Indeed, many of the grammarians just discussed acknowledge that much—usually in the form of a caveat.[49] So the problem is not that these writers completely miss the purpose for the article in this construction. The problem is that interpreters make statements that go beyond the article's limited role as a function marker.[50]

---

45. Robertson, p. 1065; cf. James L. Boyer, 'The Classification of Infinitives: A Statistical Study', *Grace Theological Journal* 6 (1985), pp. 3-27 (26).

46. Robertson, p. 1065.

47. BDF, §399, 205.

48. BDF, §399, 205.

49. E.g. Turner, *Syntax*, p. 140; BDF, §§398-399, 205. Others show that they see the article as a case-identifier; see William Douglas Chamberlain, *An Exegetical Grammar of the Greek New Testament* (New York: Macmillan, 1941), p. 105; Dana and Mantey, *Manual Grammar*, p. 212; Porter, *Idioms*, p. 194; Winer, *Grammar*, pp. 408-409, 412. Also, among grammars of classical dialects: Jannaris, *An Historical Greek Grammar*, pp. 482-83; Smyth, p. 451.

50. It is precisely this sort of over-interpretation of the article's meaning that leads to the misinterpretation of biblical texts such as N.T. Wright's anaphoric reading of the articular infinitive in Phil. 2.6; see his 'ἁρπαγμός and the Meaning of Philippians 2.5-11', *JTS* NS 37 (1986), pp. 321-52 (344). The same piece appeared subsequently in Wright's

c. *Underestimating the Article's Significance*

While I argue that the article does not *substantivize* the infinitive or make an *anaphoric* reference, I do not mean to suggest that the authors of the New Testament chose the articular infinitive over the anarthrous infinitive for no reason at all. The opposite error of overestimating the article's significance is underestimating its syntactical value. Once again, errors in this direction go at least as far back as Winer's seminal work: 'We certainly cannot assume any distinction in *meaning* between the infinitive with, and the infinitive without the article'.[51] Winer's remark is certainly accurate in one sense, but it is also misleading in another. Yes, it is true that the article does not affect the *lexical* meaning of a given infinitive. The article does not effect a semantic change in the meaning of the infinitive.[52] However, the article does in fact alter the *structural* meaning of the articular infinitive. And since *total linguistic meaning* is the goal of interpretation, it is crucial for the critical observer to note the syntactical value of the article. Nevertheless, many interpreters do in fact say too little in their description of the articular infinitive's significance. These writers miss the fundamental role that the article plays in denoting grammatical *structure*. For instance, Boyer wonders 'if there is any' grammatical significance of the article.[53]

Scholars underestimate the article's significance in at least three ways. First, some New Testament scholars see the use of the article as the stylistic preference of the author. In this case, these grammarians like to point out that both the articular and anarthrous infinitives are used to denote a whole range of infinitival semantic functions. To this effect, Robertson notes that, 'The articular inf. has all the main uses of the anarthrous inf.'.[54] Daniel Wallace also notices the semantic overlap of the two kinds of infinitives. He divides his treatment of the infinitive into three major sections—adverbial uses, substantival uses, and independent uses—and there are articular and anarthrous infinitives represented in each section.[55] Of the substantival uses, both anarthrous and articular infinitives are found in the subject, direct object, appositive, and epexegetical slots. Anarthrous and articular infinitives also share a range of adverbial functions: purpose, result, means, time.[56]

The Climax of the Covenant: Christ and the Law in Pauline Theology (Edinburgh: T. & T. Clark, 1991; Minneapolis: Fortress Press, 1992), p. 83.

51. Winer, *Grammar*, p. 403 n. 1.

52. In fact, Porter acknowledges that there is widespread agreement on this point (Porter, *Idioms*, p. 194).

53. Boyer, 'Classification of Infinitives', p. 26.

54. Robertson, p. 1063.

55. Wallace, *Greek Grammar*, p. 587.

56. Wallace, *Greek Grammar*, pp. 609-11.

In his article on the semantic classification of infinitives, Boyer sees even more semantic overlap than Wallace: 'Every classification except one shows both articular and anarthrous constructions'.[57] From this observation Boyer concludes, 'The case of the article does not seem to be related to the classification of infinitive functions'.[58] Because the case of the article seems to be disconnected from meaning, by the end of the article Boyer speculates that the article is perhaps just a 'stylistic' preference or 'personal whim' of the author.[59] What Boyer neglects to observe is that not only does the article help to specify grammatical relations, it also often denotes a meaning that derives from the case of the neuter singular article. The argument set forth by some of the scholars of Classical Greek likely holds true for Hellenistic Greek. The notion of style is not so much driven by personal whim, but by grammatical and syntactical restraints.[60]

Second, some grammarians observe that in certain instances the normal meanings of the Greek cases lose their significance when used with the infinitive. For instance, there are writers who contend that some articular infinitives are Semitisms and as such do not conform to the normal meaning of the Greek case-system. Once again, this view can be traced back as far as Winer. In his remarks on the genitive articular infinitive, he writes, 'It would seem that the infinitive with τοῦ had come to be regarded by the Hellenists as the representative of the Hebrew infinitive with ל in its manifold rela-tions…the proper signification of the genitive was no longer thought of."[61] While it is possible that this idiom derives from some sort of formal-equivalence approach to translation going back to the LXX,[62] it is not clear that the case has lost its original significance.

Ernest Burton observes a decline in meanings normally associated with the genitive case. As a matter of fact, he claims that the genitive articular infinitive can be found as subject or object in the New Testament—functions not normally associated with the genitive case. He writes,

---

57.   Boyer, 'Classification of Infinitives', p. 25.

58.   Boyer, 'Classification of Infinitives', p. 25.

59.   Boyer, 'Classification of Infinitives', p. 26. Boyer says he is following Robertson in this, but I am not sure that Boyer has understood Robertson's analysis.

60.   Heiny, 'Articular Infinitive', p. 26; cf. Burguière, *Histoire de l'infinitif en grec*, p. 113.

61.   Winer, *Grammar*, p. 411. Allen quotes from Winer in agreement on this point (*The Infinitive in Polybius*, p. 53). Others have acknowledged the presence of a Semitism. Not all say that the case is losing its original significance: Moule, *Idiom Book*, p. 129; James Hope Moulton, *A Grammar of New Testament Greek*. II. *Accidence and Word-Formation*, by Wilbert Francis Howard (Edinburgh: T. & T. Clark, 1929), pp. 448-51; Robertson, p. 1068; Turner, *Syntax*, pp. 141, 144-45.

62.   Moulton calls such translations in the LXX 'barbarous literalness' (James Hope Moulton, *A Grammar of New Testament Greek*. I. *Prolegomena* (Edinburgh: T. & T. Clark, 3rd edn, 1908], p. 13).

> In Post-Aristotelian Greek, notably in the Septuagint and the New Testa-
> ment…[t]he Infinitive with the article in the genitive began to assume some
> such prominence… [T]he sense of its case being in some degree lost, this
> genitive Infinitive came to be used as a nominative or accusative… [T]he
> Infinitive with the article in the genitive begins to lose the sense of its genitive
> function and to be employed as a nominative or accusative.[63]

James Hope Moulton also notes the depletion of the semantic force of the
genitive article. He states that the genitive article retains 'its genitive force
almost as little as the genitive absolute'.[64] James Boyer echoes Moulton in
this regard and thereby argues that the article in the articular infinitive is not
for case identification.[65]

Third, one author regards the article as a spacer. This novel explanation
for the article in prepositional phrases comes from A.T. Robertson. Having
argued convincingly that the article is not a *substantivizer* (*contra* Winer *et
al.*), he argues that the real reason for the article did not have much to do
with meaning at all. He writes,

> As a rule the article was essential if a preposition occurred with an inf. The
> reason for this was due to the absence of division between words. It was
> otherwise almost impossible to tell this use of the inf. from that of composition
> of preposition with the verb if the two came in conjunction. Cf. ἀντὶ τοῦ
> λέγειν in Jas. 4.15.[66]

This explanation is ingeniously conceived, but does not adequately account
for the articular infinitive in every instance. First of all, if the article appears
so that the preposition will not be mistaken for a prefix to the infinitive verb,
then why is the article also employed with prepositions that do not ever get
used in composition with verbs (e.g. ἕως in Acts 8.40 and ἕνεκεν in 2 Cor.
7.12)?[67] Second of all, the article appears between the preposition and the
infinitive even when there are other intervening words (such as postpositive
δέ in Mt. 26.32 and Mk 1.14; see also Mk 5.4). We would expect the article
to be absent in such situations if it were just there to make a gap between

---

63. Burton, *Moods and Tenses*, pp. 143-44.

64. Moulton, *Prolegomena*, p. 216. With respect to ἐν τῷ with the infinitive in Luke,
Moulton writes that it is a 'grammatical Hebraism' (Moulton, *Prolegomena*, p. 14).
Moulton also writes, 'The fact that [ἐν τῷ with the infinitive] exactly translates the
Hebrew infin. with ב does not make it any worse Greek, though this naturally increases
its frequency' (Moulton, *Prolegomena*, p. 215 [compare these remarks with a sort of
retraction on p. 249]). For Moulton, even though the articular infinitive was a feature of
Attic that was passed down to the Koine, Hebrew and Aramaic still exerted influence in
Luke's writings (pp. 13-19).

65. Boyer, 'Classification of Infinitives', pp. 24-25.

66. Robertson, p. 1069.

67. Not all prepositions are used in composition with verbs, as Robertson himself
points out (Robertson, p. 636).

preposition and infinitive. In every case where there are other intervening words, the article still shows up. There is another explanation for the fact that the articular infinitive gets used every time it follows a preposition. Robertson himself provides that explanation in another section of his grammar: 'It is the *case* which indicates the meaning of the *preposition*, and not the preposition which gives the meaning to the case'.[68] While the article may help to distinguish verbs being used in composition from those that are not, it also has the syntactical force of identifying the case of the preposition.

This history of research has attempted to outline how other studies of the articular infinitive have either said too little or too much about the meaning of the articular infinitive in New Testament Greek. They have either over-estimated the *semantic* value of the article or have underestimated the *structural* meaning of the article. The goal of this book will be to avoid both errors. To reiterate, I will argue that the article is employed with the infinitive primarily as a *function* word and as a *case* marker.

4. *Methodology*

A traditional approach to the Koine Greek language treats grammar 'as if it were something known and absolute',[69] as though grammar were understood intuitively and thus should be studied and taught as such. Modern linguistics approaches the study of language in an entirely different manner. A linguistic approach seeks to describe in a scientific way the system of meaning underlying the intuitions of the native speaker of a given language(s).[70] The linguistic approach represents a relatively new departure in the study of New Testament Greek. For this reason David Alan Black writes, 'a revolution of sorts has occurred in the study of language. Today any work on New Testament Greek that ignores these new findings will not easily escape the charge of obscurantism.'[71] Therefore, it is necessary to set forth in broad strokes (1) the methodological presuppositions of modern linguistics and (2) how those presuppositions inform the procedure of my research.

---

68. Robertson is quoting F.W. Farrar's *Greek Syntax* (1876) in this statement. In the same paragraph Robertson writes, 'The notion, therefore, that prepositions "govern" cases must be discarded definitely' (Robertson, p. 554).

69. Black, *Linguistics for Students of New Testament Greek*, p. xiii.

70. Noam Chomsky, *Current Issues in Linguistic Theory* (Janua Linguarum; The Hague: Mouton, 1967), p. 28.

71. David Alan Black, 'Introduction', in David Alan Black, Katharine Barnwell, and Stephen Levinsohn (eds.), *Linguistics and New Testament Interpretation: Essays on Discourse Analysis* (Nashville: Broadman, 1992), pp. 10-14 (11). Black writes elsewhere: 'Both the content and the spirit of traditional instruction in grammar are being challenged in fundamental ways by the revolution in language scholarship brought about by modern linguistic research' (*Linguistics for Students of New Testament Greek*, p. xiii).

a. *Methodological Presuppositions of Modern Linguistics*[72]

(1) *Modern linguistics emphasizes spoken language over written language.* This item immediately presents a problem to the student of New Testament Greek since the very language we wish to investigate no longer exists as it did two thousand years ago. All we have to work with are the various written texts. However, this disadvantage does not undermine the linguistic investigation of Koine Greek. For we can assume the written language to be a formalized representation of what was actually spoken at one time: 'Writing is merely a form of talk—talk that has been caught in flight and pinned down on paper so that the words can be *heard* (not merely seen) again'.[73] Therefore we should not conclude too quickly that the linguistic investigation of dead languages is a futile enterprise.[74] The methodological point that needs to be made here is that when we are dealing with the written remnants of a language, we must keep ever before us the fact that the spoken language is primary. Languages originate and change as a result of articulation, not as a result of writing.[75] The written form of the language always follows the spoken.

(2) *Modern linguistics is scientific.* To say that modern linguistics is scientific is insufficient in itself.[76] In the last fifty or sixty years a debate has emerged among linguists as to what a true scientific study of language is.[77]

72. These points are a conflated summary of Porter, 'Studying Ancient Languages', pp. 151-55, and Black, *Linguistics for Students of New Testament Greek*, pp. 12-14.

73. Black, *Linguistics for Students of New Testament Greek*, p. 14.

74. Although Hockett argues that linguists must make a distinction between *language* and *writing*, even he concedes that 'the relationship between writing and language is close' (Hockett, *A Course in Modern Linguistics*, p. 4).

75. The written language is so closely connected to the spoken form that we can often explain morphological changes in a language on the basis of how words were articulated in actual speech. Black notes 'Linguists know that speech is governed by an orderly system of rules... He may show that what seems to be an "irregular" form is not irregular at all, but is in fact quite predictable in terms of the phonological rules of the language' (Black, *Linguistics for Students of New Testament Greek*, p. 42).

76. 'Modern science, however, has been re-evaluating what it means to do "objective" science. Thomas Kuhn (1970) has perhaps best illustrated the terms of this re-assessment, so that it is no longer sufficient simply to say that a discipline is scientific... [E]very discipline, including the so-called hard sciences, has methodological presuppositions which govern the behavior of the discipline... "There is no such thing as theory-neutral and hypothesis-free observation and data collection. To use a currently fashionable phrase...observation is, of necessity and from the outset, theory-laden"' (Porter, 'Studying Ancient Languages', p. 151).

77. R.H. Longman acknowledged the heart of this dispute two decades ago: 'There is today lively discussion on the degree of empiricism that should be embodied in a linguistic theory' (*General Linguistics: An Introductory Survey* [Longman Linguistics Library; New York: Longman, 3rd edn, 1980], p. 6).

One approach (made especially popular in America last century by Leonard Bloomfield[78]) emphasizes the observation of actual uses of language, be they spoken or written.[79] This approach is the legacy of Ferdinand de Saussure and of Structuralism, a linguistic movement that can be traced back to him. De Saussure speaks of the *concrete entities of language* which are the object of the linguist's study: 'The signs that make up language are not abstractions but real objects... [S]igns and their relations are what linguistics studies; they are the *concrete entities* of our science'.[80] This theory of scientific analysis advocates a thoroughgoing inductivism and only concerns itself with the observation and analysis of actual speech (written or spoken).[81] While there is obvious value in focusing one's study upon actual use of language, this is not the entire task of linguistic research.

Chomskian linguistics cautions against focusing too heavily upon empirical evidence in trying to study and understand a natural language. Chomsky argues that understanding a language goes beyond understanding a set corpus of materials:

> We can sketch various levels of success that might be attained by a grammatical description associated with a particular linguistic theory. The lowest level of success is achieved if the grammar presents the observed primary data correctly. A second and higher level of success is achieved when the grammar

78.   Walter R. Bodine calls Bloomfield one of the principal figures who shaped the direction of American descriptive linguistics, even though Bloomfield was following the 'seminal work' of de Saussure (Walter R. Bodine, 'How Linguists Study Syntax', in *idem* (ed.), *Linguistics and Biblical Hebrew* [Winona Lake, IN: Eisenbrauns, 1992], pp. 89-107 [95]).

79.   Leonard Bloomfield, *Language* (New York: Henry Holt, 1933), p. 38. He also argues that the linguist must study as if he held the presuppositions of a scientific materialist: 'A linguistic observer...must record every form he can find and not try to excuse himself from this task by appealing to the reader's common sense or to the structure of some other language or to some psychological theory, and, above all, he must not select or distort the facts according to his views of what the speakers ought to be saying' (pp. 37-38).

80.   Ferdinand de Saussure, *Course in General Linguistics* (ed. Charles Bally and Albert Reidlinger; trans. Wade Baskin; New York: Philosophical Library, 1959), p. 102 (emphasis in original).

81.   Ruth M. Kempson criticizes the 'inductivism' that was the prevalent scientific theory of Bloomfield's day: 'The job of a scientist, it was believed, was to accumulate facts without any preconceived theory and to expect that a careful sifting of the facts would in the course of time lead to the correct theory. With this emphasis on data collection, the defining property of science was thought to be its method—objective and not swayed by such subjective factors as opinion, guess, or intuition. A consequence of this concern for objectivity was that abstract theoretical constructs were only tolerated as scientific if they could be defined in terms of observable events' (Ruth M. Kempson, *Semantic Theory* [Cambridge Textbooks in Linguistics; Cambridge: Cambridge University Press, 1977], p. 47).

gives a correct account of the linguistic intuition of the native speaker, and specifics the observed data (in particular) in terms of significant generalizations that express underlying regularities in the language.[82]

In other words, observation and precise description of the hard data (i.e. Bloomfield) falls short of truly understanding a language. One must take the next step of developing a theory that accounts for the observed phenomena.

Therefore, Ruth Kempson is nearer the mark when she says that linguistic study should be 'scientific in the sense that it makes empirically testable predictions'.[83] Indeed, the focus of linguistic investigation should be upon actual written or spoken instances of a given phenomenon of language. But these data are used primarily to form hypotheses and to falsify theories. Kempson is worth quoting at length in this regard:

> A theory can only be tested by attempts to falsify it, for while it is possible to prove that a theory is false by a given set of facts, it is logically impossible to prove the truth of a theory in this way. Facts either are or are not compatible with a theory, but their being compatible can never *prove* the validity of that theory for it may be false for some independent reason. In general therefore scientific endeavour is not concerned with evidence which seems to show theories to be correct but only with evidence which might show them to be false.[84]

---

82. Chomsky, *Current Issues in Linguistic Theory*, p. 28; cf. *idem, Aspects of the Theory of Syntax* (Cambridge, MA: The M.I.T. Press, 1965), pp. 30-37; Daryl Dean Schmidt, *Hellenistic Greek Grammar and Noam Chomsky: Nominalizing Transforms* (SBLDS, 62; Chico, CA: Scholars Press, 1981), pp. 19-22. When it comes to defining 'success' in biblical interpretation, my hermeneutic presupposes that the goal of interpretation is to discern the author's intended meaning. I do not, for instance, share Daryl Schmidt's opinion that 'as the text is allowed to rightful independent existence, apart from both author and exegete, a model of language that seeks to go beyond historically accurate description will present the paradigm needed for the study of grammar' (Daryl Schmidt, 'The Study of Hellenistic Greek Grammar in the Light of Contemporary Linguistics', *Perspectives in Religious Studies* 11 [1984], pp. 27-38 [36]). Noam Chomsky developed a new method of studying language called *transformational* or *generative* grammar (TG grammar). Moisés Silva notes, 'Because transformational linguists depend heavily on native speakers (including themselves) to determine whether utterances are grammatical, this approach has not been vigorously applied to the study of ancient languages' (*God, Language, and Scripture* [Foundations of Contemporary Interpretation; Grand Rapids: Zondervan, 1990], p. 57 n. 26). Daryl Dean Schmidt, however, is an exception. He has attempted to apply this approach to Hellenistic Greek (*Hellenistic Greek Grammar and Noam Chomsky*, pp. 41-65). With respect to TG grammar, I agree with van Rensburg ('A New Reference Grammar', p. 135) that: 'The aim of grammar should not be a description of the Greek in order to enable persons to generate new texts in this language. Rather, the aim should be to serve as an aid in the linguistic interpretation of the already existing complete corpus of texts comprising the New Testament.'

83. Kempson, *Semantic Theory*, p. 1.

84. Kempson, *Semantic Theory*, p. 1.

Within this framework, the task of the linguist is to develop a theory that adequately explains a grammatical phenomenon without being falsified by the relevant body of empirical data.

(3) *Modern linguistics is systematic.* This presupposition rests on the observation that all languages exhibit an internal structure. Even though the relationship between particular forms and meaning may only be conventional, these conventions betray patterns. Black writes,

> Because language is conventional, it is also *systematic*: it can be described in terms of a finite number of linguistic units that can combine only in a limited number of ways. That is to say, languages have their own phonological, morphological, and syntactical systems, each with its own rules of permissible combinations and order. The grammar of a language, as we have seen, is concerned with the description, analysis, and formalization of these linguistic patterns.[85]

One of the chief deficiencies of some of the standard grammar books on New Testament Greek consists in their failure to take a systematic approach to language structure.[86] This book will assume that the Hellenistic Greek of the New Testament has at least two levels of *categorical constituent structure.* As Michael Palmer points out, grammarians have assumed for centuries that Greek words belong to various word-level categories such as verb, noun, adjective, adverb, and preposition.[87] But while scholars have long recognized the morphological and syntactic evidence for word-level categories,[88] it has only been since the advent of modern linguistics that they have documented the evidence for phrase-level categories.[89] My analysis of the articular infinitive rests on Michael Palmer's arguments to the effect that, 'The syntax of New Testament Greek…necessitates both word-level and phrase-level constituent categories'.[90] The word-level categories include elements such as noun (N), verb (V), adjective (A), determiner (D), and preposition (P). The phrase-level categories include noun phrase (NP), verb phrase (VP), prepositional phrase (PP), and adjectival phrase (AP).[91]

(4) *Modern linguistics emphasizes synchronic analysis.* This is not to say that the work of comparative or historical linguistics is unimportant.[92] But it

---

85. Black, *Linguistics for Students of New Testament Greek*, p. 16.
86. Stanley E. Porter and J.T. Reed, 'Greek Grammar since BDF: A Retrospective and Prospective Analysis', *Filología Neotestamentaria* 4 (1991), pp. 143-64 (146).
87. Palmer, *Levels*, p. 35.
88. Palmer, *Levels*, pp. 35-39.
89. Palmer, *Levels*, p. 39.
90. Palmer, *Levels*, p. 55.
91. Palmer, *Levels*, p. 57.
92. See Black's brief description of each in *Linguistics for Students of New Testament Greek*, pp. 10-12.

is to say that when we pursue the meaning of any particular use of language, the contemporary context is primary. Ferdinand de Saussure asserts, 'Language is a system whose parts can and must all be considered in their synchronic solidarity'.[93] De Saussure illustrates this point by comparing language analysis to a chess game:

> In a game of chess any particular position has the unique characteristic of being freed from all antecedent positions; the route used in arriving there makes absolutely no difference; one who has followed the entire match has no advantage over the curious party who comes up at a critical moment to inspect the state of the game; to describe this arrangement, it is perfectly useless to recall what had just happened ten seconds previously. All this is equally applicable to language and sharpens the radical distinction between diachrony and synchrony. Speaking operates only on a language-state, and the changes that intervene between states have no place in either state.[94]

To apply this principle to modern English, I suggest a hackneyed illustration. If a man were to state today that he is *gay*, it does not matter a whit what *gay* meant in the English language one hundred years ago. Understanding the semantic range of this term over a long period of time will not aid me in describing the meaning of his utterance today. The current (synchronic) context must prevail in my interpretation. This principle holds true for all aspects of understanding language (semantics, syntax, phonology, and so forth).[95]

(5) *Modern linguistics is descriptive not prescriptive.* This point flows naturally from the foregoing discussion. As in any scientific discipline, in linguistic analysis we do not dictate *a priori* what should be. We merely analyze what is. Most students of Greek are familiar with the prescriptive approach to language study.[96] Not only is the prescriptive approach the preferred method of instruction from our earliest formal language study in primary school, but it is also the way many students are introduced to Greek

---

93. De Saussure, *Course in General Linguistics*, p. 87.

94. De Saussure, *Course in General Linguistics*, p. 89.

95. 'The structural linguist...may be considered a reformer of existing descriptive but not altogether strictly synchronic grammars' (Haiim B. Rosén, *Early Greek Grammar and Thought in Heraclitus: The Emergence of the Article* [Proceedings of the Israel Academy of Sciences and Humanities, 7.2; Jerusalem: Israel Academy of Sciences and Humanities, 1988], p. 24).

96. 'In the eighteenth century, the spread of education led many dialect-speakers to learn the upper-class forms of speech. This gave the authoritarians their chance: they wrote *normative grammars*, in which they often ignored actual usage in favor of speculative notions. Both the belief in "authority" and some fanciful rules (as, for instance, about the use of *shall* and *will*) still prevail in our schools' (Bloomfield, *Language*, p. 7 [emphasis in original]).

grammar. While learning English, young students are taught what the correct and incorrect uses of their native language are. How many of us have been rebuked for ending a sentence with a preposition? Modern linguistics is not concerned with such prescriptive rules, but simply with observing patterns in language. As the linguist observes these patterns changing over time, he does not make a value judgment about whether such change is good or bad.[97] As Porter writes, 'Linguistic change is not to be equated with corruption'.[98] Therefore, one style or stage of a language is not better or worse than any another, just different.

b. *Methodology for the Current Thesis*
The scientific nature of the linguistic enterprise requires a scientific methodology.[99] That is, we need to develop a procedure that gives prime consideration to the linguistic evidence and that can construct an adequate explanation for the evidence. In this book, the evidence consists of the various uses of the articular infinitive in the New Testament.[100] This does not mean that we are unconcerned with how the articular infinitive relates to other instances of the infinitive in the New Testament or in the Hellenistic Greek language system as a whole. On the contrary, these related issues will receive attention in due course. However, this book will concentrate on New Testament usage. Having narrowed the scope of research to the New Testament,[101] we

97. Robert A. Hall Jr, *Leave Your Language Alone!* (Ithaca, NY: Linguistica, 1950), pp. 9-28.

98. Porter, 'Studying Ancient Languages', p. 154.

99. Cf. Richard J. Erickson, 'Linguistics and Biblical Language: A Wide-Open Field', *JETS* 26 (1983), pp. 257-63 (258).

100. Matthew Brook O'Donnell points out that the New Testament is comprised of four of the seven genres of a selected corpus of Hellenistic Greek: letter, biography, history, and apocalyptic. Not represented in the New Testament are philosophy, geography, and speeches. O'Donnell also divides Hellenistic texts by 'Style/Formality': vulgar, non-literary, literary, and Atticistic. The New Testament contains three of the four: vulgar, non-literary, and literary. See Matthew Brook O'Donnell, 'Designing and Compiling a Register-Balanced Corpus of Hellenistic Greek for the Purpose of Linguistic Description and Investigation', in Stanley E. Porter (ed.), *Diglossia and Other Topics in New Testament Linguistics* (JSNTSup, 193; Studies in New Testament Greek, 6; Sheffield: Sheffield Academic Press, 2000), pp. 255-87 (286-87). I cite O'Donnell in order to point out that my selected corpus (the New Testament) comprises a fairly representative sample of Hellenistic Greek and that my thesis can be falsified by enough counter-examples from outside my corpus.

101. I can imagine someone raising the following objection: Is it legitimate to select the New Testament as the object of linguistic investigation? After all, New Testament Greek is but a narrow slice of the broader phenomenon of Hellenistic Greek. In this regard, J.J. Janse van Rensburg writes, 'It is not possible to speak about *New Testament Greek* as if it comprises a certain kind of Greek. The books of the New Testament came

can describe the procedure for research as follows: (1) to construct an abstract system (hypothesis) that explains the reason for the articular infinitive in New Testament Greek; (2) to investigate the consequences of setting up such a system; (3) to reject the system if it predicts certain facts that do not in fact obtain; and (4) to substitute an alternative system which is compatible with the facts.[102]

(1) *Making a preliminary hypothesis*. The first methodological step, formulating a hypothesis, has already been taken. As stated above, the point of this book is to ask and answer one question: 'What is the linguistic explanation for the article appearing with the infinitive in New Testament Greek?' My preliminary hypothesis is that the article is primarily a *function* word and not a *content* word and that the article appears with the infinitive in order to mark the infinitive's case and function. There are a variety of reasons why the case of an infinitive might need to be identified in New Testament Greek. These reasons must be demonstrated on a case by case basis. Although it remains to be seen whether or not this thesis will stand as is, it is important to note that a preliminary look at the basic New Testament data supports my contention.

Investigating the hypothesis against the data. The next step will be to test the hypothesis against the New Testament data. I have collected a database of every use of the infinitive in the New Testament (2289 occurrences).[103] I have further divided the data into two groups: anarthrous infinitives (1965 occurrences) and articular infinitives (324 occurrences).[104] Of the anarthrous

into existence over too long a period of time, and—in linguistic terms—there are too many individual authors with, in many cases, divergent backgrounds' ('A New Reference Grammar', p. 135). However, I contend that this focus on the New Testament is not too narrow. My focus on the New Testament is just a point of departure for making generalizations about Hellenistic Greek as a whole (even though my goal is to understand the New Testament). These generalizations about New Testament usage will certainly be subject to comparison with the linguistic features of Hellenistic Greek. 'The grammar of the language of the New Testament is best studied as a subset of Hellenistic Greek (HG) grammar' (Schmidt, 'The Study of Hellenistic Greek Grammar', p. 27). Furthermore, see the note immediately preceding this one.

102. Kempson, *Semantic Theory*, p. 1.

103. A computer search of the GRAMCORD database produced this number. The statistics that follow are the result of my own search of the GRAMCORD database and of a comparison of these results with Votaw and Boyer.

104. 'Most grammars that break down the inf. down [sic] by structural categories have two broad groupings, anarthrous and articular. This follows Votaw's scheme' (Wallace, *Greek Grammar*, p. 589 n. 2; cf. Clyde Votaw, *The Use of the Infinitive in Biblical Greek* [Chicago: Clyde Votaw, 1896], pp. 5-6, 7, 19). Robertson takes exception

infinitives, 66 are governed by the conjunctions ὡς or ὥστε[105] (5 and 61 occurrences respectively).[106] There are eleven anarthrous infinitives governed by the conjunction/conjunction-particle πρίν/πρὶν ἤ (8 and 3 occurrences respectively).[107]

I have observed that the articular infinitives fall into two broad categories: those governed by a preposition (200 occurrences[108]) and those not governed by a preposition (124 occurrences[109]). These two categories of articular infinitives form the objects under consideration in this study. They are represented graphically in the Appendix (Tables 16 and 17). The articular infinitive appears in the nominative, genitive, dative, and accusative cases. In this study, I define *case* according to form, not function. In Greek, *case* is best understood as the inflectional variation (in nouns, adjectives, pronouns, etc.)

with this approach and does not divide his treatment between articular and anarthrous infinitives (Robertson, p. 1058).

105.   Martin J. Higgins, 'New Testament Result Clauses with Infinitive', *CBQ* 23 (1961), pp. 233-41.

106.   Following ὡς: Lk. 9.52; Acts 20.24; 1 Cor. 7.25; 2 Cor. 10.9; Heb. 7.9. Following ὥστε: Mt. 8.24, 28; 10.1 (×2); 12.22 (×2); 13.2, 32 (×2), 54 (×2); 15.31, 33; 24.24; 27.1, 14; Mk 1.27, 45; 2.2, 12 (×2); 3.10, 20 (×2); 4.1, 32, 37; 9.26; 15.5; Lk. 4.29; 5.7; 12.1; 20.20; Acts 1.19; 5.15 (×2); 14.1; 15.39; 16.26; 19.10, 12 (×3), 16; Rom. 7.6; 15.19; 1 Cor. 1.7; 5.1; 13.2; 2 Cor 1.8; 2.7 (×2); 3.7; 7.7; Phil. 1.13; 1 Thess. 1.7, 8; 2 Thess. 1.4; 2.4; Heb. 13.6; 1 Pet. 1.21.

107.   Following πρίν: Mt. 26.34, 75; Mk 14.72; Lk. 22.61; Jn 4.49; 8.58; 14.29; Acts 2.20. Following πρὶν ἤ: Mt. 1.18; Mk 14.30; Acts 7.2.

108.   Mt. 5.28; 6.1, 8; 13.4, 5, 6, 25, 30; 20.19 (×3); 23.5; 24.12; 26.2, 12, 32; 27.12, 31; Mk 1.14; 4.4, 5, 6; 5.4 (×3); 6.48; 13.22; 14.28, 55; 16.19; Lk. 1.8, 21; 2.4, 6, 21, 27, 43; 3.21; 5.1 (×2), 12, 17; 6.48; 8.5, 6, 40, 42; 9.7, 18, 29, 33, 34, 36, 51; 10.35, 38; 11.1, 8, 27, 37; 12.5, 15; 14.1; 17.11, 14; 18.1, 5, 35; 19.11 (×2), 15; 22.15, 20; 23.8; 24.4, 15 (×2), 30, 51; Jn 1.48; 2.24; 13.19; 17.5; Acts 1.3; 2.1; 3.19, 26; 4.2 (×2), 30 (×2); 7.4, 19; 8.6 (×2), 11, 40; 9.3; 10.41; 11.15; 12.20; 15.13; 18.2, 3; 19.1, 21; 20.1; 23.15; 27.4, 9; 28.18; Rom. 1.11, 20; 3.4, 26; 4.11 (×2), 16, 18; 6.12; 7.4, 5; 8.29; 11.11; 12.2, 3; 15.8, 13 (×2), 16; 1 Cor. 8.10; 9.18; 10.6; 11.21, 22 (×2), 25, 33; 2 Cor. 1.4; 3.13; 4.4; 7.3 (×2), 12; 8.6, 11; Gal. 2.12; 3.17, 23; 4.18; Eph. 1.12, 18; 6.11; Phil. 1.7, 10, 23 (×2); 1 Thess. 2.9, 12, 16; 3.2; (×2), 5, 10 (×2), 13; 4.9; 2 Thess. 1.5; 2.2 (×2), 6, 10, 11; 3.8, 9; Heb. 2.8, 17; 3.12, 15; 7.23, 24, 25; 8.3, 13; 9.14, 28; 10.2, 15, 26; 11.3; 12.10; 13.21; Jas 1.18, 19 (×2); 3.3; 4.2, 15; 1 Pet. 3.7; 4.2.

109.   Mt. 2.13; 3.13; 11.1 (×2); 13.3; 15.20; 20.23; 21.32; 24.45; Mk 9.10; 10.40; 12.33 (×2); Lk. 1.9, 57, 73, 77, 79; 2.6, 21, 24, 27; 4.10, 42; 5.7; 8.5; 9.51; 10.19; 12.42; 17.1; 21.22; 22.6, 31; 24.16, 25, 29, 45; Acts 3.2, 12; 4.18 (×2); 5.31; 7.19; 9.15; 10.25, 47; 13.47; 14.9, 18; 15.20; 18.10; 20.3, 20 (×2), 27, 30; 21.12; 23.15, 20; 25.11; 26.18 (×2); 27.1, 20; Rom. 1.24; 6.6; 7.3, 18 (×2); 8.12; 11.8 (×2), 10; 13.8; 14.13, 21 (×2); 15.22, 23; 1 Cor. 7.26; 9.10; 10.13; 11.6 (×2); 14.39 (×2); 16.4; 2 Cor. 1.8; 2.1, 13; 7.11; 8.10 (×2), 11 (×3); 9.1; 10.2; Gal. 3.10; Phil. 1.21 (×2), 22, 24, 29 (×2); 2.6, 13 (×2); 3.10, 21; 4.10; 1 Thess. 3.3; 4.6 (×2); Heb. 5.12; 10.7, 9, 31; 11.5; Jas 5.17; 1 Pet. 3.10; 4.17; Rev. 12.7.

that encompasses various syntactical functions or relationships to other words.[110]

Rejecting the hypothesis. After carefully analyzing each instance of the articular infinitive in New Testament Greek, the next step will be to verify or refute the hypothesis in light of the evidence. The burden of this investigation will be to ascertain whether the function of each articular infinitive is somehow made explicit or *marked* by the presence of the article. For instance, if the subject of a given sentence would be otherwise unclear without the presence of the nominative neuter singular article, then it stands to reason that the article appears with the infinitive in order to *mark* the infinitive as the subject of the sentence. Therefore, in such a scenario the article would clearly be considered a *function* word. However, it is plausible that some uses of the article may have more than a structural significance. If in fact the article is found to have more than a structural significance and my hypothesis does not obtain, it will be rejected.

Refining the hypothesis. If the hypothesis proves partially adequate, then a revised hypothesis will be proposed to account for the data. If the hypothesis proves wholly inaccurate, a new one will be sought that adequately accounts for the New Testament data. This process of rejecting, refining, or rewriting the hypothesis or aspects of the hypothesis will be ongoing as each case-form (nominative-accusative, genitive, or dative) is studied. As will be shown below, the chapters of this book will consider each case-form in turn.

Having pursued this methodology, the result will be twofold: (1) a detailed syntax of the articular infinitive in New Testament Greek, and (2) an answer to the question posed at the outset, 'What is the linguistic explanation for the article appearing with the infinitive in New Testament Greek?' These results will be important to the study of New Testament Greek for two reasons. First, the purpose of the article with the infinitive will be clarified in such a way that careful exegetes will be able to avoid the dual errors of making too much or too little of the article. Second, a detailed syntactical explanation of the articular infinitive will bring the study of the infinitive up to date with the most current linguistic methods. Such a comprehensive coverage of each articular infinitive will serve as a useful reference for anyone wishing to understand a particular use of the articular infinitive.

Having introduced my thesis in this introductory chapter, the argument of this book will develop as follows. Chapter 2 will outline the use of the Greek

110. Wallace, *Greek Grammar*, p. 34; *contra* Robertson, p. 448: 'This method of interpretation…accents sharply the blending of the forms while insisting on the integrity of the case-ideas'. There is much more to be said concerning Greek case in the introduction to Chapter 3.

article as a function-marker and case-identifier elsewhere in New Testament Greek. The examination will include how the article functions in connection with other indeclinable substantives. Chapters 3 and 4 will be an inductive study of the articular infinitive in New Testament Greek. This inductive study is broken down by the major formal characteristic that divides articular infinitives: those governed by prepositions (Chapter 4) vs. those that are not governed by prepositions (Chapter 3). Chapter 5 will set the results of my study against analogous constructions in the LXX to see if my thesis is consistent with this body of literature. Chapter 6, the concluding chapter, will set forth a summary of the implications that my study has for New Testament Greek grammar and for exegesis in the New Testament. This chapter will be followed by six appendices and a bibliography.

2

THE ARTICLE AS A FUNCTION MARKER
IN NEW TESTAMENT GREEK

1. *Introduction*

Robertson's well-worn dictum concerning the Greek article still holds true: 'The article is never meaningless in Greek… Its free use leads to exactness and finesse.'[1] Robert W. Funk agrees and highlights, 'The importance of the syntax of the article for the theology of Paul'.[2] Yet in spite of the important role that it plays in our understanding of the New Testament, the article remains one of the most neglected and abused areas of Greek language study.[3] Daniel Wallace writes, 'In spite of the fact that the article is used far more frequently than any other word in the Greek New Testament (almost 20,000 times, or one out of seven words), there is still much mystery about its usage'.[4] The most comprehensive account of the Greek article in the New Testament is about two hundred years old and, though still valuable, in desperate need of revision.[5] Although more recent treatments have appeared,[6]

1.   Robertston, 756; cf. Gildersleeve, *Syntax of Classical Greek*, II, p. 216; Wallace, *Greek Grammar*, pp. 207-208.

2.   Funk, 'The Syntax of the Greek Article', p. 252.

3.   Wallace, *Greek Grammar*, p. 207.

4.   Wallace, *Greek Grammar*, p. 207. D.A. Carson exhibits this tendency: 'I suspect that some uses [of the article] are determined more by the "feel" of the speaker or writer of the language than by unambiguous principles' (*Exegetical Fallacies* [Grand Rapids: Baker Book House, 2nd edn, 1996], p. 79). Carson is correct to point out the errors that commentators have made in interpreting the Greek article, but to suggest that something so amorphous as 'feel' to be a guide in interpretation is not helpful.

5.   Thomas Fanshaw Middleton, *The Doctrine of the Greek Article Applied to the Criticism and Illustration of the New Testament* (London: Gilbert & Rivington, new edn, 1833). I looked at Southern Baptist Theological Seminary's fragile copy of the first edition (1813), but for this study I used the 1833 edition exclusively.

6.   Apart from the standard grammars, some of the more significant items include: Cignelli and Bottini, 'L'articolo nel greco biblico'; Frank Eakin, 'The Greek Article in the First and Second Century Papyri', *AJP* 37 (1916), pp. 333-40; Gildersleeve, *Syntax of*

significant gaps in our understanding still persist.[7] David Sansone concurs: 'While there is a great deal of value in these standard grammars, their treatment of the definite article cannot be regarded as complete or authoritative, and…it needs to be supplemented both by further work of a traditional nature and by the application of more recent linguistic methods'.[8] If this judgment be accurate with reference to the use of the article in general, it is no less true with respect to the use of the article with the infinitive in particular.

Yet before we can account for the use of the article with the infinitive, we must summarize the broader usage of the article in New Testament Greek. Such is the purpose of this chapter. The primary goal will be to apply crucial insights from modern linguistics concerning the article's status as a *determiner*[9] and to explain how the article functions as such in New Testament Greek. I will argue that the article is syntactically and semantically different from the other Greek determiners. The syntactic and semantic differences lead us to the conclusion that the Greek article is often employed with no semantic value as a determiner. In these cases, the article appears as a function word, and it functions as such when used in connection with the infinitive. The argument will proceed in four parts. First, I will define what a determiner is. Second, I will observe the syntactic difference between the Greek article and the other Greek determiners. Third, I will mark the semantic difference between the Greek article and the other Greek determiners.

Classical Greek, II; Stephen H. Levinsohn, *Discourse Features of New Testament Greek: A Coursebook on the Information Structure of New Testament Greek* (Dallas: SIL International, 2nd edn, 2000), pp. 148-67; Rosén, *Early Greek Grammar and Thought in Heraclitus*; Sansone, 'Towards a New Doctrine of the Article in Greek'; F. Völker, *Syntax der griechischen Papyri: Der Artikel* (Münster: Druck der westfälischen Vereinsdruckerei, 1903).

7. It is noteworthy that in Stanley E. Porter's chapter on the Greek article in *Idioms of the Greek New Testament* there is no discussion of the semantic category of *definiteness* as it is being debated among general linguists, nor is there any acknowledgment of the Greek article's status as a determiner (*Idioms*, pp. 103-14).

8. Sansone, 'Towards a New Doctrine of the Article in Greek', p. 191. Although Robert W. Funk's 1953 dissertation on the article in Paul's writings ('The Syntax of the Greek Article') represents a pre-modern linguistic approach, his 1973 three-volume grammar is a thoroughgoing application of *structuralist* principles to the study of the Hellenistic Greek of the New Testament (*A Beginning–Intermediate Grammar*). Therefore, it is his 1973 *Grammar* that has been the most helpful in the present study (Funk, *A Beginning–Intermediate Grammar*, II, pp. 85-89, 555-60).

9. I agree with Michael Palmer that there is ample morphological and syntactic justification for using 'word-level' categories such as *determiner* in describing the Greek language (Palmer, *Levels*, pp. 35-39). 'A *word-level category* is a set of words which share a common set of linguistic (especially morphological and syntactic) properties' (p. 38).

Fourth, I will sum up the results of these observations and give a preliminary statement of their relevance to the article's use with the infinitive in the New Testament.

2. *A Definition of Determiner*

The word *determiner* is likely a term with which many scholars of New Testament Greek are unfamiliar. The term has only come into currency in grammatical discussions since the advent of modern linguistic approaches to language study. Because the standard grammar books of New Testament Greek reflect a pre-modern linguistic perspective,[10] it is not a term that has made its way into the jargon of the New Testament discipline. In contrast to the situation in New Testament studies, the term has become common fare in the vernacular of general linguistics. In his dictionary of modern linguistic terminology, Hadumod Bussmann defines *determiner* as a:

> Category of words that specify a noun more closely. In English these include articles, demonstrative pronouns, and other words which previously were grouped with pronouns… Determiners specify the accompanying N semantically and restrict its reference. Thus the determiner makes the N explicit, that is, it makes it 'known' through the speech situation.[11]

It is important to notice that this description focuses on the semantic force of *determiners*—that is, that a *determiner* in some sense specifies the noun with which it is associated. David Crystal emphasizes an additional element in his definition of a *determiner*:

---

10. Daryl D. Schmidt has shown that the study of grammar in the modern era has passed through several momentous periods, each period having been ushered in by a fundamental change in linguistic theory (*Hellenistic Greek Grammar and Noam Chomsky*, p. 1; cf. Palmer, *Levels*, p. 5). Schmidt identifies at least four distinct phases of linguistic theory in the modern era: (1) *Rationalist* in the first half of the nineteenth century, (2) *Comparative-Historical* in the second half of the nineteenth century, (3) *Structuralist* in the first half of the twentieth century, and (4) *Transformational-generative*, that is, *Chomskian*, in the second half of the twentieth century (Schmidt, *Hellenistic Greek Grammar and Noam Chomsky*, p. 3). He argues that the study of Hellenistic Greek grammar has followed the same pattern, 'though always one revolution behind that in linguistics' (p. 1). Thus, the current reference grammars for the study of New Testament Greek do not reflect the *Structuralist* and *Chomskian* revolutions in linguistic theory that occurred in the twentieth century. The grammar books of BDF, Moulton–Howard–Turner, and Robertson all reflect the *Comparative-Historical* approach, a linguistic theory current in the latter half of the nineteenth century (Palmer, *Levels*, p. 7).

11. Hadumod Bussmann, *Routledge Dictionary of Language and Linguistics* (trans. Gregory Trauth and Kerstin Kazzazi; London: Routledge, 1996; originally published as *Lexikon der Sprachwissenschaft* [Stuttgart: Kröner Verlag, 2nd edn, 1990]), p. 121.

> A grammatical element whose main role is to co-occur with nouns to express such semantic notions as quantity, number, possession, and definiteness; for example, *the, a, this, some, my, much.* These words 'determine' the way in which the noun is to be interpreted—*a car* vs. *the car* vs. *my car,* etc. The term is sometimes extended to include other types of word [*sic*] within the noun phrase (such as adjectives).[12]

Notice that Crystal's definition contains two crucial elements—namely, a syntactic element and a semantic element. Syntactically, the main characteristic of a determiner is that it co-occurs with nouns (or noun phrases). Semantically, the main characteristic of a determiner is that it actually alters the meaning of the noun with which it co-occurs with respect to quantity, number, possession, and definiteness.

With Crystal's definition in mind, consider the difference in meaning between the two uses of *child* in the following sentences.

1.   The teacher spanked *the* child.
2.   The teacher spanked *this* child.

The sentences are identical except for the two italicized *determiners* co-occurring with the noun *child.* On the one hand, the article *the* determines the noun *child* as definite in the first sentence. On the other hand, the demonstrative *this* determines the noun *child* as near and definite in the second sentence. While in sentence number 1 the determiner *the* specifies that the *child* has been identified, in sentence number 2 the determiner *this* specifies that the identified child is near. The co-occurrence of the determiners *the* and *this* with the noun *child* effects these semantic changes with respect to definiteness and near/far reference.

Recent studies in general linguistics have raised questions concerning such conventional descriptions of *determination.* These studies have demonstrated that determiners do not mark for quantity, number, and possession (as Crystal alleges above). Rather, *determination* refers strictly to the devices used to mark noun phrases as definite. Heinz Vater's work in this area is critical. He argues that, 'determination and quantification are different functions'.[13] In other words, Vater shows the syntactic and semantic dissimilarity between words like the/this/that (i.e. *determiners*) and all/every/one (i.e. *quantifiers*).[14]

---

12.   David Crystal, *A Dictionary of Language* (Chicago: University of Chicago Press, 2nd edn, 2001), pp. 84-85.

13.   Heinz Vater, 'Determination and Quantification', in Violetta Koseska-Toszewa and Danuta Rytel-Kuc (eds.), *Semantyka a konfrontacja językowa* (Warsaw: Slawistyczny Osrodek Wydawniczy, 1996), pp. 117-30 (117).

14.   'Determination and quantification are different semantic phenomena with a different syntactic behavior' (Vater, 'Determination and Quantification', p. 120). Vater bases his remarks on examples from English, German, and Polish.

Syntactically, quantifiers such as adjectives in general can be used in strings of recursive combinations, whereas determiners cannot. In other words, determiners differ from other types of modifiers in that they cannot be combined with other determiners, though they can be combined with other kinds of modifiers. To illustrate in English, 'all the big red wooden wheels' is perfectly grammatical. The sentence contains a recursive combination of what Vater would call a determiner ('the'), a quantifier ('all'), and adjectives ('big', 'red', 'wooden'). Yet 'the that one red wagon' is not grammatical. The modifiers 'the' and 'that' cannot be combined in association with the same head noun. The definite article and the two demonstratives are the only three words that consistently follow this pattern of not being used in combination. This observation about the syntactic behavior of *the*, *this*, and *that* is one of the reasons that Vater considers these three as a separate class of words, namely, determiners: 'According to my observations, members of open classes (like nouns and adjectives, in some languages also verbs) can be combined (cf. a beautiful black wooden box), whereas members of closed classes (prepositions, determiners, etc.) cannot'.[15] The fact that the/this/that can be combined with words like all/every/one indicates that we are dealing with two different classes of words (i.e. determiners and quantifiers, respectively).[16]

Semantically, determiners only determine for definiteness, not for other elements such as quantity, number, and indefiniteness. John A. Hawkins's definition of *definiteness* has exerted some considerable influence in the way that linguists characterize definiteness. Hawkins writes, 'According to my location theory the speaker performs the following acts when using the definite article. He (a) introduces a referent (or referents) to the hearer; and (b) instructs the hearer to locate the referent in some shared set of objects…; and he (c) refers to the totality of the objects or mass within this set which satisfy the referring expression.'[17] Heinz Vater considers Hawkins's definition to be the best available[18] and summarizes it as follows:

> Marking [a noun phrase] as definite means to locate its referent(s) in a set of objects shared by the speaker and the hearer. This set of objects is located in the minds of speaker and hearer… It is obvious that marking a DP [or Noun]

15. Vater, 'Determination and Quantification', p. 120 n. 7.

16. Vater, 'Determination and Quantification', p. 120. Vater contends elsewhere that 'for syntactic as well as for semantic reasons, the traditional class of determiners must be subdivided into the two classes of determiners…and quantifiers' ('Zur Abrenzung der Determinantien und Quantoren', in *idem* (ed.), *Zur Syntax der Determinantien* [Studien zur deutschen Grammatik, 31; Tübingen: Gunter Narr Verlag, 1986], p. 30).

17. John A. Hawkins, *Definiteness and Indefiniteness: A Study in Reference and Grammaticality Prediction* (London: Croom Helm; Atlantic Highlands, NJ: Humanities Press, 1978), p. 167.

18. Vater, 'Determination and Quantification', p. 121.

as definite is not confined to the definite article but is a function of the so-called 'demonstrative' determiners as well.

Thus, it should be emphasized that determiners are markers for definiteness, but the speaker can also instruct the listener to interpret a referent as definite without using such a marker. The marking conventions are language specific.[19]

Vater offers three crucial observations. First, he affirms Hawkins's definition of definiteness. Contrary to Violetta Koseska-Toszewa who argues that determination and quantification belong on the same semantic axis,[20] Vater shows determination and quantification are distinct semantic functions.[21] Second, he identifies the words commonly used in languages to mark for definiteness: the definite article and the demonstratives. Third, he observes that such markers are not necessary for an item to be considered definite.

This recent work in general linguistics has made more specific the way in which determiners co-occur with and semantically alter their head noun. Yet, the usage of the Greek article in the New Testament does not wholly conform to this general description of determiners. To be specific, the *semantic change* of marking definiteness does not always result from the article's *co-occurrence* with nouns in the New Testament. In this sense, the article differs from the other Greek determiners. The co-occurrence of other Greek determiners *always* effects a semantic change to the nouns with which they co-occur.[22] This crucial semantic and syntactic difference will be elaborated in the following sections.

3. *Syntactic Difference between the Article and Other Greek Determiners*

In the Greek of the New Testament, determiners are defined by a syntactic element—namely, co-occurrence with nominals. Yet, we observe that the article's co-occurrence differs from the co-occurrence of other determiners. As in general linguistics, scholars of the Hellenistic Greek of the New Testament disagree as to the precise nature of that co-occurrence. Consequently,

19.   Vater, 'Determination and Quantification', p. 122.
20.   'Definiteness is defined as uniqueness, while existential and universal quantification cover the contents of indefiniteness' (Violetta Koseka-Toszewa, *The Semantic Category of Definiteness/Indefiniteness in Bulgarian and Polish* [Warsaw: Slawistyczny Osrodek Wydawniczy, 1991], p. 8).
21.   Vater ('Determination and Quantification', p. 121) shows that languages do not in fact mark for indefiniteness: 'It can be shown that determination means marking a DP for definiteness and that there are not markers for indefiniteness'.
22.   The only exception to this 'always' is when the determiner is used independently as a noun. Then, of course, it does not determine or modify anything. The same is true with the Greek article.

there is disagreement as to what kinds of words should be classed as determiners. David Alan Black offers a description that resembles Crystal's inclusive definition. Black observes that determiners are grammatical elements (1) that co-occur with nominals; (2) that agree in case, gender, and number with a head noun; (3) that can be used interchangeably with one another; and (4) that are non-recursive modifiers, that is, that cannot be used in combination.[23] The first two elements of the definition (*co-occurrence* and *grammatical agreement*) are traits that determiners have in common with adjectives and that place them in the same category of words with adjectives—that is, determiners and adjectives are both *modifiers*.[24] According to Black, the latter two elements taken together (*interchangeability* and *non-recursiveness*) are what distinguish determiners from adjectives.

To clarify what is meant by non-recursiveness, we say that there is a certain class of modifiers that cannot be used in combination with each other in order to modify the same head noun.[25] Whereas one class of modifiers can be combined repeatedly in one clause to modify one head noun (i.e. adjectives), another class of modifiers cannot (i.e. determiners). An example of the former is found in Rom. 12.2 where we find a long string of modifiers added on to a noun phrase, τὸ θέλημα τοῦ θεοῦ, τὸ ἀγαθὸν καὶ εὐάρεστον καὶ τέλειον.[26] This is normal for modifiers of this class. Yet determiners do not behave in this way. Determiners cannot be found in such recursive strings. Thus non-recursive modifiers are classified separately from adjectives because of the syntactical observation that they are never used in combination with one another.

David Alan Black sets forth a list of words that fall into this non-recursive, but interchangeable category. He observes that the following New Testament words are not found in combination with each other when modifying the same head noun, though they are interchangeable with one another: the article ὁ, ἡ, τό; the demonstratives οὗτος and ἐκεῖνος; the indefinite pronoun τις; the modifier πᾶς; and the pronoun αὐτός.[27] In his list of determiners, Robert W. Funk includes all of Black's words along with three

---

23. Black, *Linguistics*, pp. 108-09.

24. Funk, *A Beginning–Intermediate Grammar*, II, pp. 528-29. Bloomfield differs in his delineation of grammatical elements. He makes *adjective* the overarching category and divides the category between *descriptive* and *limiting* adjectives. In his scheme a *determiner* is a type of *limiting* adjective (Bloomfield, *Language*, pp. 202-203). Bloomfield's designation may work for contemporary English, but Funk's terminology is more useful for Hellenistic Greek.

25. Funk, *A Beginning–Intermediate Grammar*, II, pp. 528-29; Black, *Linguistics*, pp. 108-109.

26. David Alan Black uses this text as an example of recursiveness in *Linguistics*, pp. 108-109.

27. Black, *Linguistics*, p. 108.

additional ones, ἕκαστος, ἄλλος, and ἕτερος.[28] Black's qualification, however, 'when modifying the same head noun', is crucial. It is important because these words can occur in combination when one is the head noun. Thus in the New Testament we find the following kinds of combinations in which one determiner is the head noun:

Mt. 6.32:   πάντα γὰρ ταῦτα
Acts 24.15:   αὐτοὶ οὗτοι
Phil. 1.6:   αὐτὸ τοῦτο
Rom. 9.17:   εἰς αὐτὸ τοῦτο

In each of the above three examples, οὗτος is the head term and αὐτός is the modifier. But we never find both as modifiers of the same head noun. According to Black, this pattern distinguishes these terms as a special class of word (i.e. determiners).

David Alan Black's description of determiners, however, admits one crucial exception. The Greek article is the lone word from this class that is used in combination with other determiners, even when the determiners are governed by the same noun.[29] Consider the following examples that demonstrate this exception:

Mt. 26.44:   τὸν αὐτὸν λόγον
Lk. 2.8:   ἐν τῇ χώρᾳ τῇ αὐτῇ
Lk. 10.12:   τῇ πόλει ἐκείνῃ
Jn 9.24:   οὗτος ὁ ἄνθρωπος
Acts 20.18:   τὸν πάντα χρόνον
Rom. 8.16:   αὐτὸ τὸ πνεῦμα

Such uses of the Greek article demonstrate that the article is a special case and cannot be accounted for in Black's description except by an arbitrary exception clause. He writes, 'All of these forms—articles, demonstrative pronouns, indefinite pronouns, and so forth—come under the general heading of *determiners*, and all are included in this class because they may be used interchangeably, but cannot be used in combination (except with the article)'.[30] Black's exception clause indicates that the syntactical behavior of the article does not conform to his own definition of what a determiner is.

---

28.   Funk allows for words that do not fit Black's formal criterion, which excludes those words that are used in combination when modifying the same head noun. For this reason, Funk labels ἕκαστος, ἄλλος, and ἕτερος as determiners also (Funk, *A Beginning–Intermediate Grammar of Hellenistic Greek*, II, pp. 585-92). Because Funk does not give a consistent, formal criterion by which to distinguish determiners from other kinds of modifying adjectives, Black's analysis is better than Funk's.

29.   Black, *Linguistics*, p. 108.

30.   Black, *Linguistics*, p. 108.

A more syntactically consistent description appears in Michael Palmer's *Levels of Constituent Structure in New Testament Greek*. Palmer's definition of a determiner is superior to the more inclusive definition above in that it admits no exceptions. Palmer defines *determiners* as a

> group of words which have context-sensitive gender but do not allow an immediately preceding syntactically related article... While the sequence [Article][Article] does occur, it does not occur where the gender inflection of both articles is determined by the same noun. Similarly, οὗτος and ἐκεῖνος never occur in the corpus immediately preceded by an article whose gender is determined by the same noun which determines their own gender... While no determiner may be immediately preceded by an article governed by the same noun, some determiners may themselves immediately precede such an article.[31]

Only three Greek words fit Palmer's description of a determiner: the article ὁ, ἡ, τό and the demonstratives οὗτος and ἐκεῖνος. Palmer's definition of the situation in Hellenistic Greek comports nicely with what Heinz Vater has discovered in general linguistics—namely, that determiners have a different syntactic behavior from quantifiers. Palmer observes the significant syntactic differences between ὁ-ἡ-τό/οὗτος/ἐκεῖνος and a set of modifiers which are otherwise fairly similar, τις/πᾶς/αὐτός/ἕκαστος/ἄλλος/ἕτερος. Thus Palmer only classifies ὁ-ἡ-τό/οὗτος/ἐκεῖνος as determiners.

Yet even Palmer's definition gives an indication that the Greek article is a special case among the other two determiners. While the article is interchangeable with words like οὗτος and ἐκεῖνος, for whatever reason it is the only determiner that is found in combination with other determiners. Observe the following examples representative of the common usage in the New Testament.

Mt. 3.1:	ταῖς ἡμέραις ἐκείναις
Mt. 13.54:	ἡ σοφία αὕτη
Mt. 26.12:	τὸ μύρον τοῦτο
Mk 7.23:	πάντα ταῦτα τὰ πονηρά
Jn 9.24:	οὗτος ὁ ἄνθρωπος
Rom. 12.2:	τῷ αἰῶνι τούτῳ

The article's use in combination with other determiners is a crucial syntactic difference from other determiners. While οὗτος and ἐκεῖνος are never combined with one another in any order, the article does combine with οὗτος and ἐκεῖνος in every instance of an attributive demonstrative pronoun. Thus the article gets combined with demonstratives throughout the New Testament. In this way, the syntax of the article is distinguished from the demonstratives.

---

31. Palmer, *Levels*, pp. 37, 111 n. 25.

4. *Semantic Difference between the Article and Other Greek Determiners*

In addition to syntactic distinctions, the article also differs semantically from other determiners. While the demonstratives always mark their related noun as definite, the article does not.[32] As noted above, in the Greek of the New Testament we observe a common semantic element among determiners—namely, a change in meaning that results from co-occurrence with nominals. Generally speaking, the article and the demonstratives in Greek determine nominals as *definite*, though their presence is not required in order for nominals to be definite.

In the case of the demonstratives οὗτος and ἐκεῖνος, we cannot find a single instance in which the noun that governs the demonstrative is not both *definite* and *located*. I use the word *definite* in its most generic sense—that is, that the noun has been identified in a set of objects that are shared in the minds by the speaker and the hearer.[33] I use the word *located* to emphasize the fact that the demonstratives, in addition to signifying definiteness, have an added semantic element, 'οὗτος does, as a rule, refer to what is near or last mentioned and ἐκεῖνος to what is remote'.[34] For instance, consider οὗτος in Jn 4.15: κύριε, δός μοι τοῦτο τὸ ὕδωρ. In this case, the demonstrative οὗτος marks the 'water' as present or near in the discourse.[35] Also, consider ἐκεῖνος in Mt. 7.2: ἔπνευσαν οἱ ἄνεμοι καὶ προσέπεσαν τῇ οἰκίᾳ ἐκείνῃ, καὶ οὐκ ἔπεσεν. The 'house' is considered remote in the sense that it is distinguished from the house previously mentioned that was destroyed. The demonstrative ἐκεῖνος marks the house not as remote physically, but as remote in the discourse.[36] Whether the nearness or remoteness is literal or a feature of the discourse, the point is that the demonstratives invariably mark their head noun as both *definite* and *located* in every instance that they are used. The demonstratives always bear a semantic load.

The article differs significantly from demonstratives in this respect. The article can but does not always have semantic weight as a determiner. When the article does carry a semantic element, it marks its head noun as definite. Once again, I use the word *definite* in a generic sense—that is, that the noun

32.   My thesis is not undermined even if one does not agree with me in limiting the determiners along the lines of Vater's and Palmer's definition (i.e. to ὁ-ἡ-τό/οὗτος/ ἐκεῖνος). Even if we classify such words as τις/πᾶς/αὐτός/ἕκαστος/ἄλλος/ἕτερος as determiners, the semantic distinction from the article still stands. Whereas the article sometimes bears no semantic force, these other words always do.

33.   Vater, 'Determination and Quantification', p. 122.

34.   Robertson, p. 702.

35.   BDAG, *s.v.* οὗτος, p. 741.

36   'Pert. to an entity mentioned or understood and viewed as relatively remote in the discourse setting' (BDAG, *s.v.* ἐκεῖνος, p. 301).

has been identified in a set of objects that are shared in the minds by the speaker and the hearer. The authors of the New Testament employ the article to *identify* (and thereby definitize) objects in a number of different ways. The article is used to identify a noun as previously mentioned (*anaphoric*), as present at the moment of speaking (*deictic*), as in a class by itself (*par excellence*), as one of a kind (*monadic*), as well-known though perhaps not previously mentioned (*well-known*), etc.[37]

Yet there are many uses of the article in the New Testament in which these semantic notions are not readily apparent. Daniel Wallace explains, 'When the article is used as a grammatical function marker, it may or may not also bear a semantic force. But even when it does bear such a force, the grammatical (structural) use is usually prominent.'[38] In other words, any given use of the article can best be described as falling on a spectrum of significance. At one end of the spectrum is *syntactical value* and at the other end of the spectrum is *semantic value*. Many uses of the article comprise a combination of both syntactical and semantic considerations. However, there are many uses in which the syntactical element predominates and in which the semantic notion is completely absent.

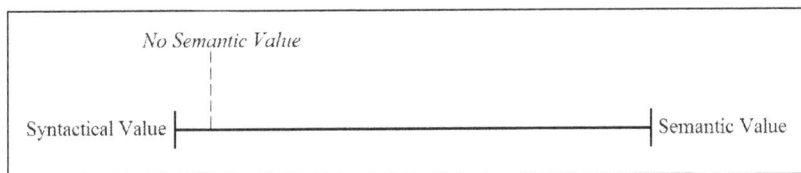

Figure 1. *The Article's Spectrum of Significance*

Robert Funk agrees that there are many uses of the article in which the article's semantic force is completely absent, thereby falling on the far left of the spectrum in Fig. 1. Funk writes that in such situations, 'the article functions more or less exclusively as a grammatical device, i.e., where it is lexically entirely empty'.[39] He elaborates, 'The article in Greek is often a purely grammatical device and should be assigned only grammatical "meaning"'.[40] As a syntactical marker at the simplest level, the article assists in

37. I do not mean for this list of the article's semantic range to be all-inclusive. Yet I do intend for it to be representative of the way in which the standard grammars approach the article. Here I have chosen Daniel Wallace's list as representative of the ways in which the grammars describe the article's semantic significance (*Greek Grammar*, pp. 216-27; cf. Funk, *A Beginning–Intermediate Grammar*, II, pp. 555-56).

38. Wallace, *Greek Grammar*, p. 238.

39. Funk, *A Beginning–Intermediate Grammar*, II, p. 557. However, Funk's use of Jn 8.37 as an example of a purely grammatical use of the article is incorrect. This text is actually an example of the article's function as a determiner.

40. Funk, *A Beginning–Intermediate Grammar*, II, p. 558.

identifying the gender, case, and number of the head noun and in identifying word groups.[41]

What uses of the article in the New Testament fall on the far left of this spectrum? Daniel Wallace devotes a section of his grammar to this very question. Wallace observes at least nine ways in which the article is employed in the New Testament to denote a purely grammatical relation with little or no semantic force.[42] This tracing of the article's use as a function word begs the question as to what are the contextual-syntactical characteristics that lead one to conclude that a given use of the article is purely grammatical. Therefore, we will investigate four such uses of the article and create a description of the syntactic features that compel the use of the article as a function word.

First, the use of the article to denote adjectival positions is a purely syntactical use of the article.[43] Any time an adjective follows an article that is syntactically related to a head noun, that adjective stands in an attributive relation to the head noun. Observe the phrases in Table 1.

Table 1. *Attributive Positions*

First Attributive Position	τὴν ἁγίαν πόλιν (Mt. 4.5)
	τοὺς κακοὺς ἐργάτας (Phil. 3.2)
Second Attributive Position	ὁ ὀφθαλμός σου ὁ δεξιός (Mt. 5.29)
	τὰ ἔργα τὰ καλά (1 Tim. 5.25)
	τῆς δωρεᾶς τῆς ἐπουρανίου (Heb. 6.4)
Third Attributive Position[44]	στολὴν τὴν πρώτην (Lk. 15.22)
	εἰρήνην τὴν ἐμήν (Jn 14.27)
	ἀσθενεστέρῳ σκεύει τῷ γυναικείῳ (1 Pet. 3.7)
Fourth Attributive Position	ἐν πνεύματι ἁγίῳ (Mk 1.8)
	ζωὴν αἰώνιον (Jn 3.16)
	ἔργον ἀγαθόν (Phil. 1.6)
	ὕδωρ ζῶν (Jn 4.10)

When an article precedes the noun, that article has the semantic effect of making that noun definite. However, when an article follows a noun, it does not definitize the noun or the following adjective. So in texts that reflect the first attributive position, the article has the dual effect of definitizing the head noun and setting the adjective in an attributive relation to that noun. In the second attributive position, the first article definitizes the head noun, while the second article appears only to mark the adjective as being in an attributive relation to the head noun. In the third attributive position, the head noun is not marked with an article as being definite, while the following

41. Funk, *A Beginning–Intermediate Grammar*, I, p. 86.
42. Wallace, *Greek Grammar*, pp. 238-43.
43. Wallace, *Greek Grammar*, p. 239.
44. 'The third attributive position—a frequent construction with participles, but not with adjectives' (Wallace, *Greek Grammar*, p. 618).

article serves only to mark the adjective as being in an attributive relation to the head noun. In the fourth attributive position, the head noun is not marked with an article as definite.[45]

We can illustrate the significance of the article in these different situations using the spectrum (see Fig. 2). Only the articles that precede the adjective and the noun in the first attributive position and the articles that precede the noun in the second attributive position carry their full semantic weight.

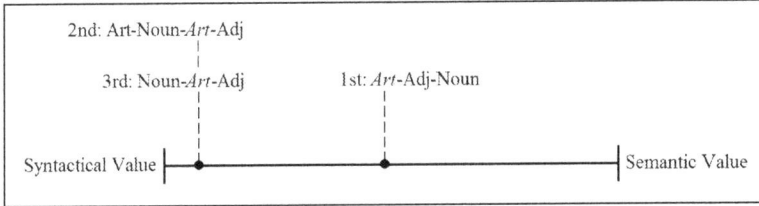

Figure 2. *The Attributive Article's Value on the Spectrum of Significance*

That the article only appears as a syntactical marker with no semantic value as a definitizing determiner in the second and third attributive positions is borne out by certain texts in which the head noun is clearly indefinite in the third attributive position. Texts that show the third attributive position fall into two categories: (1) noun–article–adjective, (2) noun–article–participle. In the first category (noun–article–adjective), the vast majority of the anarthrous nouns are proper nouns.[46] In the handful of texts[47] that employ a non-proper head noun in the third attributive position, that head noun can be construed as indefinite. Consider the following texts.

Lk. 15.22:
ταχὺ ἐξενέγκατε *στολὴν τὴν πρώτην* καὶ ἐνδύσατε αὐτόν, καὶ δότε δακτύλιον εἰς τὴν χεῖρα αὐτοῦ καὶ ὑποδήματα εἰς τοὺς πόδας

Quickly bring out a special[48] robe and put it on him, and put a ring on his hand and sandals on his feet.

Jn 14.27:
Εἰρήνην ἀφίημι ὑμῖν, *εἰρήνην τὴν ἐμὴν* δίδωμι ὑμῖν

Peace I leave with you; A peace which is from me I give to you.

45. In Greek, definite nouns are often anarthrous after prepositions (Robertson, p. 791; Moulton, *Prolegomena*, p. 82).
46. Mt. 4.13; 23.35; 26.69; Mk 14.10; 15.40; Acts 5.37; 13.14; Rom. 16.5, 8, 9, 10, 12, 13; Phlm. 1.1; 3 Jn 1.1; Rev. 14.8; 16.19; 17.5; 18.2. Some texts that match this construction are actually appositional phrases, not attributive: Acts 24.24; Eph. 6.21; Col. 1.7; 4.7; Phlm. 1.1; Rev. 18.21. I used the GRAMCORD search engine and database to locate these texts.
47. Wallace says that there are 'a couple dozen' such instances, but I only found six: Lk. 15.22; Jn 14.27; Acts 2.20; 1 Tim. 4.8; 1 Pet. 3.7; Rev. 15.1.
48. 'Special' as a rendering of πρῶτος comes from BDAG, *s.v.* πρῶτος, p. 893 (2.a).

Acts 2.20:

ὁ ἥλιος μεταστραφήσεται εἰς σκότος καὶ ἡ σελήνη εἰς αἷμα, πρὶν ἐλθεῖν ἡμέραν κυρίου *τὴν μεγάλην* καὶ *ἐπιφανῆ*

The sun shall be turned into darkness, And the moon into blood, Before the great and glorious day of the Lord shall come.

1 Tim. 4.8:

ἡ δὲ εὐσέβεια πρὸς πάντα ὠφέλιμός ἐστιν ἐπαγγελίαν ἔχουσα *ζωῆς τῆς νῦν* καὶ *τῆς μελλούσης*

But godliness is profitable for all things, because it has a promise of life in the present and in [life] to come.[49]

1 Pet. 3.7:

Οἱ ἄνδρες ὁμοίως, συνοικοῦντες κατὰ γνῶσιν ὡς ἀσθενεστέρῳ *σκεύει τῷ γυναικείῳ*, ἀπονέμοντες τιμὴν ὡς καὶ συγκληρονόμοις χάριτος ζωῆς εἰς τὸ μὴ ἐγκόπτεσθαι τὰς προσευχὰς ὑμῶν

Husbands likewise, live with [your wives] according to knowledge, as with a weaker female vessel; and grant her honor as a fellow heir of the grace of life, so that your prayers may not be hindered.

Rev. 15.1:

ἀγγέλους ἑπτὰ ἔχοντας *πληγὰς ἑπτὰ τὰς ἐσχάτας*

Seven angels who had seven plagues, [which are] last.

In all but one of these texts (Acts 2.20), the context clearly indicates that the anarthrous head noun is indefinite. In Lk. 15.22, στολήν is clearly set in parallel to the nouns δακτύλιον and ὑποδήματα, both of which are indefinite. In Jn 14.27, the two parallel anarthrous uses of εἰρήνην are most likely to be read not as definite but as qualitative.[50] In 1 Tim. 4.8, the anarthrous ζωή is also qualitative, a nuance which is typical for this term in the New Testament.[51] In 1 Pet. 3.7, the anarthrous σκεύει is parallel with the anarthrous συγκληρονόμοις, which best translates as indefinite. In Rev. 15.1, the anarthrous head noun is quantified by ἑπτὰ, not determined (and thereby definitized) by τάς.

Because the head nouns in all these texts are not definite, we can conclude that the article does not bear its normal semantic load—that is, the article does not determine any noun or adjective as definite in the third attributive

49.   The pattern here is of course Noun–Article–Adverb with the Adverb functioning adjectivally.

50.   With this use of εἰρήνη the author emphasizes the quality, nature, or essence of peace as opposed to communicating that εἰρήνη has unique referential identity (Wallace, *Greek Grammar*, pp. 244-45).

51.   Wallace, *Greek Grammar*, p. 245: 'ζωή is a typically abstract term in the New Testament'.

position. Nor does the article have any lexical meaning. The definiteness or indefiniteness of the head noun is determined by other considerations, not by the presence of the attributive article. The article carries primarily grammatical meaning and fulfills a syntactic function, thereby setting it on the far left of the spectrum above. In this case, the article sets the adjective in attributive relation to its head noun. In this sense, the article is a function word.[52] The article marks the function of the adjective with respect to its head noun.[53]

Second, the article often appears with indeclinable nouns in the New Testament without any semantic effect on the head noun. There are at least 741 instances of indeclinable nouns in the New Testament.[54] The vast majority

52. Bussmann, *Routledge Dictionary of Language and Linguistics*, pp. 175-76.

53. There are at least eleven examples of participles in the third attributive position in which the head noun is most likely not definite: Jn 5.2; Acts 7.35; 10.41; 11.21; 20.19; Rom. 2.9; Gal. 3.21; 4.27; Heb. 9.3; Jas 4.12; 1 Pet. 3.7. The vast majority of participles in the third attributive position have proper names as their head nouns: Mt. 1.16; 4.18; 10.2; 11.14; 23.16, 24, 37: 26.25; 27.3, 17, 22; 28.5; Mk 1.4; 6.14, 24; Lk. 1.19; 2.5; 6.15; 8.2; 11.51; 13.34; 22.3; 23.49; Jn 1.18; 11.2, 16; 18.2, 5, 14; 21.2; Acts 1.16, 23; 9.17; 11.13; 12.12, 25; 13.1; 15.22; 19.17; Rom. 4.17, 34; 16.22; 1 Cor. 12.6; Gal. 1.3, 4; Col 4.11; 1 Thess. 1.10; 2.4; 5.9, 10; 1 Tim. 6.13, 17; 2 Tim. 4.1; 1 Pet. 1.21; Rev. 22.8. Likewise, the vast majority of adjectives in the third attributive position have proper names as their head nouns: Mt. 4.13; 23.35; 26.69; Mk 14.10; 15.40; Acts 5.37; 13.14; Rom. 16.5, 8, 9, 10, 12, 13; Phlm. 1.1; 3 Jn 1.1; Rev. 14.8; 16.19; 17.5; 18.2. When proper nouns govern modifiers in the third attributive position, the article clearly does not make the head noun definite. Proper nouns are definite with or without the article.

54. I arrived at this number using the GRAMCORD search engine. I scrolled through all of the nouns in GRAMCORD's UBS Dictionary and selected all the nouns that were marked as indeclinable. I came up with the following list of texts, many of which references contain more than one indeclinable noun: Mt. 1.1, 2, 3, 4, 5, 6, 7, 8, 9, 10, 12, 13, 14, 15, 16, 17, 18, 19, 20, 23, 24; 2.1, 5, 6, 8, 12, 13, 16, 18, 19, 20, 21, 22, 23; 3.9; 4.13, 15; 5.18, 22; 8.10, 11; 9.27, 33; 10.6, 23, 25; 11.21; 12.3, 23, 24, 27; 13.55; 15.22, 24, 31, 39; 16.17; 19.28; 20.29, 30, 31; 21.1, 5, 9, 11, 15; 22.32, 42, 43, 45; 23.7, 8, 35; 24.15, 37, 38; 26.2, 17, 18, 19, 25, 36, 49; 27.9, 19, 33, 42, 46, 56, 57, 59, 61; 28.1; Mk 1.9; 2.25, 26; 3.17, 22; 5.41; 6.45; 7.11; 8.22; 9.5; 10.46, 47, 48, 51; 11.1, 10, 11, 21; 12.26, 29, 35, 36, 37; 14.1, 12, 14, 16, 32, 36, 45; 15.22, 32, 34, 43, 45; Lk. 1.5, 7, 13, 15, 16, 19, 24, 26, 27, 30, 32, 33, 34, 36, 38, 39, 40, 41, 46, 54, 55, 56, 57, 68, 69, 73, 80; 2.4, 5, 11, 15, 16, 19, 25, 32, 34, 36, 39, 41, 51; 3.8, 23, 24, 25, 26, 27, 28, 29, 30, 31, 32, 33, 34, 35, 36, 37, 38; 4.16, 22, 25, 27; 6.3; 7.9, 11; 9.10; 10.13, 30, 39, 42; 11.15, 18, 19, 51; 13.4, 16, 28; 16.22, 23, 24, 25, 29, 30; 17.26, 27; 18.35, 38, 39; 19.1, 9, 29; 20.37, 41, 42, 44; 22.1, 7, 8, 11, 13, 15, 30; 23.50; 24.13, 21; Jn 1.31, 38, 44, 45, 46, 47, 48, 49; 2.1, 11, 13, 23; 3.2, 10, 23, 26; 4.5, 6, 12, 31, 46; 5.2; 6.4, 25, 31, 42, 49; 7.42; 8.33, 37, 39, 40, 52, 53, 56, 57, 58; 9.2, 7, 11; 11.2, 8, 19, 20, 28, 31, 32, 45, 54, 55; 12.1, 3, 13, 15, 21; 13.1; 18.1, 28, 39; 19.13, 14, 17, 38; 20.16, 18; 21.2; Acts 1.6, 14, 16, 19, 23; 2.16, 25, 29, 34, 36; 3.13, 24, 25; 4.10, 25, 27, 36; 5.21, 31, 34; 7.2, 4, 8, 9, 10, 11, 12, 13, 14, 15, 16, 17, 18, 21, 23, 29, 30, 32, 37, 38, 40, 42, 43, 45, 46; 9.4, 15, 17, 36, 40; 10.36, 38; 12.4; 13.1, 17, 19, 20, 21, 22, 23, 24, 26, 34, 36; 15.14, 16; 18.2, 18, 26; 22.3, 7, 13; 26.14; 27.16; 28.15, 20; Rom. 1.3; 4.1, 2, 3, 6, 9, 12, 13, 16; 5.14; 8.15; 9.6, 7, 10, 13, 17,

of indeclinable nouns are proper names (e.g. ᾿Αβραάμ, ᾿Ισαάκ, ᾿Ιακώβ, Βηθλέεμ, Δαυίδ), but there are also many that are not proper (e.g. πάσχα, ῥακά, ῥαββί).[55] In the New Testament, we observe both articular and anarthrous uses of indeclinable nouns in the nominative, genitive, dative, and accusative cases. The article is not required to mark the indeclinable noun as standing in an oblique case, not even when following a preposition (unlike the infinitive after a preposition, which requires an article). For instance, in the phrase πέμψας αὐτοὺς εἰς Βηθλέεμ (Mt. 2.8) no article is required to mark Βηθλέεμ as an accusative. Nor is the article required to mark a genitive relation between an indeclinable and a head noun as in ὁ θεὸς ᾿Αβραὰμ καὶ ᾿Ισαὰκ καὶ ᾿Ιακώβ (Acts 7.32), though sometimes it does appear as in τὴν σκηνὴν τοῦ Μόλοχ (Acts 7.43).

There are at least two situations in which the article is grammatically obligatory: (1) in the dative case not following a preposition, and (2) in distinguishing the function of indeclinables appearing in the same clause or sentence with one another. With respect to the first situation, every use of an indeclinable noun in a dative relation is marked for being in the dative case. Sometimes the dative case is marked by the presence of a preposition that only takes the dative case, as in ἐν ᾿Ισαὰκ κληθήσεταί σοι σπέρμα (Rom. 9.7).[56] Sometimes the dative case is marked with an article, as in τῷ δὲ Αβραὰμ ἐρρέθησαν αἱ ἐπαγγελίαι (Gal. 3.16).[57] Sometimes the dative case is marked using both article and preposition, as in ἐν τῷ ῾Ωσηέ (Rom. 9.25).[58] What is clear is that the dative is always clearly marked. When the indeclinable noun in the dative case follows a dative preposition, the article is not required. In every other instance the dative article is syntactically obligatory.

25, 27, 29, 31, 33; 10.19, 21; 11.1, 2, 4, 7, 9, 25, 26; 15.12; 16.3; 1 Cor. 5.7; 10.18; 15.22, 45; 16.19, 22; 2 Cor. 3.7, 13; 6.15; 11.22; Gal. 3.6, 7, 8, 9, 14, 16, 18, 29; 4.6, 22, 24, 25, 28; 6.16; Eph. 2.12; Phil. 3.5; 1 Tim. 2.13, 14; 2 Tim. 2.8; 3.8; 4.19; Tit. 3.13; Heb. 2.16; 4.7; 5.4, 6, 10; 6.13, 20; 7.1, 2, 4, 5, 6, 9, 10, 11, 15, 17; 8.8, 10; 9.4, 5; 11.4, 5, 7, 8, 9, 17, 18, 20, 21, 22, 24, 28, 30, 31, 32; 12.16, 22, 24; Jas 2.21, 23, 25; 5.4, 11; 1 Pet. 2.6; 3.6, 20; 2 Pet. 1.1; 2.5, 15; 1 Jn 3.12; Jude 1.9, 11, 14; Rev. 1.8; 2.14, 17, 20; 3.7; 5.5; 7.4, 5, 6, 7, 8; 9.11; 12.7; 14.1; 16.16; 20.8; 21.6, 12; 22.13, 16.

55.   I count at least 19 non-proper indeclinable nouns, some of which are loan-words (ἀββά, βοανηργές, ἐλωΐ, ἠλί, ἰῶτα, κορβᾶν, μάννα, μαράνα θά, ὄναρ, πάσχα, ῥακά, ῥαββί, ῥαββουνί, σαβαώθ, σίκερα, ταλιθά), some of which are not (ἄλφα, δώδεκα, ὦ).

56.   Cf. Mt. 2.1, 5, 16, 18; Lk. 2.5; 11.15, 18, 19; Jn 2.1, 11; 3.23; Acts 1.14; 7.2, 4, 16; Rom. 9.7, 33; Heb. 4.7; 7.1; 11.18; 1 Pet. 2.6.

57.   Cf. Mt. 1.18; 2.19; 3.9; Mk 15.45; Lk. 1.55, 57; 3.8; Jn 1.31; 4.5; Acts 1.6; 5.31; 7.13, 17, 40; 13.23; Rom. 4.9, 13; 9.17; 11.4, 25; Gal. 3.8, 16, 18; Heb. 6.13; 1 Pet. 3.6; Rev. 2.14.

58.   Cf. Mt. 8.10; 9.33; 12.24, 27; Lk. 2.34; 4.25, 27; 7.9; 13.4; Jn 2.23; 18.39; Rom. 9.25; 1 Cor. 15.22; Gal. 3.9.

With respect to the second situation, the article is used to distinguish subject from direct object when both are indeclinable nouns. For instance, in Matthew's genealogy of Jesus, one would have great difficulty in distinguishing the subject from the direct object if the accusative article were absent. For example, in the sentence Ἀβραὰμ ἐγέννησεν τὸν Ἰσαάκ (Mt. 1.2), the accusative article marks Ἰσαάκ as the direct object of the verb ἐγέννησεν. Without the article it would be impossible to tell which noun is the subject and which is the direct object. Daniel Wallace notes that the same kind of phenomenon appears in Jn 4.5, 'πλησίον τοῦ χωρίου ὃ ἔδωκεν Ἰακὼβ τῷ Ἰωσήφ [*sic*]... Without the dat. article, it would be possible to misconstrue Ἰωσήφ as the subject of ἔδωκεν. The article serves no other purpose than clarifying the roles of Joseph and Jacob.'[59] What we see in the dative uses of the article and in certain accusative uses is that the article appears only as a function word and effects no semantic change to its head noun.

Third, the article appears in the predicate position with the demonstrative pronoun to denote an attributive relation. As Daniel Wallace describes, 'Only when [demonstrative pronouns] are in predicate position to an *articular* noun can demonstratives be considered dependent and attributive'.[60] This usage is so routine that we need not collate an exhaustive list of examples. However, it is important to note that in phrases that have demonstrative pronouns in an attributive relation to a head noun, the article is semantically superfluous because the demonstrative pronoun is a *definitizer* in its own right. The article need not appear except to mark an attributive relation. Thus the article has no semantic weight; it only has grammatical meaning.

Fourth, the article often distinguishes subject from predicate noun while effecting no demonstrable semantic difference to the head noun. For example, in Mt. 12.8 we read, κύριος γάρ ἐστιν τοῦ σαββάτου ὁ υἱὸς τοῦ ἀνθρώπου. The nominative article ὁ marks υἱός as the subject while not definitizing the christological phrase 'Son of Man'. As the following texts demonstrate, the phrase 'Son of Man' is definite with or without the article.

Jn 5.27:
καὶ ἐξουσίαν ἔδωκεν αὐτῷ κρίσιν ποιεῖν, ὅτι υἱὸς ἀνθρώπου ἐστίν.

Heb. 2.6:
διεμαρτύρατο δέ πού τις λέγων· τί ἐστιν ἄνθρωπος ὅτι μιμνήσκῃ αὐτοῦ,
ἢ υἱὸς ἀνθρώπου ὅτι ἐπισκέπτῃ αὐτόν;

59. Wallace, *Greek Grammar*, p. 241.
60. Wallace, *Greek Grammar*, p. 241 (emphasis in original). Robertson considers the phrase μιᾶς ταύτης φωνῆς (Acts 24.21) to be the only attributive usage of οὗτος with an anarthrous noun in the entire New Testament (Robertson, p. 702). Cf. Gen. 17.8; Lev. 25.10; Num. 35.7 (LXX).

Rev. 1.13:

καὶ ἐν μέσῳ τῶν λυχνιῶν ὅμοιον υἱὸν ἀνθρώπου ἐνδεδυμένον ποδήρη
καὶ περιεζωσμένον πρὸς τοῖς μαστοῖς ζώνην χρυσᾶν.

Rev. 14.14:

καὶ εἶδον, καὶ ἰδοὺ νεφέλη λευκή, καὶ ἐπὶ τὴν νεφέλην καθήμενον
ὅμοιον υἱὸν ἀνθρώπου, ἔχων ἐπὶ τῆς κεφαλῆς αὐτοῦ στέφανον χρυσοῦν
καὶ ἐν τῇ χειρὶ αὐτοῦ δρέπανον ὀξύ.

These texts demonstrate that the article is not necessary to make 'Son of
Man' definite. Therefore, the article must be employed for something other
than a semantic purpose. In Mt. 12.8 that purpose is clear. The article is
obligatory in Mt. 12.8 in order to distinguish subject from predicate nominative. Thus we can conclude that when the article is used to distinguish
subject from predicate nominative, it is not necessarily used in order to make
a semantic change to the head noun. The article distinguishes the subject
from the object or the object from the complement.

The above examples of the article's use as a function word demonstrate
how the article differs semantically from the other two determiners. The
article is frequently used with little or no semantic weight. Yet the other two
determiners always bear the semantic weight of definitizing and locating
their head noun.

5. *Conclusion and Relevance to the Articular Infinitive*

In past treatments of the articular infinitive, grammarians have explained the
article's use and non-use as a function of whether the author wishes to
determine the nominal head as in some sense definite. This approach
encounters problems, however, when it tries to explain instances in which a
nominal head appears with the article and does not appear to be *determined*
as definite. We have just explored four such situations in which the article
appears as a function word. In these kinds of situations, the grammars have a
difficult time explaining why the article appears. As David Sansone notes,
'The standard grammars sometimes give the impression that we can never
know, in some instances, why the article is used or is not used'.[61] He cites
Smyth as an example of this tendency, 'The generic article is frequently
omitted, especially with abstracts...without appreciable difference in meaning'.[62] Further, Sansone notes:

> Now, it may be the case that there is no appreciable difference in meaning
> between, say, ἡ ἐλπίς and ἐλπίς but...to say that there is no appreciable
> difference in meaning is not the same as saying that the two can be used

61.   Sansone, 'Towards a New Doctrine of the Article in Greek', p. 192.
62.   Smyth, §1126.

interchangeably. For there may be determinants other than 'meaning' that affect the use of the article, and these determinants need to be investigated more thoroughly than has been done in the past.[63]

Among the 'determinants' that Sansone proposes are both *semantic* and *syntactic* considerations.[64]

What I have shown above is that when syntactic 'determinants' require it, the article can be used with no semantic change to the head noun. The rest of this book proceeds from the assumption that when it can be demonstrated that the article is syntactically required, one should not look for any further semantic significance of the article. In these situations, the article appears as a function word with no semantic weight. In this way I am following the methodological assumption of Haiim B. Rosén in his work on the Greek article in Heraclitus:

> The recognition of grammatical features is also essential for the exegete or semanticist, that is, for one whose objective is to explain the meaning of an expression or text, since…only a total elimination of all grammatical features permits us to arrive at true semantic statements… [T]he first step of linguistic analysis aimed at defining the function of a given element of expression is to exclude all its uses in environments where it appears to be compulsory or grammatically induced.[65]

While the use of the article with nouns in general is motivated by both semantic and syntactic considerations, the use of the article with the infinitive in particular is motivated by syntactic considerations only. When all the grammatically induced uses of the article with the infinitive are taken out of consideration, no other examples remain to be considered. Thus the articular infinitive in the New Testament consistently falls on the far left of the spectrum of significance.

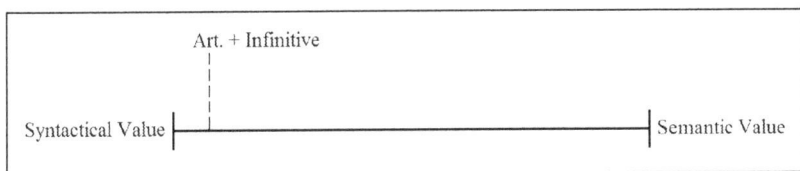

Figure 3. *The Articular Infinitive on the Spectrum of Significance*

The analysis in the following chapters will show that the article does not determine the infinitive as definite (be it *individual, generic, par excellence,*

---

63. Sansone, 'Towards a New Doctrine of the Article in Greek', p. 192.

64. Sansone ('Towards a New Doctrine of the Article in Greek', p. 205) concludes that an adequate explanation of the use and non-use of the article 'requires the application of semantic, syntactic, pragmatic, psychological, and even historical categories'.

65. Rosén, *Early Greek Grammar and Thought in Heraclitus*, pp. 30, 37.

anaphoric, etc.), thereby effecting a semantic change to the infinitive. Therefore it is unhelpful to say that the article is used with the infinitive in exactly the same way that it is used with other nouns. With other nouns, the article's significance is all over the spectrum. With the infinitive, it is only on the left side. There are a number of reasons why this is the case, and these reasons will be taken up as the following chapters unfold.

3

ARTICULAR INFINITIVES NOT FOLLOWING PREPOSITIONS IN THE NEW TESTAMENT

1. *Introduction*

In this chapter we will survey the usage of the articular infinitives of the New Testament that do not follow prepositions. So far, I have made two important observations concerning the semantic effect that the article has on the infinitive. In Chapter 1, I observed that the article does not *nominalize* the infinitive in the sense that the infinitive is somehow less of a noun without the article and more of a noun with the article. The infinitive is a noun with or without the article.[1] In Chapter 2, I argued that the article does not have the semantic effect of definitizing the infinitive but appears for syntactical reasons only. Having set forth in previous chapters what the article does not do, we can now press forward into what the article does do when it appears before the infinitive.

In order to understand the article's meaning in connection with the infinitive, we have to consider the phenomenon that linguists call *markedness*. *Markedness* is an analytical principle that linguists use, whereby pairs of linguistic features, seen as oppositions, are given values of positive (i.e. marked) or negative/neutral (i.e. unmarked). In its most generic sense, the distinction between *marked* and *unmarked* relates simply to the presence or absence of a particular characteristic.[2] In thinking about the articular infini-

---

1. 'The addition of the article made no essential change in the inf. It was already both substantive and verb' (Robertson, p. 1063). In this respect, the articular infinitive differs from the substantival participle. More often than not, the participle needs the article if it is to be considered a noun, even though it is inflected for gender, case, and number. Such is not the case with the infinitive, which is not inflected for gender, case, and number.

2. Crystal, *A Dictionary of Language*, p. 212. Cf. Bussmann, *Routledge Dictionary of Language and Linguistics*, p. 294: 'The concept of markedness is concerned with the distinction between what is neutral, natural, or expected (= unmarked) and what departs from the neutral (= marked) along some specified parameter. It was introduced in linguistics by the Prague School (L. Trubetzkoy, R. Jakobson) for evaluating the members of an oppositional pair as 'marked' (having some kind of feature) or "unmarked" (having no features)'.

tive, this distinction becomes very important since we are trying to discover why an author would select to use an articular infinitive over and against the anarthrous infinitive. In the New Testament's 2289 uses of the infinitive, 1965 are anarthrous, and only 324 are articular. Clearly the normal *unmarked* state is the anarthrous infinitive, as it far outnumbers the infinitive *marked* with the article.[3] We have already seen in Chapter 2 that the article is not *marking* the semantic notion of definiteness. So now we have to investigate what significance the article does contribute to the marked construction, even though that significance may not be easily rendered in English translation. In this chapter I will show that the article *marks* two grammatical features: (1) it marks the case[4] of the infinitive and/or (2) it marks a syntactical function that can best be made explicit by the presence of the article.

Before turning to specific New Testament texts, I need to set forth three assumptions underlying my approach to the issue of *case* in Greek. First, I must properly distinguish my task in this study of Greek cases from that of proponents of *case theory* or *case grammar*. Ever since Charles J. Fillmore's important essay 'The Case for Case', Chomskian linguists have more or less adopted an approach to case that assumes a 'difference between deep and surface structure'.[5] For Fillmore and his successors, the grammatical category known as *case* does not refer to the inflectional variation in a noun

---

3. This observation holds not only for the New Testament, but also for Greek litera-ture in general. From a diachronic perspective, one can see that the articular infinitive was in fact extremely rare in Homeric Greek, the dramatists, and Herodotus (eighth–fifth centuries BCE). Only with Thucydides and after does the articular infinitive begin to be used more widely (see Table 15 in the Appendix).

4. We know that the case of a given noun is typically made explicit by inflection. At other times, nouns are not inflected for case and their syntactical function in the sentence must be deduced from the context. For example, there are numerous examples of inde-clinable foreign loan-words that are not inflected for case yet are clearly employed as if they were. In Mt. 1.1, for example, 'Abraham' and 'David' are indeclinable but they are clearly employed as if they were marked as a genitives: Βίβλος γενέσεως ʼΙησοῦ Χριστοῦ υἱοῦ Δαυὶδ υἱοῦ ʼΑβραάμ. Such is the case with numerous anarthrous infi-nitives. To give an example of what is a routine usage in the New Testament, we can observe Mt. 1.20: μὴ φοβηθῇς παραλαβεῖν Μαρίαν τὴν γυναῖκά σου ('Do not fear to take Mary as your wife'). Clearly παραλαβεῖν is the direct object of φοβηθῇς, even though the infinitive is not marked as accusative (this is just one example from a long list compiled by Votaw, *The Infinitive in Biblical Greek*, pp. 31-40). There are many such examples throughout the New Testament in which the case is not explicit yet the function of the indeclinable substantive can be deduced from context. We can observe many situations in which it is grammatically necessary for the case of the indeclinable infinitive to be made explicit. In this chapter we will explore why it is necessary for the case function of the infinitive to be made explicit in certain contexts.

5. Charles J. Fillmore, 'The Case for Case', in Emmon Bach and Robert T. Harms (eds.), *Universals in Linguistic Theory* (New York: Holt, Rinehart & Winston, 1968), pp. 1-88 (21).

(i.e. surface structure), but to an 'underlying syntactic-semantic relationship' (i.e. deep structure) that is quite distinct from morphological form.[6] Fillmore's work has spawned a whole generation of linguistic scholarship based on a distinction between form and function in its approach to case.[7] Simon Wong, for instance, has sought to bring the observations of Fillmore to bear upon the Greek cases of the New Testament.[8] Wong's description of his task follows Fillmore rather closely: 'While most traditional grammars always refer "case" to the morphological case forms of the surface structure, in Case Theory it refers to the underlying semantic roles, independent of their surface form'.[9] Wong, therefore, distinguishes 'syntactic case' (a formal category that is based upon inflectional variation) and 'semantic case' (a semantic category that is based upon a finite set of possible relations of noun to verb).

Case Grammar has by no means become the uniform approach to case among linguists in general or among New Testament Greek scholars in particular. Probably the most significant difficulty with case grammar has been the inability of case grammarians to come up with an agreed upon set of 'innate' case roles. According to case theory, there is indeed a finite set of case roles that appear across different languages, but no consensus has been reached as to how many case roles there are and how they should be defined. To this effect, Barry Blake assesses the case grammar of Fillmore:

> To establish a universal set of semantic roles is a formidable task. Although some roles are demarcated by case or by adpositions in some languages, in many instances they have to be isolated by semantic tests. *There are no*

6. Fillmore, 'The Case for Case', p. 21. Before Fillmore, linguists assumed that a division between subject and predicate comprised the deep structure of all sentences in all languages (p. 17). Fillmore denied that the underlying structure of all sentences is subject-predicate. Instead, he argued that 'the sentence in its basic structure consists of a verb and one or more noun phrases, each associated with the verb in a particular case relationship' (p. 21).

7. Ironically, this a debate that has already taken place among scholars of New Testament Greek, albeit within the framework of a whole other set of linguistic assumptions. At the heart of Robertson's eight-case system is the assumption that case should be defined as a matter of function, not morphological form. Not having been convinced by Robertson's arguments in favor of defining case in terms of grammatical function, the majority of New Testament scholars today adopt a five-case system. It is not surprising, therefore, that this Chomskian reincarnation of an old issue has not really caught on among scholars of the New Testament.

Simon Wong, though advocating a functional approach to case, acknowledges that there are only five inflectional cases in Koine and Hellenistic Greek: 'What Case is This Case? An Application of Semantic Case in Biblical Exegesis', *Jian Dao* 1 (1994), pp. 49-73 (59).

8. Wong, 'What Case is This Case?', pp. 49-73.

9. Simon Wong, *Classification of Semantic Case-Relations in the Pauline Epistles* (ed. D.A. Carson; SBG, 9; New York: Peter Lang, 1997), p. xvii.

> *agreed criteria and there is certainly no consensus on the universal inven-tory...* There tends to be agreement on salient manifestations of roles like agent, patient, source and instrument, but problems arise with the classifica-tion of relationships that fall between the salient ones.[10]

It is for this same reason that Bernard Comrie rejects 'Case Grammar and its latest off-shoots', because 'any endeavour that depends on establishing a prior definitive inventory of case functions is likely to have to wait a long time—certainly indefinitely, perhaps everlastingly—for its inception'.[11] This critique is at the heart of Stanley Porter's refutation of Fillmore's and Wong's work. Porter's cleverly titled essay, 'The Case for Case Revisited',[12] observes that it is always possible to posit more case roles, depending on how fine a semantic distinction one wants to make.[13] In fact, Wong increases Fillmore's original eight semantic cases to fifteen. Porter contends for a more traditional approach, 'one that makes a useful linkage between form and function'.[14]

When I refer to *case* in the present study, I am not referring to underlying semantic roles that employ various surface structures. In fact, I use the term *case* in the traditional sense to refer to the morphological forms that are employed to denote various semantic roles. While case grammar may be profitably utilized as a tool for lexicography[15] or perhaps in translating the Bible,[16] it is not as useful when one begins with a given morphological form (in this study case inflection) and tries to describe how that form encodes

10.   Barry J. Blake, *Case* (ed. J. Bresnan *et al.*; Cambridge Textbooks in Linguistics; Cambridge: Cambridge University Press, 1994), pp. 67-68 (my emphasis).

11.   Bernard Comrie, 'Form and Function in Identifying Cases', in Frans Plank (ed.), *Paradigms: The Economy of Inflection* (Empirical Approaches to Language Typology, 9; New York: Mouton de Gruyter, 1991), pp. 41-55 (45).

12.   An obvious throw-back to Fillmore's initial work: Stanley E. Porter, 'The Case for Case Revisited', *Jian Dao* 6 (1996), pp. 13-28.

13.   Porter, 'The Case for Case Revisited', p. 19.

14.   Porter, 'The Case for Case Revisited', p. 13.

15.   This is in fact the stated goal of Wong's recent application of Case Theory to the New Testament: 'To stimulate the ongoing research of New Testament lexicography, so as to include another kind of lexical information in a dictionary entry of a verb' (*Classi-fication of Semantic Case-Relations*, p. 2).

16.   Consider the following problem that a translator might face. Suppose a translator has the task of rendering a Greek sentence that uses the passive voice into a language that does not even have a passive voice. In this instance, a translator might use semantic case notions as the basis of his translation. He can identify the *agent/instrument* and the *event* in the passive-voice Greek sentence and construct an appropriate active voice sentence into the receptor language. Though this process may be useful in translation, I would argue that it is not as useful when one is trying to describe the characteristics of a single language (my colleague at the Criswell College, LeRoy Metts, stimulated my thinking on this use of case grammar).

various semantic and syntactic meanings in a given language (which is the approach of the present study). This leads me to my second assumption concerning case.

Second, in order to give a proper description of the Greek cases, I would like to introduce some terminology that distinguishes the Greek nominative and accusative cases from the Greek genitive and dative cases. There is an older use of the terms *semantic case* and *grammatical case* that has nothing to do with the terms' meaning in case grammar. Yet even this older use of the term has been variable in the literature. Sometimes the distinction is labeled as *semantic* vs. *syntactic case, semantic* vs. *grammatical* case,[17] or *concrete* vs. *grammatical* case.[18] In any event, the distinction being drawn is the same. The distinction is between inflectional morphemes that encode primarily syntactic functions (thus being called *syntactic* or *grammatical* case) and inflectional morphemes that encode both syntactic and semantic data (thus being called *semantic* or *concrete* case). Consider the use of the terms in the *Routledge Dictionary of Language and Linguistics*:

> The syntactic cases such as nominative and accusative encode primary syntactic functions such as subject and object and do not have any specific semantic function. On the other hand, [semantic] cases like ablative, instrumental, and locative generally represent adverbials which have a more specific semantic content.[19]

In the above entry from the *Routledge Dictionary*, the definition of *semantic* and *syntactic* cases has nothing to do with the definitions associated with those terms in case grammar. Rather, the syntactic cases primarily denote grammatical structure while semantic cases encode grammatical structure and a semantic element as well. References to this older use of the terminology appear elsewhere in the literature on case, even among those who are well-acquainted with case grammar.[20]

---

17. Blake, *Case*, pp. 32-34.

18. Jerzy Kuryłowicz, *The Inflectional Categories of Indo-European* (Indogermanische Bibliothek; Heidelberg: Carl Winter, 1964), p. 179.

19. Bussmann, *Routledge Dictionary of Language and Linguistics*, p. 63.

20. For instance, though Blake is well-aware of case grammar and the innovations of the Fillmore school (*Case*, pp. 67-75), he nevertheless utilizes the older terminology when he discusses the various problems that have been associated with describing case systems (pp. 32-33). For Blake, the terms *grammatical case* and *semantic case* are merely ways of describing the meanings associated with inflectional variation (pp. 32-33). Likewise, Kuryłowicz writes, 'The traditional distinction between the "grammatical" and the "concrete" cases is based…on the difference between *syntactical* and *semantic* functions. Putting aside the voc. and the nom., all case-forms share both kinds of functions, but the syntactical function is *primary* with "grammatical" and *secondary* with "concrete" case, semantic function being, on the contrary, primary with "concrete" and secondary with "grammatical" cases… The "grammatical" cases are represented by the nom. acc.

I would like to use the terms *semantic case* and *grammatical case* in this older sense as a way of grouping the morphological cases. Yet, I fear that the overlap with case grammar might cause confusion, and I want to be careful to distinguish my task from that of the case grammarians. So, in the present study, I will use the terms *content cases* and *syntactic cases*. The *syntactic cases* (nominative and accusative) are those morphological cases that encode primarily syntactical function. The *content cases* (genitive and dative) are those morphological cases that encode both syntactic and semantic data.[21] Thus, as I shall be following J.P. Louw's approach to Greek case, we shall see that observing the 'ground meaning' of a *content* case is much more significant than trying to observe the same for a *syntactic* case.

Third, I need to outline a coherent methodology for studying the cases. Grammarians disagree about the proper method for studying cases. Structural linguists contend that a case has one fundamental meaning while those schooled in the comparative-historical method shun the idea of a primary meaning for a given case. Karl Brugmann, for instance, rejects the possibility of our ascertaining a 'fundamental meaning' of the Greek case-forms (*Grundbedeutung der Kasusformen*), preferring rather to describe the 'original meaning' (*Gebrauchsumfang*).[22] In keeping with his historical approach, he sought to explain the cases by appealing to the oldest meaning. In this way, Brugmann employs diachronic material to account for synchronic facts with the result that he was able to group together usages of a case while not giving an explanation of the cases' meanings.[23]

gen., the "concrete" ones by the instr. abl. loc., whereas the position of the dat. stays uncertain' (Kuryłowicz, *The Inflectional Categories of Indo-European*, p. 179). Blake's and Kuryłowicz's use of the terms are consistent with that of the *Routledge Dictionary*.

21.   I do not intend to enter into the debate about whether or not the adnominal genitive and pure dative are best understood as belonging to the *syntactic* cases (e.g. Kuryłowicz, *The Inflectional Categories of Indo-European*, p. 179; Blake, *Case*, pp. 32-33.). For the purposes of this study, I will proceed from a position that commands widespread agreement among linguists. The nominative and accusative are *syntactic* cases while the dative and genitive are *content* (or *semantic/concrete*) cases.

22.   'Daher ist auch die wirkliche Grundbedeutung der Kasusformen unbekannt… Was man gewöhnlich die Grundbedeutung oder den Grundbegriff der Kasus nennt, ist der Gebrauchsumfang, den sie in derjenigen Zeit der idg' (Karl Brugmann, *Griechische Grammatik (Lautlehre, Stammbildungs- und Flexionslehre und Syntax)* (Handbuch der klassischen Altertums-Wissenschaft; Munich: C.H. Beck, 1900), p. 374. He is followed by Eduard Schwyzer and Albert Debrunner, *Griechische Grammatik auf der Grundlage von Karl Brugmanns Griechische Grammatik. II. Syntax und syntaktische Stilistik* (Handbuch der Altertumswissenschaft; Munich: C.H. Beck, 1950), p. 56: 'Statt von Grundbegriffen der indogermanischen Kasus spricht man besser von gemeinsamem Gebrauchsumfang'.

23.   J.P. Louw, 'Linguistic Theory and the Greek Case System', *Acta Classica* 9 (1966), pp. 73-88 (74).

In contrast, the approach of structuralist linguistics has been to regard each case as having 'one fundamental meaning which may be actualized in different ways'.[24] As J.P. Louw shows, 'The structural method understands by "fundamental meaning" the essential semantic function of a case which is not the source of its various contextual usages, but which comprises its connotation, its potentiality'.[25] The structuralist method is not so much interested in the historical question of ascertaining the original meaning of a case (à la Brugmann, Schwyzer), but is concerned to identify the fundamental meaning which gives rise to the various actualizations of a case in various stages of a language's history.[26] In my explanation of the articular infinitives of the New Testament, I will assume a structuralist approach as it is unfolded in J.P. Louw's important article, 'Linguistic Theory and the Greek Case System'. That is, I will explain the usage of the articular infinitive by describing the fundamental meaning of each case and how those meanings are actualized in various New Testament contexts. Therefore, the following sections are divided by case,[27] and each section is introduced by an explanation of the

24. Louw, 'Linguistic Theory', p. 75.

25. Louw, 'Linguistic Theory', pp. 75-76. Louw's definition of the 'fundamental meaning' of a case resembles what Daniel Wallace calls the 'unaffected meaning' or the 'ontological meaning' of a grammatical unit: 'By "unaffected" [or ontological] is meant the meaning of the construction in a vacuum-apart from contextual, lexical, or other grammatical intrusions' (Wallace, *Greek Grammar*, p. 2). Thus, Wallace begins his discussion of the nominative and genitive cases with a description of the 'unaffected' meaning of those cases (pp. 37, 76).

Wallace gives no explanation as to why the other three cases are not given similar consideration. He gives an introduction to each but does not include a heading on the 'unaffected' meaning. Perhaps the omission reflects his otherwise eclectic approach to language study. Wallace's grammatical method draws mainly from the insights of more traditional grammar, and occasionally from the contributions of modern structuralist approaches. Wallace does not employ Chomskian advances in his grammar, though he is certainly aware of it. Stanley Porter notes, 'Wallace almost shuns advances in modern linguistics' (Stanley E. Porter, 'The Basic Tools of Exegesis: A Bibliographical Essay', in *idem* [ed.], *Handbook to the Exegesis of the New Testament* [New Testament Tools and Studies; Leiden: E.J. Brill, 1997], pp. 23-41 [30]).

26. 'This method by no means discards or replaces the comparative-historical method (almost traditional among Classicists), but actually encompasses it, defining the essence of a case in terms of a principle or a conception within the range of which the various usages (being contextual applications thereof, or rather *allowing* various contextual applications) can be explained, either in their synchronic occurrence, or in their historical development, or in their fusion with the usages of other cases. This "essence of a case" in not *a* meaning of the case, but its *semantic function in the sentence*' (Louw, 'Linguistic Theory and the Greek Case System', p. 76 [emphasis in original]).

27. I have already defined *case* as the inflectional variation in a noun. As such, *case* is a matter of form rather than function. It therefore may seem inconsistent to divide the neuter nominative and accusative articular infinitives in my presentation since both are

semantics of that case. Another important feature of Louw's approach is that he assumes a close association between case-functions and case-forms. Thus, the present study, along with that of Louw, will not be building upon the work of the case grammarians.

2. *Nominative Articular Infinitives*

a. *Semantics of the Nominative Case*

There is wide agreement among linguists that the nominative case is a *syntactic* case functioning primarily to encode the grammatical subject and the mere nominal idea.[28] In most languages, the nominative is not marked morphologically and consists of the bare stem. In such languages, the nominative owes its status as a case to the existence of marked cases (hence, *nominative* vs. *oblique* cases).[29] Greek and other Indo-European languages are atypical in having a marked nominative in most paradigms.[30] Having no apparent semantic force connecting it to the rest of the sentence (as the dative 'to, for', or the genitive 'of'), Barry J. Blake describes the nominative 'as the case used outside syntax, the case used in naming, the case used in talking about a lexeme'.[31] The 'ground meaning' of the nominative is there-fore not semantic, but syntactic. It is for this reason that the ancient gram-marians called this case the πτῶσις ὀνομαστική or the 'naming case'.[32] J.P. Louw notes that the Greek nominative 'fully corresponds' to such definitions, 'Not only is the frequently contextual function of the nominative as subject explicable, but also the "absolute" uses'.[33]

Porter gives perhaps the best definition of the significance of the nomi-native case. He draws together the various descriptions that have been given into a coherent explanation, and is worth quoting at length:

---

identical in form. However, I would argue with Bernard Comrie that it is proper to distinguish *distributional* cases. The accusative and nominative do represent distinct *distributional* cases. In other words, even though the nominative article is not formally distinguished from the accusative article in the neuter, it is distinguished in the masculine and feminine, thereby signaling a *distributional* case (Comrie, 'Form and Function in Identifying Cases', p. 45).

28. Louw, 'Linguistic Theory and the Greek Case System', p. 79: 'The mere nominal idea is stated by the nominative without relation to the sentence'.

29. Blake, *Case*, p. 31.

30. Blake, *Case*, p. 31.

31. Blake, *Case*, p. 32. Blake goes on to give a short definition of the nominative: 'The nominative is the case used in isolation and is usually morphologically unmarked. It is the case in which the subject is normally encoded' (p. 32).

32. Robertson, p. 456.

33. Louw, 'Linguistic Theory and the Greek Case System', p. 78.

Grammarians have debated the essential semantics of the nominative case, suggesting it variously as the case of the subject (a syntactical category of restricted applicability), as the naming case (a functional category, again somewhat restricted in use), or as the 'unmarked' or purely nominal case, in other words, as the case that simply designates. This is similar to seeing the nominative case as the naming case, but without the implication of specificity. *The semantic designation of the nominative case as purely nominal circum-scribes the fundamental meaning which allows the various syntactical and contextual configurations in which it is used.* These include its frequent use as subject or as an independent clause, as well as other independent uses.[34]

Porter's definition corroborates my observation that the nominative is a *syntactic* case. It merely names the nominal idea without necessarily specifying a relation to the rest of the sentence. However, when a predicate is present, the nominative will encode the grammatical subject.

Table 2. *Nominative Articular Infinitives Not Governed by a Preposition*

	Nominative τό	*Totals*
Matthew	15.20; 20.23	2
Mark	9.10; 10.40; 12.33 (×2)	4
Romans	4.13; 7.18 (×2); 14.21 (×2)	5
1 Corinthians	7.26; 11.6 (×2)	3
2 Corinthians	7.11; 8.11; 9.1	3
Philippians	1.21 (×2), 22, 24, 29 (×2)	6
Hebrews	10.31	1
Totals	24	24

b. *Discussion of Texts*
In all the instances of the nominative articular infinitive, the article functions to mark the infinitive as the subject of the sentence in which it stands.[35] This usage is in keeping with the *non-defining* character of this syntactical case. There are at least 304 instances in the New Testament in which infinitives function as the syntactical subjects of the sentences in which they stand. In the vast majority of these examples (280 to be exact), the infinitive is anarthrous.[36] Only 24 examples of the infinitive as subject are articular.[37]

---

34. Porter, *Idioms*, pp. 83-84 (emphasis in original).

35. The only exception to this usage among the nominative articular infinitives is Rom. 4.13: Οὐ γὰρ διὰ νόμου ἡ ἐπαγγελία τῷ ᾿Αβραὰμ ἢ τῷ σπέρματι αὐτοῦ, τὸ κληρονόμον αὐτὸν εἶναι κόσμου, ἀλλὰ διὰ δικαιοσύνης πίστεως. In this text, the articular infinitive is not itself the subject but is in apposition to the subject (Votaw, *The Infinitive in Biblical Greek*, p. 35). The article marks it clearly as such.

36. See Table 18 in the Appendix for a complete listing of the texts. Votaw incorrectly includes Acts 23.30; 2 Cor. 9.5; Phil. 2.25; 2 Pet. 1.13; and Rev. 13.10 in his list of anarthrous subject infinitives (Votaw, *The Infinitive in Biblical Greek*, pp. 31-40).

37. See Table 19 in the Appendix for a complete listing of the texts.

These statistics show that the article is not obligatory in order for an infinitive to be understood as the syntactical subject. Most of the time, one can deduce that the anarthrous infinitive is the subject without the article marking it as nominative.[38] But there are several situations in which the article becomes important as a structural marker.

First, the article can be necessary in order to distinguish the subject from the predicate nominative. This is certainly the case with the two articular infinitives in Phil. 1.21, Ἐμοὶ γὰρ τὸ ζῆν Χριστὸς καὶ τὸ ἀποθανεῖν κέρδος. If the neuter articles were absent in this text, it would not be at all clear how the infinitives function in this context. If we were to utilize the normal rules for distinguishing subject from predicate nominative, then Χριστός would certainly be considered the subject in the absence of the neuter article. One might allege that ζωῆς and θανάτου (Phil. 1.20) immediately present themselves as plausible antecedents of the articles preceding the infinitives (τὸ ζῆν... τὸ ἀποθανεῖν). But to understand these articles as definite (and thereby anaphoric) would be a mistake because an anaphoric article would be semantically superfluous in this text. The author does not need an anaphoric article to clarify his continued exposition of his 'living' and 'dying'. Paul feels no compulsion to use the anaphoric article with the infinitive in similar contexts (cf. Paul's judging in 1 Cor. 5.3, 12). For this reason, the grammatical explanation of the article as a function word seems most satisfactory. The article helps to distinguish the subject from the predicate nominative without marking the infinitive as definite (and thereby anaphoric). The neuter article appears for the same reason in Mk 9.10, τί ἐστιν τὸ ἐκ νεκρῶν ἀναστῆναι. In this text, the article also functions to enclose the prepositional phrase within the infinitive phrase.

Second, the article often keeps the subject-infinitive from being confused with an infinitive that modifies a predicate adjective. In Mt. 20.23 (par. Mk 10.40), for instance, we read, τὸ δὲ καθίσαι ἐκ δεξιῶν μου καὶ ἐξ εὐωνύμων οὐκ ἔστιν ἐμὸν [τοῦτο] δοῦναι.[39] In this instance, if the article were absent, it would be difficult to decipher which infinitive is the subject and which is epexegetical to ἐμόν. There are contexts in which the anarthrous infinitive is epexegetical to a predicate adjective (Mt. 9.5 [×2]; Mk 2.9 [×2]; Lk. 5.23 [×2]). The existence of such texts introduces the possibility for confusion when the infinitive is not supposed to be construed in connection

---

38. This fact is most clearly seen in the 154 instances in which the infinitive is the subject of an impersonal verb such as δεῖ or ἔξεστιν. In each instance, the infinitive is anarthrous.

39. The editors of NA[27] admit that τοῦτο has a comparatively weak textual basis and only give it a 'C' rating (Bruce M. Metzger, *A Textual Commentary on the Greek New Testament* [Stuttgart: Deutsche Bibelgesellschaft/German Bible Society, 2nd edn, 1994], p. 42). I agree with the text of Westcott–Hort, which leaves it out.

with the predicate adjective. The neuter article removes the potential syntactic ambiguity by showing καθίσαι to be the subject and δοῦναι to be modifying the adjective ἐμόν. This explanation accounts for the article's appearance in at least six other texts:

Rom. 14.21:
καλὸν τὸ μὴ φαγεῖν κρέα μηδὲ πιεῖν οἶνον μηδὲ ἐν ᾧ ὁ ἀδελφός σου προσκόπτει

1 Cor. 7.26:
Νομίζω οὖν τοῦτο καλὸν ὑπάρχειν διὰ τὴν ἐνεστῶσαν ἀνάγκην, ὅτι καλὸν ἀνθρώπῳ τὸ οὕτως εἶναι

1 Cor. 11.6:
εἰ γὰρ οὐ κατακαλύπτεται γυνή, καὶ κειράσθω· εἰ δὲ αἰσχρὸν γυναικὶ τὸ κείρασθαι ἢ ξυρᾶσθαι, κατακαλυπτέσθω

2 Cor. 9.1:
Περὶ μὲν γὰρ τῆς διακονίας τῆς εἰς τοὺς ἁγίους περισσόν μοί ἐστιν τὸ γράφειν ὑμῖν

Phil. 1.24:
τὸ δὲ ἐπιμένειν [ἐν] τῇ σαρκὶ ἀναγκαιότερον δι' ὑμᾶς

Heb. 10.31:
φοβερὸν τὸ ἐμπεσεῖν εἰς χεῖρας θεοῦ ζῶντος

In all of these texts (some with a verb and some verbless), the neuter article marks the infinitive(s) as the syntactical subject. In Rom. 14.21, the article also functions to substantivize the third element in the threefold compound subject. In 1 Cor. 7.26, the neuter article distinguishes the function of εἶναι from the preceding infinitive ὑπάρχειν by clarifying εἶναι as the subject of the second clause. In Heb. 10.31, the neuter article is necessary to mark ἐμπεσεῖν as subject of a new independent clause. Without the article, φοβερόν could be misinterpreted as the complement of the object τὸν λαόν of the verb κρίνω (see the preceding verse, 10.30).[40] Also, without the article, the infinitive might be mistaken as *complementary* with κρίνω, 'The Lord has *decided* that his people should fall into the hands of the Living God'.[41]

Third, the article functions to clarify the infinitive as subject so that it will not be mistaken as standing in an adverbial relation to the main verb. The pair of infinitives in Rom. 7.18 have articles that perform this duty, τὸ γὰρ θέλειν παράκειταί μοι, τὸ δὲ κατεργάζεσθαι τὸ καλὸν οὔ. In this text,

40. Cf. Acts 13.46; 16.15; 26.8; Rom. 2.27 for κρίνω with the object-complement construction.
41. κρίνω often takes a *complementary* infinitive, thus giving it the sense of 'decide'; cf. Acts 3.13; 20.16; 21.25; 25.25; 27.1; 1 Cor. 2.2; 7.37; Tit. 3.12.

the article is necessary to mark the infinitive as subject because παράκειμαι can be followed by the anarthrous infinitive with an *ecbatic* sense (cf. Jdt. 3.2, 3; perhaps 2 Macc. 12.16; *3 Macc.* 7.3). The article removes the ambiguity. If Paul had not used the article in this text to clarify the infinitive as the subject, then it would have been syntactically possible to translate the infinitives adverbially, 'It is present in order to desire for me, but not in order to do the good'. Such an understanding is perhaps unlikely, but the presence of the definite articles removes any potential confusion about how these infinitives are functioning in this sentence. In Phil. 1.29, we find a similar example of this usage, ὑμῖν ἐχαρίσθη τὸ ὑπὲρ Χριστοῦ, οὐ μόνον τὸ εἰς αὐτὸν πιστεύειν ἀλλὰ καὶ τὸ ὑπὲρ αὐτοῦ πάσχειν. In this instance, the neuter article is necessary to set the infinitive in apposition to the grammatical subject, τὸ ὑπὲρ Χριστοῦ. In 2 Cor. 8.11, the article is necessary to mark ἐπιτελέσαι as subject of a new clause so that it would not be misinterpreted as in an attributive relation to the genitive article governing the previous infinitive, νυνὶ δὲ καὶ τὸ ποιῆσαι ἐπιτελέσατε, ὅπως καθάπερ ἡ προθυμία τοῦ θέλειν, οὕτως καὶ τὸ ἐπιτελέσαι ἐκ τοῦ ἔχειν. In all of these texts, the definite articles provide the structural clues we need to identify the infinitive as subject. The article appears for syntactical reasons associated with the nominative case, not to mark the infinitives as definite.

3. *Genitive Articular Infinitives*

a. *Semantics of the Genitive Case*
The name *genitive* comes from the Latin *casus genitivus*, meaning 'the case of origin', a mistaken translation of the Greek γενικὴ πτῶσις, 'case denoting the class'.[42] The pure genitive most commonly limits the meaning of substantives, adjectives, and adverbs by denoting the class to which a person or thing belongs.[43] Yet, the genitive case is what Smyth calls a 'composite' or 'mixed' case in that it encompasses both ablative and pure genitive functions.[44] The ablative and genitive functions were morphologically distinguished in earlier Indo-European languages, but not in Greek.[45] In the

42. Smyth, §1289.a.
43   Smyth, §1289.a.
44. Smyth, §1289.a., §1279; Funk, *A Beginning–Intermediate Grammar*, I, p. 71. I have already defined *case* in Chapter 1 according to form not function. *Case* refers to the inflectional variation (in declinable words) that encompasses various syntactical functions or relationships to other words.
45. Robertson, pp. 491-92; Smyth, §1279; Funk, *A Beginning–Intermediate Grammar*, I, p. 71 n. 1; Wallace, *Greek Grammar*, pp. 33-34; Moulton, *Prolegomena*, pp. 60-61; cf. Moule, *Idiom Book*, p. 30: 'Certain common N.T. words ending in -θεν and denoting *origin* are, although classed as adverbs, recognized…as "quasi-ablative"'.

Classical, Hellenistic, and Koine Greek dialects, the syntactical functions of the ablative were taken over by one form.

As a content case, this one genitive form encodes two main semantic notions—that of *restriction* (pure genitive) and of *separation* (ablative).[46] With reference to the former, the primary function of the pure genitive is to mark an attribute of a noun.[47] As such, it primarily functions like an adjective. Moule writes, 'The chief thing to remember is that the Genitive often practically does the duty of an adjective, distinguishing two otherwise similar things'.[48] It is for this reason that Wallace calls this use of the genitive the 'Adjectival Genitive', saying that 'this broad category really touches the heart of the genitive'.[49] The standard grammars describe many nuances of the pure genitive (e.g. possessive, partitive, attributive, etc.), but it is best to see these nuances as contextual applications of the primary meaning of the genitive case. As Louw writes, 'The notion of restriction can be applied with reference to the object *itself* (partitive) or to its *adjunct* (pertaining to)… Therefore: on the semantic level we can define the genitive as connoting restriction, but this connotation has two planes of application on the contextual level.'[50] Thus the idea of restriction is closely akin to the *partitive* genitive.

With reference to the latter, the primary function of the ablative genitive is to encode various types of adverbial relations.[51] In Greek, the ablative genitive denotes the adverbial notion of *separation*.[52] The ablative genitive is rarely used with nouns,[53] and most often used in connection with prepositions, verbs, and adjectives.[54] In the Hellenistic Greek of the New Testament, the ablative genitive is being replaced by ἐκ and ἀπό with the genitive.[55]

We can summarize the significance of the genitive case as follows. Semantically, the genitive case denotes either *restriction* or *separation*. Syntactically, the genitive case encodes either an adjunct of a noun or an

---

46. This is the terminology of Louw, 'Linguistic Theory and the Greek Case System', p. 84, which is used by Porter, *Idioms*, p. 92. Others prefer 'limitation' or 'description'; cf. Young, *Intermediate New Testament Greek*, p. 23; Smyth, §1289; Wallace, *Greek Grammar*, p. 77; Funk, *A Beginning–Intermediate Grammar*, I, p. 71.

47. Bussmann, *Routledge Dictionary of Language and Linguistics*, p. 185.

48. Moule, *Idiom Book*, p. 38.

49. Wallace, *Greek Grammar*, p. 78.

50. Louw, 'Linguistic Theory and the Greek Case System', p. 85 (emphasis in original).

51. Bussmann, *Routledge Dictionary of Language and Linguistics*, p. 1.

52. Louw, 'Linguistic Theory and the Greek Case System', p. 86; cf. Robertson, p. 514.

53. Robertson, p. 514.

54. Robertson, pp. 515-17.

55. Wallace, *Greek Grammar*, p. 107.

adjunct of a verb phrase. Yet, the ablative meaning is not connected exclusively to adverbial uses, nor is the *restriction* meaning connected exclusively to the adnominal uses. J.P. Louw notes that even though the idea of restriction is most commonly associated with adnominal uses, the partitive notion 'resembles the ablative very closely'.[56] The partitive, therefore, belongs on the same semantic axis as the ablative. Thus, the significance of the genitive article can be plotted on two intersecting axes: a semantic axis and a syntactic axis.

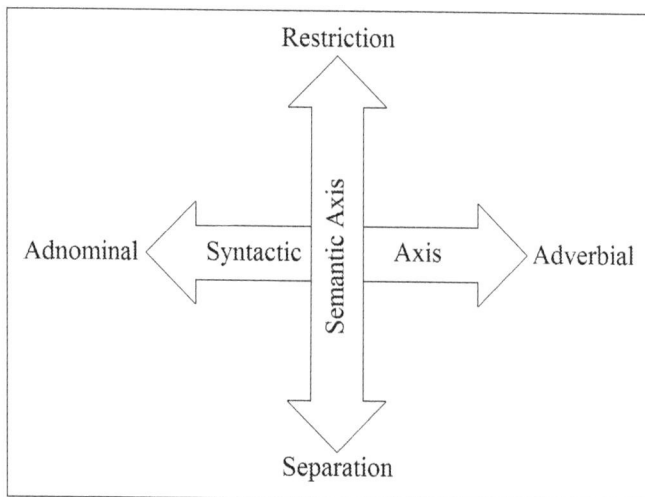

Figure 4. *Four Quadrants Representing*
the Semantic Possibilities of the Genitive Case

The result is that any given use of the genitive articular infinitive falls in one of the four quadrants in Figure 4. The adnominal genitive can connote either *restriction* or *separation*, as can the adverbial genitive. The following analysis of the New Testament data divides the uses of the articular infinitive between the adnominal and adverbial uses.

My thesis concerning the meaning of the article with the infinitive is that the article is a function word, appearing for one of two reasons: (1) to mark the case of the infinitive or (2) to mark some other syntactical function that can only be made explicit by the presence of the article. Every instance of the genitive articular infinitive appears to be grammatically induced in one or both of these ways. With regard to the genitive articular infinitives that do not follow prepositions, the article is employed in order to mark the case of the infinitive and thereby also a meaning associated with its case: either a pure genitive meaning (*restriction*) or an ablative meaning (*separation*).

56. Louw, 'Linguistic Theory and the Greek Case System', pp. 85-86.

Having demonstrated that the article is grammatically motivated in every instance of the articular infinitive, it will be clear that the article has no semantic value as a definitizing determiner.[57]

Table 3. *Genitive Articular Infinitives Not Governed by a Preposition*

	Genitive τοῦ	*Totals*
Matthew	2.13; 3.13; 11.1 (×2); 13.3; 21.32; 24.45	7
Luke	1.9, 57, 73, 77, 79; 2.6, 21, 24, 27; 4.10, 42; 5.7; 8.5; 9.51; 10.19; 12.42; 17.1; 21.22; 22.6, 31; 24.16, 25, 29, 45	24
Acts	3.2, 12; 5.31; 7.19; 9.15; 10.25, 47; 13.47; 14.9, 18; 15.20; 18.10; 20.3, 20 (×2), 27, 30; 21.12; 23.15, 20; 26.18 (×2); 27.1, 20	24
Romans	1.24; 6.6; 7.3; 8.12; 11.8 (×2), 10; 15.22, 23	9
1 Corinthians	9.10; 10.13; 16.4	3
2 Corinthians	1.8; 8.11	2
Galatians	3.10	1
Philippians	3.10, 21	2
Hebrews	5.12; 10.7, 9; 11.5	4
James	5.17	1
1 Peter	3.10; 4.17	2
Revelation	12.7	1
Totals	80	80

b. *Discussion of Texts*

There are at least four texts in which some grammarians have alleged that the genitive case's meaning has completely dissolved and in which the genitive articular infinitive appears to function as the syntactical subject:[58]

Lk. 17.1:

ἀνένδεκτόν ἐστιν τοῦ τὰ σκάνδαλα μὴ ἐλθεῖν, πλὴν οὐαὶ δι᾽ οὗ ἔρχεται

It is inevitable that stumbling blocks should come, but woe to him through whom they come.

57. This line is a restatement of a critical methodological assumption that I set forth in Chapter 2. When it can be demonstrated that the article is syntactically required, one should not look for any further semantic significance of the article (Rosén, *Early Greek Grammar and Thought in Heraclitus*, pp. 30, 37).

58. Robertson writes, 'In the LXX also we see τοῦ and the inf. used as the subject of a finite verb in complete forgetfulness of the case of τοῦ... One must recall the fact that the inf. had already lost for the most part the significance of the dative ending -αι and the locative -ι (-ειν). Now the genitive τοῦ and the dative -αι are both obscured and the combination is used as subject nominative' (Robertson, pp. 1067-68). 'This is the extreme development of the use of the infinitive with τοῦ, in which its original gentival character is not only lost but entirely forgotten' (Votaw, *The Infinitive in Biblical Greek*, p. 28). Cf. Burton, *Moods and Tenses*, p. 159; Moule, *Idiom Book*, p. 129.

Acts 10.25:

Ὡς δὲ ἐγένετο τοῦ εἰσελθεῖν τὸν Πέτρον, συναντήσας αὐτῷ ὁ Κορνήλιος πεσὼν ἐπὶ τοὺς πόδας προσεκύνησε

And when it came about that Peter entered, Cornelius met him, and fell at his feet and worshiped.

Acts 27.1:

Ὡς δὲ ἐκρίθη τοῦ ἀποπλεῖν ἡμᾶς εἰς τὴν Ἰταλίαν, παρεδίδουν τόν τε Παῦλον καί τινας ἑτέρους δεσμώτας ἑκατοντάρχῃ ὀνόματι Ἰουλίῳ σπείρης Σεβαστῆς

And when it was decided that we should sail for Italy, they proceeded to deliver Paul and some other prisoners to a centurion of the Augustan cohort named Julius.

1 Cor. 16.4:

ἐὰν δὲ ἄξιον ᾖ τοῦ κἀμὲ πορεύεσθαι, σὺν ἐμοὶ πορεύσονται

And if it is fitting for me to go also, they will go with me.

While it may be argued that the genitive infinitive is the *logical* subject in these texts, one is hard-pressed to find any justification for treating a genitive substantive as the *syntactical* subject. In Lk. 17.1 and 1 Cor. 16.4, the genitive infinitive is not the subject but is the adjunct of the predicate adjective. This usage is attested in similar syntactical arrangements in texts where the syntactical subject is clearly not the genitive infinitive.[59] Porter suggests that all four of these instances may be more broadly considered 'as appositional uses of the genitive, restating or rephrasing the action being spoken of'.[60] This interpretation comports with the frequent 'epexegetic' use of the infinitive, 'specifying or defining the modified element (whether a word or a phrase)'.[61] In Acts 10.25 and 27.1, the modified element would be the entire verb phrase.[62] The point is that one can find a reasonable explanation of the genitive case in these four texts without resorting to an interpretation that

59. Nigel Turner lists two texts that are analogous to Lk. 17.1 and 1 Cor. 16.4 in this respect (*Syntax*, p. 141): ὦ ἀνόητοι καὶ βραδεῖς τῇ καρδίᾳ τοῦ πιστεύειν ἐπὶ πᾶσιν οἷς ἐλάλησαν οἱ προφῆται ('O foolish men and slow of heart to believe in all that the prophets have spoken', Lk. 24.25); ἡμεῖς δὲ πρὸ τοῦ ἐγγίσαι αὐτὸν ἕτοιμοί ἐσμεν τοῦ ἀνελεῖν αὐτόν ('And we for our part are ready to slay him before he comes near', Acts 23: 15). Burton acknowledges this interpretation as a possibility, but is much less certain about it (Burton, *Moods and Tenses*, p. 160). Yet Blass states without qualification that in 1 Cor. 16.4, the genitive infinitive is an adjunct of the predicate adjective (BDF §400[3]).
60. Porter, *Idioms*, p. 196.
61. Porter, *Idioms*, p. 198.
62. James L. Boyer also argues that Acts 10.25 contains a subject infinitive ('Classification of Infinitives', p. 4 n. 9). Wallace disputes his interpretation, saying that Boyer's 'one example of a gen. articular inf. as subject…is better treated as indicating contemporaneous time' (Wallace, *Greek Grammar*, p. 589 n. 1).

amounts to an arbitrary suppression of the meaning of the genitive case. If these texts can be explained in a way that is consistent with the norms of language of the genitive case, then the burden of proof lies with the interpreter who wishes to read these examples as anomalous uses of the genitive.

Having shown that genitive articular infinitive is never properly understood as subject, we can argue that the 81 genitive examples of this construction encode a meaning associated with the genitive case form. As such, we see two broad patterns of usage of the genitive articular infinitive: adnominal (i.e. pure genitive) and adverbial (i.e. ablative).[63] In other words, the genitive article marks the infinitive either as an adjunct of a noun[64] or as an adjunct of a verb phrase.[65]

(1) *Adverbial uses of the genitive articular infinitive.* Many genitive articular infinitives encode the notion of *purpose.* This particular semantic nuance is perhaps a surprising feature of the genitive case, as one would notice that *purpose* is the semantic opposite of *cause*, a notion frequently associated with the ablatival genitive.[66] Whereas *purpose* emphasizes the *end* of an action, *cause* indicates the *beginning* or ground of an action. Yet Smyth rightly notes that *purpose* and *cause* are not mutually exclusive concepts. He writes, 'Allied to the genitive of cause is the genitive of purpose in τοῦ with the infinitive...and in expressions where ἕνεκα is usually employed'.[67] Two important observations are made in this statement from Smyth: (1) the semantic notions of *cause* and *purpose* appear together in the genitive infinitive, and (2) the genitive infinitive is often a synonym of ἕνεκα plus the infinitive. Louw and Nida's lexicon captures the fundamental idea of the preposition ἕνεκεν as 'A marker of cause or reason, often with the implication of purpose in the sense of "for the sake of"—"on account of, because of"',[68] or conversely, 'A marker of purpose, with the frequent implication of

---

63. See Table 20 in the appendix for a complete categorization of genitive articular infinitives in chart form.

64. In this category, I include the four instances in which the genitive articular infinitive is an adjunct of an adjective: Lk. 17.1; 24.25; Acts 23.15; 1 Cor. 16.4. This procedure is in line with Louw: 'The notion of restriction can be applied with reference to the object *itself*...or to its *adjunct*' (Louw, 'Linguistic Theory and the Greek Case System', p. 85).

65. I am following Votaw's categories and analysis of the texts very closely in the following sections and in Table 20 of the Appendix, though I have excluded the category of subject (*The Use of the Infinitive in Biblical Greek*, pp. 31-40).

66. Though Smyth says that 'the genitive of cause is partly a true genitive, partly ablatival' (Smyth, §1405.a). I think Smyth's statement confirms what I argued above—that the notions of *separation* and *restriction* belong on the same semantic axis.

67. Smyth, §1408.

68. L&N, *s.v.* ἕνεκεν, I, p. 781.

some underlying reason—"in order that, for the sake of, for"'.[69] Louw and Nida assert that both *cause* and *purpose* are indicated by ἕνεκεν.[70] Smyth's remark helps us to see that we should be expecting the same dual sense in the genitive infinitive of purpose. For instance, in Mt. 2.13 we read, μέλλει γὰρ Ἡρῴδης ζητεῖν τὸ παιδίον τοῦ ἀπολέσαι αὐτό ('For Herod is about to seek the child in order to destroy him'). In this text it is clear that destroying the child Jesus is both the *reason for* and the *purpose* of Herod's 'seeking'. Likewise, Lk. 1.73-74 reads, ὅρκον ὃν ὤμοσεν πρὸς Ἀβραὰμ τὸν πατέρα ἡμῶν, τοῦ δοῦναι ἡμῖν ἀφόβως...λατρεύειν αὐτῷ ('The oath which he swore to our father Abraham so that he might give to us...to serve him without fear'). In this text, the *goal* of serving God fearlessly is the *reason for* God's oath. This dual sense is seen in all the genitive infinitives of purpose.[71]

The genitive articular infinitive often functions as the object of a verb.[72] In the New Testament, we find that the genitive object-infinitive follows the same pattern of usage found among non-infinitival objects in the genitive case. BDF lists eleven adverbial uses of the genitive case, many of which have to do with certain classes of verbs that take genitive objects.[73] Three of

69. L&N, *s.v.* ἕνεκεν, I, p. 785.

70. This sense is clearly implied in 2 Cor. 7.12: ἄρα εἰ καὶ ἔγραψα ὑμῖν, οὐχ ἕνεκεν τοῦ ἀδικήσαντος οὐδὲ ἕνεκεν τοῦ ἀδικηθέντος ἀλλ' ἕνεκεν τοῦ φανερωθῆναι τὴν σπουδὴν ὑμῶν τὴν ὑπὲρ ἡμῶν πρὸς ὑμᾶς ἐνώπιον τοῦ θεοῦ ('Therefore, even though I wrote to you, I did it not for the sake of the one who offended nor for the sake of the one who was offended but *for the sake of* having your earnestness on my behalf revealed to you before God'). This text will be discussed in more detail in Chapter 4.

71. Mt. 2.13; 3.13; 11.1 (×2); 13.3; 21.32; 24.45; Lk. 1.73, 77, 79; 2.24, 27; 4.42; 5.7; 8.5; 9.51; 12.42; 22.31; 24.29, 45; Acts 3.2; 5.31; 7.19; 13.47; 14.18; 18.10; 20.30; 23.20; 26.18 (×2); Rom. 6.6; 11.10; Phil. 3.10; Heb. 10.7, 9; 11.5. McKay and Porter suggest the possibility that some of these genitive infinitives be considered a genitive of *result*, resembling the meaning of ὥστε plus the infinitive (K.L. McKay, *A New Syntax of the Verb in New Testament Greek: An Aspectual Approach* [SBG, 5; New York: Peter Lang, 1994], p. 129: 'Consequence'; Porter, *Idioms*, p. 199: 'Resultative'). In my opinion, the following texts might contain genitive infinitives of result: Lk. 24.16; Acts 3.12; 10.47; 20.20 (×2), 27. In any case, it is well-known that there is very little semantic difference between *result* and *purpose*. Votaw includes another category: 'Genitive Object of Verbs of Commanding, Promising and the Like' (Votaw, *The Infinitive in Biblical Greek*, p. 23). Under this classification would appear the genitive infinitives in Lk. 4.10; Acts 15.20; 21.12. But in all three of these texts, the idea of purpose is still manifest.

72. Robertson, pp. 1068, 1085.

73. The eleven uses are: (1) the partitive genitive with verbs of touching, (2) with verbs meaning to touch or take hold of, (3) with verbs meaning to strive after, to desire, to reach, or to obtain, (4) with verbs meaning to fill or to be full of, (5) with verbs of perception, (6) with verbs for smelling, (7) with verbs for remembering and forgetting, (8) with verbs of emotion, (9) the genitive of separation, (10) the genitive of price and value, and (11) the genitive dependent upon prepositions in compound verbs (BDF §§169-81).

these uses are found with the genitive articular infinitive: (1) the partitive genitive, (2) the genitive of separation, and (3) the genitive dependent upon prepositions in compound verbs.[74]

In the first category of genitive objects is included texts that have verbs that govern partitive genitives. Smyth's remarks on this use of the genitive are instructive: 'A verb may be followed by the partitive genitive if the action affects the object only in part. If the *entire* object is affected, the verb in question takes the accusative'.[75] Smyth's observation certainly apply in Lk. 1.9, ἔλαχε τοῦ θυμιᾶσαι ('he received the burning of incense').[76] In this text, 'the burning of incense' was a responsibility shared by the priests; therefore Zacharias' fulfillment of his priestly duty is only a *part* of this larger service as a whole. Also, we note that the verb λαγχάνω governed the genitive case in Classical Greek and that Lk. 1.9 represents a holdover of that older idiom.[77]

In the second category of genitive objects, BDF specifies that the main prepositions used in composition that require a genitive object are ἀπό, ἐκ, and κατά.[78] Smyth adds to this list πρό, ὑπέρ, and ἐπί: 'Many verbs compounded with ἀπό, πρό, ὑπέρ, ἐπί, and κατά take the genitive when the compound may be resolved into the simple verb and preposition without change in the sense… In general, prose, as distinguished from poetry, repeats the preposition contained in the compound; but κατά is not repeated'.[79] The verb ἐξαπορέω is a good example of a verb that takes a genitive object without the preposition repeated. ἐξαπορέω is a strengthened form of ἀπορέω, 'to be in great doubt *or* difficulty'.[80] We can discern two prepositions used in this compound verb, both of which take the genitive case. Thus it is natural for us to see the genitive articular infinitive following this verb in 2 Cor. 1.8, ὥστε ἐξαπορηθῆναι ἡμᾶς καὶ τοῦ ζῆν ('so that we despaired even of life').[81] The prefixed prepositions ἐξ and ἀπό make clear that the articular infinitive is an ablatival genitive of *separation*.[82]

---

74. BDF §§169, 180, 181.

75. Smyth §1341.

76. For the purposes of explaining the syntax of this verse, I chose a literal translation of λαγχάνω and did not render the idiom 'to be chosen by lot'.

77. Cf. LXX Wis. 8.19. BDF §400(3).

78. BDF §181.

79. Smyth §1384: 'Many verbs compounded…take the genitive when the compound may be resolved into the simple verb and preposition without change in the sense'.

80. LSJ, *s.v.* ἐξαπορέω, p. 586.

81. Two genitive infinitives of purpose/result also fall into this category. The verb καταπαύω is a verb formed with κατά. In Acts 14.18 we read, κατέπαυσαν τοὺς ὄχλους τοῦ μὴ θύειν αὐτοῖς ('They restrained the crowds from offering sacrifice to them'). In the middle voice, the compound verb ὑποστέλλω also takes a genitive object, and this is exactly how the verb appears in Acts 20.20 and 20.27: οὐδὲν ὑπεστειλάμην τῶν συμφερόντων τοῦ μὴ ἀναγγεῖλαι ὑμῖν καὶ διδάξαι ὑμᾶς…οὐ γὰρ ὑπεστειλάμην

In the third category of genitive objects is Rom. 15.22, Διὸ καὶ ἐνεκο-πτόμην τὰ πολλὰ τοῦ ἐλθεῖν πρὸς ὑμᾶς ('For this reason I have often been hindered from coming to you'). This genitive of separation comes after a verb of hindering.[83] Thus this category is similar to what Votaw categorizes as an object after a verb of hindering.[84] In a figurative sense, this use of the genitive emphasizes the *separation from* the object or activity in view. In this case, Paul is 'separated from' coming to the Romans—that is, he was hindered. In Lk. 24.16, the genitive infinitive follows κρατέω, a verb that in the passive voice means 'to hinder' or 'to prevent': οἱ δὲ ὀφθαλμοὶ αὐτῶν ἐκρατοῦντο τοῦ μὴ ἐπιγνῶναι αὐτόν.[85] The same type of "separation" is also in view here, but in this case the 'eyes' are 'separated' from knowledge of Jesus. Other texts in this category are Lk. 4.42; Acts 14.18; 20.20 (×2), 27.

I already alluded to the *epexegetical* use of the genitive infinitive at the beginning of this section on adverbial uses.[86] This category of usage of the genitive case is well-attested in the standard grammars and need not be belabored here,[87] except to point out with Porter that this use of the genitive infinitive restates or rephrases the action being spoken of.[88] It does not restate or rename a *substantive* as is normally the case. This is a true adverbial usage. So we read in Gal. 3.10, ἐπικατάρατος πᾶς ὃς οὐκ ἐμμένει πᾶσιν τοῖς γεγραμμένοις ἐν τῷ βιβλίῳ τοῦ νόμου τοῦ ποιῆσαι αὐτά. In this text, τοῦ ποιῆσαι αὐτά is an epexegetical expansion[89] of the verb

τοῦ μὴ ἀναγγεῖλαι (BDAG, *s.v.* ὑποστέλλω, p. 1041; LSJ, *s.v.* ὑποστέλλω, p. 1895). ὑποστέλλω takes an accusative object in the active voice, but in the intransitive middle voice it is always followed by the genitive.

82.   In 2 Cor. 1.8, the article also *marks* the second infinitive as the 'object' of the verb ἐξαπορηθῆναι: ὥστε ἐξαπορηθῆναι ἡμᾶς καὶ τοῦ ζῆν. If the article were absent, it would be very easy to misconstrue ζῆν as joined by καὶ in a coordinate relationship with ἐξαπορηθῆναι. The genitive article removes any ambiguity on this score. Thus the article is truly a function marker in this verse as well.

83.   This category corresponds to BDF §180(6), which includes verbs of 'ceasing' or 'resting'.

84.   Votaw, *The Infinitive in Biblical Greek*, p. 24.

85.   Votaw notes that the negative μή does not reverse the meaning of the phrase as an English double negative would (Votaw, *The Infinitive in Biblical Greek*, p. 24). The genitive infinitive following a verb of hindering appears with μή in at least one-third of the instances in the New Testament and the LXX (Votaw, *The Infinitive in Biblical Greek*, p. 24). Cf. Acts 14.18; 20.20 (×2), 27; 2 Cor 1.8.

86.   I noted that Acts 10.25 and 27.1 are epexegetical genitives, not subject-genitives.

87.   For example, BDF §167: 'Genitive of content and appositive genitive'; Robertson, p. 498: 'Apposition or Definition'; Wallace, *Biblical Greek*, p. 95: 'Epexegetical Genitive'; Zerwick, §45, 16: 'Epexegetic genitive'.

88.   Porter, *Idioms*, p. 196.

89.   It could be argued that this infinitive phrase expresses *result* (e.g. Robertson, p. 1067), but this interpretation arises more from the logic of the sentence than from the syntax. My interpretation does not exclude the notion of *result*.

phrase ἐμμένει πᾶσιν τοῖς γεγραμμένοις. Similarly, we read in Jas 5.17, προσευχῇ προσηύξατο τοῦ μὴ βρέξαι ('He prayed with a prayer of not raining'). In this text, the genitive infinitive is an epexegetical expansion upon Elijah's prayer.[90]

(2) *Adnominal uses of the genitive articular infinitive.* Adnominal genitive articular infinitives are the second most frequent use of this construction (the first being *purpose*). We have already seen how the partitive notion appears with adverbial uses of the genitive infinitive, and this partitive idea also appears in connection with nouns. Concerning this construction, K.L. McKay has aptly pointed out that,

> The genitive of the articular infinitive is found with expressions implying separation (ablatival genitive) and in dependence on nouns (descriptive genitive)... Occasionally the genitive of an articular infinitive is found in constructions in which an anarthrous infinitive is normal, and where there seems to be no need for the genitive... In all these the genitive is probably partitive...indicating that the preceding activity is in some way seen as part of that expressed by the infinitive.[91]

McKay's point is that even in those texts that appear to be expressing purpose, the sense is probably partitive. Yet we note that in texts such as 1 Cor. 10.13, the genitive articular infinitive is often rendered as purpose (ποιήσει σὺν τῷ πειρασμῷ καὶ τὴν ἔκβασιν τοῦ δύνασθαι ὑπενεγκεῖν, 'He will also provide a way out so that you can stand up under it' [NIV]). McKay's literal translation probably captures the heart of what Paul intended, 'He will provide with the temptation a way of escape *so that* you might be able (...a way of escape consisting in the ability) to bear up'.[92] McKay shows that in this text the genitive actually defines τὴν ἔκβασιν, and the idea of purpose (or consequence) actually arises from the logic rather than the grammar of the sentence.[93] The point of the genitive in this text is to modify or *restrict* the noun τὴν ἔκβασιν. A literal rendering of Lk. 1.57 shows the same adnominal usage, Τῇ δὲ Ἐλισάβετ ἐπλήσθη ὁ χρόνος τοῦ τεκεῖν αὐτὴν καὶ ἐγέννησεν υἱόν ('For Elizabeth, the time of her giving birth was fulfilled, and she bore a son'). Here the genitive infinitive *restricts* ὁ χρόνος so as to specify what 'time' is being referred to.[94] In Lk. 10.19, the genitive infinitive *restricts* 'authority', δέδωκα ὑμῖν τὴν ἐξουσίαν τοῦ πατεῖν

90. Cf. Rom. 7.3; 1 Pet. 3.10; Rev. 12.7.
91. McKay, *A New Syntax of the Verb in New Testament Greek*, pp. 59, 55.
92. McKay, *A New Syntax of the Verb in New Testament Greek*, p. 129.
93. McKay, *A New Syntax of the Verb in New Testament Greek*, p. 129.
94. Cf. Lk. 2.6: ἐπλήσθησαν αἱ ἡμέραι τοῦ τεκεῖν αὐτήν; Lk. 2.21: ἐπλήσθησαν ἡμέραι ὀκτὼ τοῦ περιτεμεῖν αὐτόν. Other texts that include adnominal references to a period of time include Lk. 21.22; 22.6.

ἐπάνω ὄφεων καὶ σκορπίων. The notion of purpose may be a secondary implication, but the primary notion is that the genitive infinitive tells what kind of 'authority' has been given. This usage occurs mainly in Luke and Paul, with two examples in Hebrews and 1 Peter.[95]

I have already mentioned two examples in which the genitive infinitive *restricts* an adjective. Porter's translation of Lk. 17.1 captures the sense of this usage, ἀνένδεκτόν ἐστιν τοῦ τὰ σκάνδαλα μὴ ἐλθεῖν ('It is impossible for causes of stumbling not to come').[96] We might render 1 Cor. 16.4 in a similar way, ἐὰν δὲ ἄξιον ἦ τοῦ κἀμὲ πορεύεσθαι ('And if it is fitting for me to go also'). In both of these texts the genitive infinitive *restricts* the predicate adjective.[97] Likewise notice Acts 23.15, ἡμεῖς δὲ πρὸ τοῦ ἐγγίσαι αὐτὸν ἕτοιμοί ἐσμεν τοῦ ἀνελεῖν αὐτόν ('And we are ready to slay him before he comes near'). A very clear example of this usage occurs in Lk. 24.25 where εἰμί does not appear: ὦ ἀνόητοι καὶ βραδεῖς τῇ καρδίᾳ τοῦ πιστεύειν ἐπὶ πᾶσιν οἷς ἐλάλησαν οἱ προφῆται. In this text, the genitive infinitive tells in what respect the hearers were 'foolish and slow in heart'.

4. *Dative Articular Infinitive*

a. *Semantics of the Dative Case*
Grammarians have found it very difficult to describe the *Grundbedeutung* ('primary' or 'essential meaning') of the dative case-form and have typically reverted to a definition that consists of the dative's *Gebruachsumfang* ('earliest meaning'). Even those who take a modern linguistic approach have found it extremely difficult to identify what is the semantic essence of the dative case and have had to resort to giving an historical description of the dative's earliest use. As is widely known, the pre-history of the Koine dative reveals a gradual morphological coalescing of three of the original eight Indo-Germanic case-forms—the dative, locative, and instrumental.[98] For this reason, instead of setting forth one primary meaning of the Koine dative, the grammars typically describe three basic meanings of the one case-form: *interest, locative,* or *instrumental.* Even J.P. Louw's analysis of the Greek cases fails to arrive at a singular semantic description of the dative case that

---

95.   Lk. 1.57; 2.6, 21; 10.19; 21.22; 22.6; Acts 9.15; 14.9; 20.3; 27.20; Rom. 1.24; 8.12; 11.8 (×2); 15.23; 1 Cor. 9.10; 10.13; 2 Cor. 8.11; Phil. 3.21; Heb. 5.12; 1 Pet. 4.17. See Table 20 in the Appendix for the full chart.

96.   Porter, *Idioms*, p. 196.

97.   In both of these instances, word-order is not an argument against seeing the genitive as modifying the pre-verbal adjective. This word-order is attested elsewhere, and the genitive is clearly dependent upon the pre-verbal adjective. Cf. 1 Cor. 11.27: ἔνοχος ἔσται τοῦ σώματος καὶ τοῦ αἵματος τοῦ κυρίου; Mt. 6.25; Lk. 12.23; Jn 4.12; 8.53; 1 Cor. 12.23.

98.   Robertson's discussion of this matter is well-known (pp. 446-47).

comprises its 'connotation' and 'potentiality', even though such a description is the goal of his article.[99]

That is why it is difficult to understand Porter's definition, which relies on
Louw: 'The dative case is the most explicit and particular of the cases in
meaning and function, grammaticalizing the semantic feature of relation'.[100]
Porter appeals to Louw's work as the basis of his explanation of the dative
case, yet Louw does not identify relation as the fundamental semantic value
of the dative. In fact, Louw argues that the idea of relation is the semantic
essence only of the so-called 'pure dative'.[101] Louw's remarks on the locative and instrumental datives come in the following pages,[102] and Louw does
not say that relation is the fundamental meaning of the locative and instrumental usage. In fact, Louw argues that the idea of togetherness is the essence
of the locative and instrumental:[103]

> The Greek dative also represents the instrumental case which (on the semantic
> level) not necessarily denotes the instrument but rather expresses *the idea of
> togetherness*... [There are examples] in which the dative may be either loca-
> tive or instrumental according to a particular point of view, thus affording
> another indication of the fusion of cases.[104]

For Louw, the *idea of togetherness* is fundamental only to the *locative* and
instrumental datives, not the pure dative of *interest*. If we follow Louw, the
most that can be said is that the dative case form has the potential to be
employed with one of two primary meanings: (1) *relation*, that is, pure
dative, or (2) *togetherness*, that is, locative or instrumental.[105]

Nevertheless, Porter's description gets more at the heart of the semantics
of the dative case than does Louw's, and it comprises a singular *Grundbedeutung* (which is the goal of Louw's approach but which Louw does not
achieve for the dative case). Instead of seeing the dative as encoding two
discreet semantic notions (relation and togetherness), Porter would define
the dative as encoding the singular idea of *relation*, with the *instrumental*
and *locative* uses being specific contextualizations of *relation*.[106]

99. Louw, 'Linguistic Theory and the Greek Case System', p. 76.
100. Porter, *Idioms*, p. 97.
101. Louw, 'Linguistic Theory and the Greek Case System', pp. 80-81. These pages
contain comment only on the 'pure dative'.
102. Louw, 'Linguistic Theory and the Greek Case System', pp. 82-83.
103. Louw, 'Linguistic Theory and the Greek Case System', p. 83.
104. Louw, 'Linguistic Theory and the Greek Case System', p. 83.
105. Because the meaning of the dative case-form cannot be reduced beyond these
two meanings, some linguists regard the pure dative as a *syntactic* case (encoding the
indirect object) and the instrumental and locative datives as *semantic* cases.
106. In a personal e-mail correspondence (25 June 2005), Stanley Porter explained
to me the reasoning behind his divergence from Louw on this point: 'My definition of the

Table 4. *Dative Articular Infinitive Not Governed by a Preposition*

	Dative τῷ	Totals
2 Corinthians	2.13	1
Totals	1	1

b. *Discussion of Text*

The one dative example in 2 Cor. 2.13 deserves little comment because there is general agreement that the article appears to encode a meaning associated with the dative case: οὐκ ἔσχηκα ἄνεσιν τῷ πνεύματί μου τῷ μὴ εὑρεῖν με Τίτον τὸν ἀδελφόν μου. In this lone example from the New Testament, the dative case form is employed in order to signify *instrumentality* (cf. LXX [Swete's text] 2 Chron. 28.22; Eccl. 1.16; *4 Macc.* 17.20-21).[107] Votaw recognizes that *instrumentality* to some extent overlaps semantically with the categories *cause*, *manner*, *means* and includes 2 Cor. 2.13 under this threefold heading.[108] It is for this reason, perhaps, that Robertson labels this as an 'instrumental' use of τῷ and does not mention the notion of causality at all.[109] In his discussion on the 'instrumental' case, Robertson rightly observes that 'the instrumental may be used also to express the idea of cause, motive or occasion. This notion of ground wavers between the idea of association and means.'[110] This use of the instrumental/causal use of the dative case attested elsewhere in the New Testament,[111] and that is how we should read the dative articular infinitive in 2 Cor. 2.13.

5. *Accusative Articular Infinitives*

a. *Semantics of the Accusative Case*

Like the nominative, the accusative is a *syntactic* case. As such it functions primarily as a syntactical marker to encode nominals as objects. Louw argues that the best way to understand the meaning of the accusative is by

---

dative in terms of "relation" was an attempt to find a way of describing what I see as the semantics of the dative, including (if you want to) the pure, locative and instrumental. When Louw talks of togetherness, I see in that the relational dimension that applies throughout the range of usage, so my use of relation is more inclusive than his.'

107.   Robertson, pp. 1061-62; Votaw, *The Infinitive in Biblical Greek*, p. 29.

108.   Votaw, *The Infinitive in Biblical Greek*, p. 29; see also Moulton, *Prolegomena*, p. 220; Porter, *Idioms*, p. 200.

109.   Robertson, p. 1061.

110.   Robertson, p. 532.

111.   For example, Lk. 15.17: ἐγὼ δὲ λιμῷ ὧδε ἀπόλλυμαι ('I am dying here *because* of hunger'); Gal. 6.12: ἵνα τῷ σταυρῷ τοῦ Χριστοῦ μὴ διώκωνται ('in order that they might not be persecuted *because* of the cross of Christ'). For other examples, see Robertson, p. 532.

comparing it with the other cases.[112] The nominative and accusative bear similarity to one another as syntactic cases with one important difference, 'On the semantic level the mere nominal idea is stated by the nominative without relation to the sentence, while the accusative, denoting a relation, is non-defining'.[113] Like the nominative, the accusative merely names the nominal idea without defining an additional semantic element (as the dative 'to', for', or the genitive 'of'). Unlike the nominative, the accusative encodes a relation to the 'constructional chain'.[114] Porter uses the nominative–accusative comparison in his definition of the accusative and is worth quoting again at length: 'Like the nominative case, which simply expresses the nominal idea, *the accusative case in syntactically restricted (oblique) contexts expresses an idea without defining it. This fundamental meaning accounts for its several syntactical and contextual uses.*'[115] In the New Testament, we will see that the accusative articular infinitive has primarily a syntactic function of encoding the verbal or prepositional object.

b. *Discussion of Texts*
There are at least 16 instances of the accusative articular infinitive in the New Testament.[116]

112.   'In order to determine and to define the semantic level, cases should be studied comparatively, with special attention to constructions where cases compete' (Louw, 'Linguistic Theory and the Greek Case System', p. 78).
113.   Louw, 'Linguistic Theory and the Greek Case System', p. 80.
114.   Louw, 'Linguistic Theory and the Greek Case System', p. 80.
115.   Porter, *Idioms*, pp. 88-89 (emphasis in original). See pp. 88-90 for Porter's explanation of how this definition applies to the so-called *accusative of respect* and the *accusative of time or space*.
116.   Acts 25.11; Rom. 13.8; 14.13; 1 Cor. 14.39 (×2); 2 Cor. 2.1; 8.10 (×2), 11; 10.2; Phil. 2.6, 13 (×2); 4.10; 1 Thess. 4.6 (×2). Acts 4.18 is excluded from this list. The article is absent in some significant witnesses and may not belong here. 'The Alexandrian omission (only ℵ* B) of τό…was perhaps a precautionary measure, lest the reader suppose that the article was to be taken with the infinitive' (Metzger, *Textual Commentary*, p. 278). The grammatical insight behind the Alexandrian omission is probably correct because the article does go with καθόλου μή and not with the infinitives (cf. the LXX versions of the following: Amos 3.3, 4; Ezek. 13.3, 22; 17.24; Dan. 3.50). Votaw does not count it as articular, though he does say that it is the verbal object (*The Infinitive in Biblical Greek*, p. 34). I conclude that the article is original but does not go with the infinitives (cf. BDF §399[3]; C.K. Barrett, *A Critical and Exegetical Commentary on the Acts of the Apostles* [ICC; 2 vols.; Edinburgh: T. & T. Clark, 1998], II. p. 236; Hans Conzelmann, *Acts of the Apostles: A Commentary on the Acts of the Apostles* [Hermeneia; Philadelphia: Fortress Press, 1987], p. 33; against Turner, *Syntax*, p. 141). Rom 15.5: The article goes with αὐτό, not the infinitive (cf. Rom. 12.16; 2 Cor. 13.11; Phil. 2.2; 4.2). Phil. 4.2: The article goes with αὐτό, not the infinitive (cf. Rom. 12.16; 15.5; 2 Cor. 13.11; Phil. 2.2). 1 Thess. 3.3: As F.F. Bruce suggests, this example most likely should be considered as the object of the preposition εἰς in 1 Thess. 3.2 (*1 and 2 Thessalonians*

Table 5. *Accusative Articular Infinitives Not Governed by a Preposition*

	Accusative τό	*Totals*
Acts	4.18 (×2); 25.11	3
Romans	13.8; 14.13	2
1 Corinthians	14.39 (×2)	2
2 Corinthians	2.1; 8.10 (×2), 11; 10.2	5
Philippians	2.6, 13 (×2); 4.10	4
1 Thessalonians	3.3; 4.6 (×2)	3
Totals	19	19

With the exception of two texts in which the accusative article marks an appositional relation (Rom. 14.13; 2 Cor. 2.1),[117] the accusative case appears with the infinitive in order to encode the infinitive as the direct object of a transitive verb. In at least five of these texts, the accusative articular infinitive helps to clarify the meaning of the main verb. In Acts 25.11, we read, οὐ παραιτοῦμαι τὸ ἀποθανεῖν. The article with ἀποθανεῖν removes the possibility that the infinitive is indirect discourse. An accusative object with no indirect discourse leads to interpreting παραιτοῦμαι as 'refuse' or 'reject' (1 Tim. 4.7; 5.11; 2 Tim. 2.23; Tit. 3.10; Heb. 12.25). Without the article, παραιτοῦμαι might be misinterpreted as 'request' (cf. Lk. 23.23; Jn 4.9; Acts 3.14; 7.46; 13.28; Eph. 3.13; Heb. 12.19). Consider also 2 Cor. 10.2, δέομαι δὲ τὸ μὴ παρὼν θαρρῆσαι τῇ πεποιθήσει ᾗ λογίζομαι τολμῆσαι ἐπί τινας τοὺς λογιζομένους ἡμᾶς ὡς κατὰ σάρκα περιπατοῦντας. James L. Boyer includes δέομαι in his list of verbs that take an infinitive in indirect discourse.[118] When δέομαι is followed by an anarthrous infinitive, the infinitive phrase indicates indirect discourse (e.g. Lk. 8.38; 9.38; Acts 26.3). Bauer's lexicon shows that with the accusative, δέομαι refers to the accusative of the thing as distinguished from 'indirect discourse' and 'direct discourse'.[119]

In Rom. 13.8, the accusative article appears to clarify the meaning of the verb ὀφείλετε: Μηδενὶ μηδὲν ὀφείλετε εἰ μὴ τὸ ἀλλήλους ἀγαπᾶν· ὁ γὰρ ἀγαπῶν τὸν ἕτερον νόμον πεπλήρωκεν. The verb ὀφείλω requires either a *complementary* infinitive or an accusative *object*. When it is followed by a *complementary* infinitive in Paul, the sense of ὀφείλω is always 'ought,

[WBC, 45; Waco, TX: Word Books, 1982], p. 59). Thus, 'we sent Timothy…in order to establish you…in order that no one should be disturbed'.

117.   We might add 1 Thess. 4.6 to the list of appositional uses. However, I think it is more likely that the article marks the two object infinitives as asyndetically coordinated with the infinitive phrase τὸ ἑαυτοῦ σκεῦος κτᾶσθαι of 4.4. Thus there are two direct objects of the verb οἶδα of 4.4.

118.   Boyer, 'Classification of Infinitives', p. 9.

119.   BDAG, *s.v.* δέομαι, p. 218.

should, must' (Rom. 15.1, 27; 1 Cor. 5.10; 7.36; 9.10; 11.7, 10; 12.11, 14; Eph. 5.28; 2 Thess. 1.3; 2.13). When followed by an accusative *object*, the sense of ὀφείλω is always 'owe' (Rom. 13.8; Phlm. 18). Thus the article marks the infinitive as accusative object and shows that the infinitive is not *complementary*. The ὀφείλω...ἀγαπᾶν pair also occurs in Eph. 5.28 where ἀγαπᾶν is anarthrous and thus *complementary*. A similar situation is found in 2 Cor. 8.10, οἵτινες οὐ μόνον τὸ ποιῆσαι ἀλλὰ καὶ τὸ θέλειν προενή- ρξασθε ἀπὸ πέρυσι. The accusative article is necessary to mark the infini- tive as object because ἐνάρχω and related verbs can be used with the anarthrous infinitive as *complementary* (cf. Deut. 2.24, 25, 31).[120] The main point in all these texts is that the article appears in order to clarify the infini- tive's case. Thus the article emerges as a function word in such texts.

Sometimes the accusative case is made explicit by the article so that the main verb will be construed as transitive with respect to the infinitive object. Such is the case in Phil. 4.10, ἀνεθάλετε τὸ ὑπὲρ ἐμοῦ φρονεῖν. Though ἀναθάλλω is a *hapax legomenon* in the New Testament, we know from its use in the LXX that an accusative object is required in order for this verb to be considered transitive (Sir. 1.18; 11.22; 50.10; Ezek. 17.24). Without the article, the subject of ἀναθάλλω can be construed as more or less the receptor of the verbal action (cf. Ps. 27.7; Wis. 4.4; Sir. 46.12; 49.10; Hos. 8.9), a sense clearly not intended in Phil. 4.10.[121] Likewise, in Phil. 2.13 the article clarifies the sense of ἐνεργέω: θεὸς γάρ ἐστιν ὁ ἐνεργῶν ἐν ὑμῖν καὶ τὸ θέλειν καὶ τὸ ἐνεργεῖν ὑπὲρ τῆς εὐδοκίας. With accusative of thing, ἐνεργέω means 'produce, effect'. Without the accusative, ἐνεργέω is intransitive and refers to a more generic 'working'.[122] In 1 Cor. 14.39, the two accusative articles mark the two infinitives as objects of their respective imperative verbs, Ὥστε, ἀδελφοί [μου], ζηλοῦτε τὸ προφητεύειν καὶ τὸ λαλεῖν μὴ κωλύετε γλώσσαις. Without the article, the two infinitives might be taken in a final sense with ὥστε, a very common use of the infinitive in the New Testament.[123]

120.   The accusative articular infinitive in the following verse (2 Cor. 8.11) is necessary to remove any possible *final* or *ecbatic* sense from the infinitive phrase, which is the thrust of the following ὅπως clause.
121.   In the transitive sense, this verb takes 'an accusative of the thing germinated' (J. B. Lightfoot, *St Paul's Epistle to the Philippians* [repr., Peabody, MA: Hendrickson, 1993], p. 163). The intransitive sense would only occur if the genitive τοῦ reading (F G) were preferred over the accusative τό, which is probably why BDAG and BDF describe this use of ἀναθάλλω as factitive (BDAG, *s.v.* ἀναθάλλω, p. 63; BDF §101; §399[1]).
122.   BDAG, *s.v.* 'ἐνεργέω', p. 335.
123.   Mt. 8.24 (×2); 10.1 (×2); 12.22 (×2); 13.2, 32 (×2), 54 (×2); 15.31, 33; 24.24; 27.1, 14; Mk 1.27, 45; 2.2, 12 (×2); 3.10, 20 (×2); 4.1, 32, 37; 9.26; 15.5; Lk. 4.29; 5.7; 12.1; 20.20; Acts 1.19; 5.15 (×2); 14.1; 15.39; 16.26; 19.10, 12 (×3), 16; Rom. 7.6; 15.19; 1 Cor. 1.7; 5.1; 13.2; 2 Cor. 1.8; 2.7 (×2); 3.7; 7.7; Phil. 1.13; 1 Thess. 1.7, 8; 2 Thess. 1.4; 2.4; Heb. 13.6; 1 Pet. 1.21.

In all of these examples of the accusative articular infinitive, we can see that the neuter accusative article regularly occurs for a syntactical reason. It marks the infinitive as object. In a similar way, that is what is happening in Phil. 2.6, ὃς ἐν μορφῇ θεοῦ ὑπάρχων οὐχ ἁρπαγμὸν ἡγήσατο τὸ εἶναι ἴσα θεῷ. But in this text, the article marks the direct object and thereby distinguishes it from its accusative complement. Imagine for a moment the potential syntactical confusion that would result if we were to remove the definite article from the infinitive in Phil. 2.6. It would then be syntactically possible to take ἁρπαγμόν as the direct object and to take the infinitive as an adverbial phrase, 'He did not think about ἁρπαγμός so that he would not be equal with God'. This understanding of Paul's meaning might be unlikely, but it would be syntactically possible. The presence of the article clears away any possible ambiguity. These texts illustrate what I think is the case across the board with the articular infinitive in the New Testament. The article only appears with the infinitive as a *function word* or *syntactical marker*.

6. *Conclusion*

In this chapter I have sought to show that the article appears with the infinitive in order to *mark* syntactical relationships and/or to make the case of the infinitive explicit. To this end, I have shown in various contexts how the article disambiguates certain syntactical arrangements and how the case of the article contributes to the semantics of the articular infinitive phrase. The semantic effect of the article is not to *mark* the infinitive as definite, but to encode a meaning associated with the article's case. In the nominative and accusative examples, the case does not contribute a semantic element as it does with the genitive and dative examples. The nominative and accusative articles appear for syntactical reasons only. With respect to the nominative articular infinitive, the article serves the syntactical purpose of marking the infinitive as subject.[124] Similarly, the accusative article marks the infinitive as the object[125] of a transitive verb in certain contexts where this syntactical arrangement needs clarification. The genitive and dative examples of the articular infinitive occur for similarly syntactical reasons (encoding either adnominal or adverbial relations), but more so for the semantic element associated with these two content cases. The lone dative articular infinitive encodes an instrumental idea. The genitive articular infinitives encode meanings associated with the notions of *separation* and *restriction*. In none of these texts is it clear that the article somehow marks the infinitive as definite. On the contrary, the article emerges as a function word to *mark* (and thereby clarify) case and syntactical relations.

---

124.   In one text it marks the infinitive as an appositive of the subject: Rom. 4.13.
125.   In two texts it marks apposition to the object: Rom. 14.13; 2 Cor. 2.1.

4

ARTICULAR INFINITIVES FOLLOWING PREPOSITIONS
IN THE NEW TESTAMENT

1. A Methodology for Interpreting Prepositional Phrases

a. *Prepositions Governing Cases or Cases Governing Prepositions?*
Grammarians of New Testament Greek dispute whether the cases govern
prepositions or the prepositions govern the cases with respect to meaning.
Daniel Wallace argues the latter point of view. Wallace writes that it is the
'older' grammars that insist upon an understanding of case as the key to
understanding prepositions. Wallace contends that while such an approach
may be accurate for Classical Greek, it is not appropriate for the Koine
Greek of the New Testament:

> A proper grammatical method separates prepositional phrases from simple
> case uses. Whenever any of the oblique cases follows a preposition, you should
> examine the use of the *preposition*, rather than the case usage, to determine the
> possible nuances involved… [I]n Hellenistic Greek, because of the tendency
> toward explicitness, the preposition increasingly gained independent value.
> Thus, the preposition does not just clarify the case's usage; often, it *alters* it…
> [When interpreting prepositional phrases] you would err if you shut yourself
> up to the categorical *possibilities* of the naked case.[1]

Therefore, according to Wallace's method, the preposition can completely
override the meaning of a given case. For instance, when ἀπό plus the
genitive is used with a temporal nuance, it differs radically from the naked
genitive used with a temporal nuance. The preposition completely overrides
any meaning that might be inherent in the genitive case.[2] Thus Wallace
concludes, '*The use of a particular preposition with a particular case <u>never</u>
exactly parallels—either in category possibilities or in frequency of nuances
—the use of a case without a preposition*'.[3] For Wallace, any attempt to

---

1. Wallace, *Greek Grammar*, pp. 360-61.
2. Wallace, *Greek Grammar*, p. 361.
3. Wallace, *Greek Grammar*, pp. 361-62 (emphasis in original).

discern an underlying meaning for a given preposition constitutes the root fallacy.[4]

Murray J. Harris's approach has both similarities and differences with Wallace's. Harris writes: 'Strictly speaking, from the point of view of historical development, a prep. does not "govern" the case of a noun but rather adds a certain precision to the case-meaning of the noun whose case is determined by its relation to the verb or to another noun'.[5] In this statement, Harris sounds as if he is going to embrace the 'older' approach that Wallace warns against. Harris goes on, however, to explain that, 'the writers [of the New Testament] themselves probably regarded preps. as "governing" or determining the case of the noun'.[6] Yet even with this latter statement, Harris does not go as far as Wallace does in saying that the preposition 'overrides' the case in some instances or in saying that an appeal to the basic meaning of the preposition constitutes root fallacy. On the contrary, he advocates a multi-faceted approach to understanding prepositional phrases:

> In seeking to determine the meaning of a prep. phrase the New Testament exegete should (at least ideally) consider: (1) the primary meaning of the prep. in itself (i.e. the local relation) and then its range of meanings when used with a particular case; (2) the basic significance of the case that is used with the prep.; (3) the indications afforded by the context as to the meaning of the prep.; (4) the distinctive features of prep. usage in the New Testament which may account for seeming irregularities.[7]

For this book, I will employ an approach that differs from Wallace's and is more akin to Harris's. I have already pointed out my agreement with Robertson on this point in Chapter 1: 'It is the *case* which indicates the meaning of the *preposition*, and not the preposition which gives meaning to the case'.[8] This is one instance in which a diachronic understanding of the language helps in interpretation. Robertson shows that in the early stages of the Greek language the cases by themselves were sufficient to express the relationship between words. But as the language developed, the burden on the cases became too heavy to be borne by the case alone. The range of meaning that was possible with any given use of a case became so extensive, that the naked case became insufficient in many instances to specify certain meanings. Thus, the prepositions grew in use in order to clarify the meaning of a case in a given context.[9] Stanley Porter agrees: '*A preposition is governed by its case, in some way helping the case to manifest its meaning and*

---

4. Wallace, *Greek Grammar*, p. 363; *contra* Murray J. Harris, 'Prepositions and Theology in the Greek New Testament', in *NIDNTT*, III, pp. 1171-15 (1172-73).
5. Harris, 'Prepositions and Theology', III, p. 1173.
6. Harris, 'Prepositions and Theology', III, p. 1173.
7. Harris, 'Prepositions and Theology', III, p. 1173.
8. Robertson, p. 554.
9. Robertson, p. 554.

to perform more precisely its various functions… Hence prepositions were found necessary by writers and speakers to clarify case meanings and relationships.'[10] This tendency is perhaps seen most clearly in the use of ἐκ and ἀπό to denote the ablatival genitive. In the Hellenistic period, the naked genitive case-form was rarely used to denote an ablative relation. The prepositions ἐκ and ἀπό were employed to specify that the genitive case-form was denoting the ablatival notion of separation.

Robertson's (and Porter's) contention, therefore, has a profound impact on the way we go about understanding prepositions and cases: 'The case retains its original force with the preposition and this fundamental case-idea must be observed'.[11] If Robertson is correct (and in this book I will assume he is), then the proper method for studying Greek prepositions is as follows: 'To begin with the case-idea, add the meaning of the preposition itself, then consider the context. The result of this combination will be what one translates into English, for instance, but he translates the total idea, not the mere preposition.'[12] This is the approach reflected in Harris's four suggestions, and it is the approach that I will use in setting forth the significance of the articular infinitive as object of the preposition.

b. *The Article as Grammatically Obligatory in Prepositional Phrases*
Two observations lead us to the conclusion that the article is grammatically obligatory when an infinitive serves as the object of the preposition. The first observation consists of a simple description of the data as it stands in the New Testament. As has already been pointed out, every infinitive that serves as a prepositional object in the New Testament is articular. There is no exception to this pattern in the New Testament literature.[13] As a second

10. Porter, *Idioms*, p. 140. Cf. Louw, 'Linguistic Theory', p. 82: '*In Greek prepositions are used to increase the precision of the statement*' (emphasis in original).

11. Robertson, p. 567.

12. Robertson, p. 568. James A. Brooks and Carlton L. Winbery follow this method closely in their *Syntax of New Testament Greek* (Lanham, MD: University Press of America, 1979), pp. 65-69.

13. The exceptions in literature outside of the New Testament are so rare that Goodwin does not appear to be aware of them: 'The Infinitive as genitive, dative, or accusative is very often governed by prepositions, or by adverbs used as prepositions. In this case it always takes the article τοῦ, τῷ, or τό' (William W. Goodwin, *Syntax of the Moods and Tenses of the Greek Verb* [Boston and Cambridge: Sever, Francis & Co., 3rd edn, 1870], p. 197). Yet Mayser notes that there are some (Edwin Mayser, *Grammatik der griechischen Papyri aus der Ptolemäerzeit, mit Einschluss der gleichzeitigen Ostraka und der in Ägypten verfassten Inschriften*. II.1. *Satzlehre, analytischer Teil, erste Hälfte* [Berlin and Leipzig: W. de Gruyter, 1926], p. 324). Robertson agrees, 'The instances without the article are clearly very few' (Robertson, p. 1069). According to Moulton, the Greek of the New Testament follows Attic in its use of the article. Moulton says that the frequent use of εἰς πεῖν in the papyri is the result of Ionic influence. That is why this

observation, we can see that the articular infinitive is necessary after prepositions by considering two grammatical ambiguities that would result if the
anarthrous infinitive were employed following a preposition. The first
ambiguity is semantic, and the second syntactic. The first semantic ambiguity stems from the observation mentioned above that the proper method for
studying prepositions involves first identifying the case of the object and
second observing how the preposition clarifies the case usage. The meaning
of the phrase would not be clear if the case were not made explicit by the
presence of the article. The second ambiguity consists in the fact that the
syntactical relation of the infinitive to the preposition would be unclear
without the article. While the article does not substantivize the infinitive,[14] it
does mark the infinitive as object of the preposition. Thus the article in the
articular infinitive following a preposition has semantic[15] force as a case-
marker and syntactic force as a function word.

The idea that the article is a case-marker and a function word in such
situations might appear to be undermined by the appearance in the New
Testament of an analogous construction in which the article is not present. In
the New Testament we find the regular use of anarthrous indeclinable nouns
after prepositions. Consider the following examples:

Mt. 1.17:	ἀπὸ ᾿Αβραὰμ ἕως Δαυὶδ...ἀπὸ Δαυίδ
Mt. 8.11:	μετὰ ᾿Αβραὰμ καὶ ᾿Ισαὰκ καὶ ᾿Ιακώβ
Mt. 21.11:	ἀπὸ Ναζαρέθ
Mt. 24.15:	διὰ Δανιήλ
Mk 1.9:	ἀπὸ Ναζαρέτ
Mk 2.26:	ἐπὶ ᾿Αβιαθάρ
Jn 3.24:	ἀπὸ Σαμουήλ
Jn 12.21:	ἀπὸ Βηθσαϊδα

Because the article is not required with indeclinable foreign loan-words
following prepositions, texts like these (and there are many more) cause one

exception exists in the papyri and not in the New Testament (Moulton, *Prolegomena*,
p. 81). There are many textual problems with the exceptions in the LXX (e.g. Judg. 6.11;
Ps. 122.2; 1 Macc. 16.9; see Robertson, pp. 1071-72; Votaw, *The Infinitive in Biblical
Greek*, pp. 17-18). I will address these exceptions in Chapter 5.

14.   As was noted in Chapter 1, the infinitive is a substantive with or without the
article. For instance, in Phil. 3.1, the anarthrous infinitive clearly functions as the subject
of the sentence: τὰ αὐτὰ γράφειν ὑμῖν ἐμοὶ μὲν οὐκ ὀκνηρόν. The article is not needed
to mark the infinitive as a noun. See Votaw's study for a complete listing of anarthrous
infinitives that function as subjects and direct objects (*The Infinitive in Biblical Greek*,
pp. 7-10, 12).

15.   It should be kept in mind that the semantic effect of case-marking is quite distinct
from the semantic notion of marking for definiteness. While the article does specify a
case and thus a meaning associated with that case, the article does not mark for definiteness. So, it is not as if the article has absolutely no semantic value. What I argued in
Chapter 2 is that it has no semantic value *as a determiner*.

to question whether the article is really required with indeclinable infinitives that follow a preposition. The constructions seem so analogous to one another that it would seem that the syntactical markers that are required for one must be required for the other.[16]

Upon closer inspection, however, it is clear that the constructions are not analogous. Their dissimilarity is exhibited by the fact that indeclinable foreign loan-words do not form compounds with prepositions. As a result, there is little question as to the grammatical function of an anarthrous indeclinable noun following a preposition. Such a noun must be the object of the preposition,[17] even though its case is not made explicit by the presence of the article.[18] However, because of the absence of spaces between words in Greek, great ambiguity would result if only anarthrous infinitives were used following prepositions. Theoretically, there would be at least two syntactical possibilities for an anarthrous infinitive following a preposition. The first possibility is that the infinitive might be functioning as the object of the preposition. The second possibility is that the preposition may be combining with the verb to form a compound. Because of this potential ambiguity, the article is needed in order to distinguish the first situation from the second situation. The ambiguity that would result if the article were not used as a function word with infinitival prepositional objects does not appear when anarthrous indeclinable foreign loan-words are used as objects of prepositions. For this reason, indeclinable foreign nouns are not analogous to infinitives when appearing as objects of prepositions. The only thing that the two constructions have in common is that they are both indeclinable.

We can illustrate the function of the Greek article in these kinds of prepositional phrases by thinking about how English distinguishes prepositional objects from compound words. In English this distinction has both morphological[19] and phonetic aspects. Morphologically, English readers distinguish 'infields of gold' from 'in fields of gold' by the use of spaces between words. In the first phrase, we know 'infields' to be a compound word simply by observing that there is no space between the prepositional prefix 'in' and the noun 'fields'. The space separating 'in' from 'fields' in the second phrase

---

16. Mark Seifrid raised this issue in the doctoral colloquium in which I presented my dissertation prospectus.

17. While some prepositions are postpositive (Robertson, p. 553), all of the ones that we are concerned with in this study (including those used with indeclinable foreign loan-words) precede the noun to which they are syntactically related.

18. Though the case function in many instances can be easily deduced because many prepositions only take one case. Of the 201 articular infinitives that follow a preposition, about 70 per cent follow prepositions that take only one case: 74 follow εἰς, 56 follow ἐν, 9 follow πρό, 1 follows ἕως, 1 follows ἕνεκεν, 1 follows ἐκ, and 1 follows ἀντί.

19. Technically, this is a morpho-syntactic distinction because English relies so heavily upon word order.

shows us that 'fields' is intended to be the object of the preposition. English speakers also make a phonetic distinction between 'infields' and 'in fields' through the use of accent. 'Infields' is articulated with an accent on the first syllable, while 'in fields' would normally have an accent on the second. The point is that English users utilize both morphological and phonetic conventions in order to disambiguate what would otherwise be very unclear.

Table 6. *Compound Infinitives in the New Testament*[20]

Verbs Used in Composition	Number of Compound Verbs Using this Preposition	Number of Texts Containing One or More Compound Infinitives
ἀνά	65	49
ἀντί	13	1
ἀπό	82	126
διά	63	24
ἐν	34	11
εἰς	10	40
ἐκ	58	32
ἐξ	30	18
ἐπί	67	42
κατά	99	56
μετά	21	13
παρά	58	49
περί	33	30
πρό	45	14
πρός	41	35
σύν	66	26
ὑπέρ	14	2
ὑπό	30	3
Totals	829	571

Such morphological and phonetic distinctions would have been important to the authors of the New Testament since their original audience would have included both readers and hearers.[21] The original reader of a given use

20.   I gathered these statistics using the GRAMCORD database. I scrolled through all the compound verbs, added each one to a search query, and specified the retrieval of every infinitival use of compound verbs in the New Testament.

21.   Modern readers often fail to recognize this fact. The proliferation of printed Bibles in our own day makes it difficult for modern readers to relate to the oral culture that existed two millennia ago. Yet we know that both Jews and Christians of the first century relied upon the spoken word for their scriptural training, not the written (Lk. 4.16; Acts 13.15, 27; 15.21, 30-31; 2 Cor. 3.14-15; Eph. 3.4; Col. 4.16; 1 Thess. 5.27; 1 Tim. 4.13; Rev. 1.3). Robert Stein has recently reminded New Testament scholars of the importance of remembering that the New Testament materials were written with the knowledge that they were to be read aloud in the Christian assembly: 'Another important

of the articular infinitive would have needed a way to distinguish compound infinitives from infinitives as object of the preposition. Morphologically, just as the space marks the noun as the prepositional object in English, so the article marks the infinitive as prepositional object in Greek. The original hearers of the New Testament materials also would have needed such signals. The spoken article would have enabled the original hearers to make the syntactic distinction.

The statistics in Table 6 trace the usage of infinitival compound verbs in the New Testament.

In all of these texts, it would be possible to construe the infinitive as the object of the preposition were it not for the regular use of the article to distinguish infinitival prepositional objects. I will illustrate my point with an example from Mk 8.31: Καὶ ἤρξατο διδάσκειν αὐτοὺς ὅτι δεῖ τὸν υἱὸν τοῦ ἀνθρώπου πολλὰ παθεῖν καὶ ἀποδοκιμασθῆναι ὑπὸ τῶν πρεσβυτέρων καὶ τῶν ἀρχιερέων καὶ τῶν γραμματέων. We know that the original readers of this verse would have been faced with a text that did not have spaces between the words. If the article were not regularly used as a function word in prepositional phrases, would it not be syntactically possible to regard the infinitive ἀποδοκιμασθῆναι as a prepositional phrase rather than as a compound verb? Thus we might understand Mk 8.31 in one of two ways: (1) as a compound verb, 'It is necessary that Son of Man should suffer many things and be rejected by the elders and chief priests and scribes', or (2) as a prepositional phrase, 'It is necessary that the Son of Man should suffer many things, even from being tested by the elders and chief priests and scribes'. The context makes this second reading unlikely even without the article, but it would be syntactically possible if anarthrous infinitives were routinely used as objects of prepositions. However, the writers of the Hellenistic Greek of the New Testament, always use the articular infinitive when the infinitive is meant to be construed as the object of the preposition. Just as the article is employed as a function word in other syntactical arrangements in order to clarify grammatical relationships (see Chapters 2 and 3), so the neuter article with the infinitive disambiguates the function of the infinitive following the preposition.[22]

---

implication that flows out of the presupposition that Mark thought of his "readers" as "hearers" having his Gospel read to them, is that he wrote clearly enough that his hearers would be able to understand what he said *as the Gospel was being read to them...* Thus Mark, and even Paul's letters, should be interpreted in light of the ability of their hearing audiences to process the information being read to them, *as it was being read*' (Robert H. Stein, 'Our Reading of the Bible vs. the Original Audience's Hearing It', *JETS* 46 [2003], pp. 63-78 [73-74 (my emphasis)]).

22. I noted in Chapter 1 that this explanation comes from Robertson: 'As a rule the article was essential if a preposition occurred with an inf. The reason for this was due to the absence of division between words. It was otherwise almost impossible to tell this use

We can support this point further by considering the result of removing the article from those texts which use the articular infinitive as prepositional object. For example, consider the prepositional phrase at the beginning of Jas 4.15: ἀντὶ τοῦ λέγειν ὑμᾶς· ἐὰν ὁ κύριος θελήσῃ καὶ ζήσομεν καὶ ποιήσομεν τοῦτο ἢ ἐκεῖνο. As noted above, the original readers of this text would not have seen spaces between the words, so the opening phrase would have appeared as, αντιτουλεγεινυμας. Now imagine if this same phrase were to appear without the article, αντιλεγεινυμας. Whereas the first articular phrase could be understood as, 'Instead of your saying', the second anarthrous phrase could be construed in one of two ways: (1) 'instead of your saying', or (2) 'in order that you might oppose'. James's use of the article clears away the latter ambiguity by marking the infinitive as object, thereby excluding the possibility of this phrase being understood as a *final* use of the infinitive ἀντιλέγειν ('to oppose'). This kind of ambiguity would attach itself to every text that uses an infinitive after a preposition if the article were not routinely employed as a function word in this way.

We must conclude that the article with the infinitive in prepositional phrases does not carry semantic weight as a definitizing determiner. This conclusion follows from the premise set forth in Chapter 2:

> Only a total elimination of all grammatical features permits us to arrive at true semantic statements... [T]he first step of linguistic analysis aimed at defining the function of a given element of expression is to exclude all its uses in environments where it appears to be compulsory or grammatically induced.[23]

---

of the inf. from that of composition of preposition with the verb if the two came in conjunction. Cf. ἀντὶ τοῦ λέγειν in Jas. 4.15' (Robertson, p. 1069). When I began this study, I disagreed with Robertson on this point in favor of the opinion that the only reason the article appears is to mark the case of the infinitive. I have since changed my opinion on this matter. I thought that Robertson's explanation could not answer two important questions. First, if the article appears so that the preposition will not be mistaken for a prefix to the infinitive verb, then why is the article also employed with prepositions that do not ever get used in composition with verbs (e.g. ἕως in Acts 8.40, ἕνεκεν in 2 Cor. 7.12)? Second, if the article is used merely to separate the preposition from the infinitive so that the infinitive is not mistaken for a compound verb, then why does the article appear between the preposition and the infinitive even when there are other intervening words (such as postpositive δέ in Mt. 26.32 and Mk 1.14; see also Mk 5.4). I have come to the conclusion, however, that these questions should not lead us to reject Robertson's explanation but to refine it. Not only does the article appear for the reason that Robertson sets forth, but it also appears in order to mark for case. We need not make a false dichotomy, as if only one of these explanations could be correct. They are both correct. The fact that there are literally hundreds of infinitival compound verbs in the New Testament led me to the conclusion that the authors of the New Testament had to have a way to distinguish infinitives as object of a preposition from those that are simple compounds.

23. Rosén, *Early Greek Grammar and Thought in Heraclitus*, pp. 30, 37.

Because the article is required as a grammatical marker (i.e. function word) following prepositions, we should not press the article's semantic value as a definitizer in such contexts.

I have demonstrated two important methodological assumptions that must be observed in the following sections as we set forth a syntax of articular infinitives as prepositional objects. First, it is important to remember that cases govern prepositions and not vice versa. In other words, when cases are used with prepositions, the case-meaning does not dissolve into the semantic domain of the preposition. On the contrary, the prepositions merely bring to the fore a particular meaning associated with a given case. Second, because the use of the article is clearly grammatically obligatory in every instance that the articular infinitive follows a preposition, one should not impute a definitizing semantic value to the article that precedes the infinitive.

2. *Genitive Articular Infinitives Following Prepositions*

a. *Semantics of the Construction*
As noted in the previous chapter, the genitive case is what Smyth calls a 'composite' or 'mixed' case in that it encompasses both ablative and pure genitive functions.[24] This one genitive form denotes two main semantic relations, that of *restriction* (pure genitive) and of *separation* (ablative).[25] My thesis concerning the meaning of the article with the infinitive is that the article is a function word, appearing for one of two reasons: (1) to mark the case of the infinitive or (2) to mark some other syntactical function that can only be made explicit by the presence of the article. Every instance of the genitive articular infinitive appears to be grammatically induced in one or both of these ways. With respect to the genitive articular infinitive after prepositions, the article has two functions: (1) to mark the case of the infinitive and (2) to mark the infinitive as object of the preposition. After having demonstrated that the article is grammatically motivated in these two ways in every instance of the articular infinitive, it will be clear that the genitive article has no semantic value as a definitizing determiner.[26]

b. *Discussion of Texts*
There are only thirteen genitive articular infinitives following prepositions in the New Testament. There are only six prepositions represented among the

24. Smyth, §1279; Funk, *A Beginning–Intermediate*, I, p. 71.
25. Louw, 'Linguistic Theory', pp. 84, 86.
26. This line is a restatement of a critical methodological assumption that I set forth in Chapter 2. When it can be demonstrated that the article is syntactically required, one should not look for any further semantic significance of the article (Rosén, *Early Greek Grammar and Thought in Heraclitus*, pp. 30, 37).

thirteen: πρό, διά, ἕως, ἕνεκεν, ἐκ, and ἀντί.[27] As discussed in the previous chapter, we expect that the genitives would have either a pure genitive force (*restriction*) or an ablatival genitive force (*separation*).[28] The evidence will show that prepositions combine with genitive articular infinitives in order to specify an ablatival relation. Just as the genitive after ἀπό and ἐκ is increasingly replacing the 'naked' genitive form to denote the ablative idea with non-verbal substantives,[29] so certain prepositions are used to denote various ablatival notions with the genitive articular infinitive. The prepositions with the genitive case-form draw attention to the adverbial side of the infinitive and thus to an ablatival relation.

Table 7. *Genitive Articular Infinitives Governed by a Preposition*

	πρὸ τοῦ	διὰ τοῦ	ἕως τοῦ	ἕνεκεν τοῦ	ἐκ τοῦ	ἀντὶ τοῦ	*Total*
Matthew	6.8						1
Luke	2.21; 22.15						2
John	1.48; 13.19; 17.5						3
Acts	23.15		8.40				2
2 Corinthians				7.12	8.11		2
Galatians	2.12; 3.23						2
Hebrews		2.15					
James						4.15	1
Totals	9	0	1	1	1	1	13

(1) *Genitive articular infinitives following* πρό. There are nine genitive articular infinitives following the preposition πρό in the New Testament. In terms of the 'local' relation[30] exhibited by πρό, this preposition describes an

27. These six prepositions appear with genitive articular infinitives in the papyri as well as with ἄνευ, μέχρι, περί, πλήν, ὑπέρ, and χάριν (Mayser, *Grammatik*, II.1, pp. 324-28, 332-33). They begin showing up as early as the third century BCE. Hamilton Ford Allen categorizes two instances of Polybius's use of the anarthrous infinitive after πλήν as prepositional objects (Allen, *The Infinitive in Polybius*, p. 312). This categorization of Polybius's usage is misleading, however, because he says very clearly in the description that follows that in these two instances πλήν functions as an adverb, not a preposition. Cf. Mayser, *Grammatik*, II.1, p. 327.

28. Smyth, §1675.b: 'The genitive [with the preposition] is either the genitive proper...or the ablatival genitive'.

29. Wallace, *Greek Grammar*, p. 77.

30. 'Most prepositions have a fundamental sense related to being situated in, moving toward or moving away from a location. Prepositions used with the accusative case often carry a sense of motion or direction toward a location; prepositions with the genitive case often carry a sense of motion or direction away from a location; and prepositions with the dative case often carry a sense of rest. This framework in no way implies that a Greek

object as 'at rest' and 'before' or 'in front of' some other element in the context.[31] The fundamental idea of πρό is that it denotes a relationship of *precedence*. Robertson and Bauer agree that this 'before' or 'in front of' notion of πρό applies to place, time, and rank in the New Testament.[32] The result is that πρό denotes a *position before*, a *time before*, or a *rank before*.

Both Robertson and Brooks and Winbery agree that these three nuances of πρό employ the genitive case-form in order to specify an ablatival relation.[33] As discussed above, the ablatival genitive primarily denotes the idea of separation. How does the notion *separation* appear when such genitive case-forms follow πρό? With respect to 'rank', Brooks and Winbery say, 'The ablative [genitive] expresses the idea of separation in terms of rank, order, or precedence'.[34] In this way, we see πρό plus the genitive employed in Jas 5.12, Πρὸ πάντων δέ, ἀδελφοί μου, μὴ ὀμνύετε ('*Above all*, my brothers, do not swear'). In this text, the prohibition on swearing is *separated* out from (ablative notion) and *ranked before* (πρό notion) other moral obligations. With respect to 'position', the idea of *separation* is also apparent in many texts.[35] To single out one representative example, observe Acts 12.6, φύλακές τε πρὸ τῆς θύρας ἐτήρουν τὴν φυλακήν ('And guards *in front of* the door were guarding the jail'). The position of the guards is *separated* from and *before* the prison door as opposed to the two guards and

speaker or writer began by thinking of the basic sense of the preposition each time it was used. To the contrary, most usage was second nature to the native speaker, any connection between the two being long ago severed. But twentieth-century interpreters, who do not have native competence in the language, often find it useful to begin from a basic sense of the preposition. This provides a line of continuity among the various extensions of meaning. Many of these extensions are far removed from the basic sense, since their usage is based upon syntax and context. But this framework is designed to help bring more order to a potentially chaotic discussion by not multiplying categories unnecessarily' (Porter, *Idioms*, p. 142).

31. Harris, 'Prepositions and Theology', p. 1172; cf. Robertson, p. 620: 'It is simply "fore", "before". It is rather more general in idea than ἀντί and has a more varied development.' See Porter's diagram in *Idioms*, p. 170.

32. Robertson, pp. 620-21; BDAG, *s.v.* πρό, p. 864. LSJ observes this basic threefold usage in its broader accounting of Greek literature: place, time, and *other relations* (LSJ, *s.v.* πρό, p. 1465). Stanley Porter's threefold division is *locative, temporal*, and *positional* (*Idioms*, pp. 170-71).

33. Robertson, pp. 621, 1075; Brooks and Winbery, *Syntax*, p. 29. Both Robertson and Brooks and Winbery are working from an eight-case system, but this fact does not nullify the observation that the *function* of these genitive forms is ablative. Though we may define *case* differently, we agree on the function of these particular forms.

34. Brooks and Winbery, *Syntax*, p. 29. BDAG only lists two texts in the New Testament that employ πρό as a 'marker of precedence or rank': Jas 5.12, 1 Pet. 4.8 (BDAG, *s.v.* πρό, p. 864).

35. E.g. Mt. 11.10; Mk 1.2; Lk. 1.76; 7.27; 9.52; 10.1; Jn 10.8; 14.13; Acts 5.23; 12.6, 14; 13.24; Jas 5.9 (BDAG, *s.v.* πρό, p. 864).

Peter who were in the jail and behind the door. In terms of 'time', there are also many texts that denote the idea of separation.[36] Consider Mt. 8.29, ἦλθες ὧδε πρὸ καιροῦ βασανίσαι ἡμᾶς; ('Did you come here to torment us *before* the time?'). Jesus' 'tormenting' occurs at a time *separated* from an appointed time; indeed Jesus' 'tormenting' takes place *before* a day which obviously has been set for reckoning. These texts show how the ablatival genitive notion of *separation* combines with the πρό idea of *precedence* with respect to rank, position, and time.

All nine of the genitive articular infinitives governed by πρό have a temporal meaning. In other words, all nine texts employ πρό plus the genitive articular infinitive to mark a point in time that is prior to or before another point in time:[37]

Mt. 6.8:
οἶδεν γὰρ ὁ πατὴρ ὑμῶν ὧν χρείαν ἔχετε πρὸ τοῦ ὑμᾶς *αἰτῆσαι* αὐτόν.

For your Father knows of that which you have need before you ask him.

Lk. 2.21:
Καὶ ὅτε ἐπλήσθησαν ἡμέραι ὀκτὼ τοῦ περιτεμεῖν αὐτὸν καὶ ἐκλήθη τὸ ὄνομα αὐτοῦ Ἰησοῦς, τὸ κληθὲν ὑπὸ τοῦ ἀγγέλου πρὸ τοῦ *συλλημφθῆναι* αὐτὸν ἐν τῇ κοιλίᾳ.

And when the eight days of his circumcision were completed, his name was called Jesus, the [name] which he was called by the angel before he was conceived in the womb.

Lk. 22.15:
ἐπιθυμίᾳ ἐπεθύμησα τοῦτο τὸ πάσχα *φαγεῖν* μεθ' ὑμῶν πρὸ τοῦ με *παθεῖν*

I have greatly desired to eat this Passover with you before I suffer.

Jn 1.48:
πρὸ τοῦ σε Φίλιππον *φωνῆσαι* ὄντα ὑπὸ τὴν συκῆν εἶδόν σε.

Before Philip called you, while you were under the fig tree, I saw you.

Jn 13.19:
ἀπ' ἄρτι λέγω ὑμῖν πρὸ τοῦ *γενέσθαι*, ἵνα πιστεύσητε ὅταν γένηται ὅτι ἐγώ εἰμι.

From now on I tell you before it comes to pass, so that when it does occur, you may believe that I am.

36. E.g. Mt. 5.12; 8.29; 24.38; Lk. 2.21; 11.38; 21.12; 22.15; Jn 1.48; 5.7; 10.8; 11.55; 12.1; 13.1, 19; 17.5, 24; Acts 5.36; 7.4; 21.38; 23.15; Rom. 16.7; 1 Cor. 2.7; 4.5; 2 Cor. 12.2; Gal. 1.17; 2.12; 3.23; Eph. 1.4; Col. 1.17; 2 Tim. 1.9; 4.21; Tit. 1.2; Heb. 11.5; 1 Pet. 1.20; Jude 25 (BDAG, *s.v.* πρό, p. 864).

37. BDAG, *s.v.* πρό, p. 864.

Jn 17.5:
καὶ νῦν δόξασόν με σύ, πάτερ, παρὰ σεαυτῷ τῇ δόξῃ ᾗ εἶχον πρὸ τοῦ τὸν κόσμον εἶναι παρὰ σοί.

And now, you glorify me, Father, with yourself with the glory which I had with you before the world was.

Acts 23.15:
ἡμεῖς δὲ πρὸ τοῦ *ἐγγίσαι* αὐτὸν ἕτοιμοί ἐσμεν τοῦ *ἀνελεῖν* αὐτόν.

And we are ready in order that we might slay him before he comes near.

Gal. 2.12:
πρὸ τοῦ γὰρ *ἐλθεῖν* τινας ἀπὸ ᾿Ιακώβου μετὰ τῶν ἐθνῶν συνήσθιεν·

For before certain people came from James, he was eating with the Gentiles.

Gal. 3.23:
Πρὸ τοῦ δὲ *ἐλθεῖν* τὴν πίστιν ὑπὸ νόμον ἐφρουρούμεθα.

And before faith came, we were being kept under the law.

Except for Jn 13.19, all the instances of this construction have an accusative noun as the subject of the infinitive (though BDAG notes that the accusative subject of τοῦ γενέσθαι in Jn 13.19 'can easily be supplied' from the context).[38] Moreover, in all of these texts, πρό serves to clarify the ablatival function (i.e. *separation*) of the genitive infinitive in terms of one time that is prior to another.

The ablatival idea would not be clear if the preposition and/or the article were absent. In Mt. 6.8, for instance, the temporal notion of πρὸ τοῦ αἰτῆσαι would not be clear were τοῦ αἰτῆσαι employed without the preposition. The preposition πρό combines with τοῦ αἰτῆσαι to show that the Father has knowledge of a disciple's need *before* the disciple makes a request. Without this combination of πρό-τοῦ-INF, the meaning of this text would be entirely different. Luke 2.21 illustrates this difference in meaning between πρὸ-τοῦ-INF and τοῦ-INF. In the first part of the verse τοῦ-INF appears without a preposition: ὅτε ἐπλήσθησαν ἡμέραι ὀκτὼ τοῦ περι-τεμεῖν αὐτόν. We can understand this use of the genitive articular infinitive in at least one of two ways: (1) modifying the noun, that is, adnominally,[39] or (2) modifying the verb, that is, adverbially.[40] But we have argued in the

38. BDAG, *s.v.* πρό, p. 864. The subject of the infinitive is not understood to be the same as the lead verb in this instance ('I'), as is often the case with infinitives that have no expressed subject. Context makes clear that the subject of τοῦ γενέσθαι is identical with the third person singular subject of the following finite verb γένηται.

39. Votaw, *The Infinitive in Biblical Greek*, p. 33.

40. BDF §400(2): 'Certain passages exhibit a very loose relationship between the substantive and infinitive and tend toward the consecutive sense: Lk 2.21…approxi-mately = ὥστε περιτεμεῖν, ἵνα περιτέμωσιν'.

previous chapter that this example is adnominal. Yet even if we were to regard τοῦ+INF as an adverbial phrase, we would not interpret the phrase as marking a temporal association, but the consecutive notion of purpose. Thus, πρό-τοῦ-INF and τοῦ-INF denote different meanings. Πρό combines with τοῦ-INF to indicate one time that is prior to another. This temporal notion is not found in τοῦ-INF.

(2) *Genitive articular infinitive following* ἀντί. The use of the preposition ἀντί with the genitive case-form is what Brooks and Winbery label the 'Ablative of Exchange'.[41] Because the fundamental notion of ἀντί is 'set over against, opposite', this preposition came to have a three-fold usage: (1) *equivalence*, that is, one object set over against another as its equivalent; (2) *exchange*, that is, one object, opposing or distinct from another, is given or taken in return for the other; (3) and *substitution*, that is, one object that is distinguishable from another, which is given or taken instead of the other.[42] The preposition comports nicely with the ablatival genitive idea of separation because it deals with objects that are 'distinct' from one another.

The lone example of this construction in the New Testament is in Jas 4.15: ἀντὶ τοῦ λέγειν ὑμᾶς· ἐὰν ὁ κύριος θελήσῃ καὶ ζήσομεν καὶ ποιήσομεν τοῦτο ἢ ἐκεῖνο. *Substitution* is the idea conveyed by ἀντί plus the genitive in this verse.[43] The infinitive phrase in this text is widely mistranslated as, 'Instead you ought to say'.[44] This translation is unfortunate because it does not render the genitive infinitive τοῦ λέγειν as the object of the preposition ἀντί, and thus does not stress strongly enough the connection with Jas 4.13. The rendering of vv. 13 and 15 should be more along the lines of, 'Come now you who are saying...instead of what you are saying [you ought to say]...'[45] The point is that what James's hearers were 'saying' is *separated* or *distinct* from what they should be 'saying'. They need to substitute the way they are speaking with the way that James commands them to speak.

(3) *Genitive articular infinitives following* διά. BDF notes that the use of the articular infinitive with an attributive adjective is extremely rare in Greek literature,[46] but that is exactly what we find in Heb. 2.15: καὶ ἀπαλλάξῃ

41. Brooks and Winbery, *Syntax*, p. 30.

42. Harris, 'Prepositions and Theology', p. 1179.

43. Moule, *Idiom Book*, p. 128; Porter, *Idioms*, p. 201; Harris, 'Prepositions and Theology', p. 1179. Turner agrees that the idea is substitution in Jas 4.15, but he also notes that the construction is causal in Ezek. 29.9; 34.7-9; 36.3 (Turner, *Syntax*, p. 144).

44. NASB, NIV, NKJV, NRSV, RSV.

45. Douglas J. Moo, *The Letter of James* (Pillar New Testament Commentary; Grand Rapids: Eerdmans, 2000), p. 204.

46. BDF §398. Paul Ellingworth, *The Epistle to the Hebrews: A Commentary on the Greek Text* (NIGTC; Grand Rapids: Eerdmans, 1993), p. 175: 'Διὰ παντὸς τοῦ ζῆν,

τούτους, ὅσοι φόβῳ θανάτου διὰ παντὸς τοῦ ζῆν ἔνοχοι ἦσαν δουλείας ('and might deliver those who through fear of death were subject to slavery through all their living'). In my translation, I have attempted a formal equivalence rendering so that the force of the attributive παντός might clearly be seen in relation to the verbal noun τοῦ ζῆν. With the genitive case, διά is a marker of extension through an area or object.[47] When διά plus the genitive has reference to time, the idea is that of extension through time such that it refers to the whole period of time to its very end. Thus Bauer's rendering of this phrase is typical, 'throughout the lifetime'.[48] The idea of *extension* inherent in διά combines well with the notion of *separation* inherent in the genitive case. In this instance, the 'separation' is the beginning point of time from the end point of time. This is the lone use of this construction in the New Testament with the preposition διά.

(4) *Genitive articular infinitive following* ἕως. At the most fundamental level, ἕως is a 'marker of a limit reached'.[49] It is used as a preposition and as a conjunction in the New Testament. As an improper preposition, it is very often used as a temporal marker in order to mark the end-limit of a period of time. As such, it can focus attention on (1) the end of the action, *until, till*, or (2) the continuance of the action, *while*.[50] Acts 8.40 employs ἕως plus the genitive articular infinitive in the former sense, εὐηγγελίζετο τὰς πόλεις πάσας ἕως τοῦ ἐλθεῖν αὐτὸν εἰς Καισάρειαν ('He was evangelizing all the cities until he came into Caesarea'). The underlying semantic idea of the preposition ἕως comports well with the ablative notion of *separation*.[51] The preposition combines with the ablatival genitive to focus attention of the

"throughout (their) life", is an example, unique in the New Testament and very rare elsewhere, of an infinitive with an attributive in the same case… The use of τὸ ζῆν as synonymous with ὁ βίος is classical.'

47. BDAG, *s.v.* διά, p. 223.
48. BDAG, *s.v.* διά, p. 224.
49. BDAG, *s.v.* ἕως, p. 423. Though BDAG lists 'marker of a limit reached' as one among many possible meanings, this is the most fundamental idea of ἕως. Cf. Porter, *Idioms*, p. 180: 'until'.
50. LSJ, *s.v.* ἕως, p. 751. BDAG's discussion of this preposition would have been more helpful if it would have recognized this basic two-fold division. BDAG lists five categories of meaning, each of which could be subsumed under one of these two headings: (1) marker of contemporaneousness, or (2) marker of a limit reached (BDAG, *s.v.* ἕως, pp. 422-24). The former sense is far less frequent (e.g. Mt. 14.22; 26.36; Jn 9.4).With respect to the latter, the 'limit reached' idea often refers to a point in time, but it can also refer to place (e.g. Lk. 2.15; 2 Cor. 12.2), last item in a series (e.g. Mt. 20.8; 22.36), or the upper limit of measure (e.g. Mt. 18.21).
51. *Contra* Robertson and Brooks and Winbery (Robertson, p. 643; Brooks and Winbery, *Syntax*, p. 68). Why they would consider this a pure genitive is inexplicable to my mind.

endpoint of a period of time that is *separated* from the beginning of the time of the action of the verbal idea it modifies.

(5) *Genitive articular infinitive following* ἕνεκεν. So far, we have been following Harris's fourfold methodology for studying prepositional phrases: (1) to identify the primary meaning or local relation denoted by the preposition itself and its range of meanings when used with a particular case; (2) to identify the basic significance of the case that is used with the preposition; (3) to take into account special features of the context as to the meaning of the preposition; and (4) to make a note of any distinctive features of the preposition's usage in the New Testament which may account for seeming irregularities. Yet with ἕνεκεν, it is difficult to identify a primary local relation. This is probably due to the fact that not all of the improper prepositions exhibit such a primary meaning. For this reason, Harris warns, 'It is not always possible to trace clearly this basic spatial sense (the "root meaning") in extended metaphorical uses of the preps.'.[52]

Whether ἕνεκεν ever exhibited a fundamental local relation, we cannot be certain. Its usage in the New Testament and in literature contemporary to the New Testament shows that its principal usage was not to denote a local relation, but an *ideal* relation.[53] That is, the preposition ἕνεκεν primarily served to make clear a logical connection. The logical connection that it signifies is as close as we can come to arriving at a fundamental meaning. This logical relationship has been variously characterized by lexicographers and grammarians as a marker of 'cause', 'reason', or 'purpose'.[54] The only problem with these glosses is that they are logically antithetical. To say that A happens *because* B happens (*causus*) is entirely different from saying that A happens *so that* B happens (*propter*).[55]

Instead of positing a range of antithetical usages, Louw and Nida's lexicon gives a description of ἕνεκεν that best captures its fundamental sense: 'A marker of cause or reason, often with the implication of purpose in the

52. Harris, 'Prepositions and Theology', p. 1172.

53. I am using Harris's terminology, though he only covers the prepositions that are used in composition (Harris, 'Prepositions and Theology', pp. 1172-73).

54. BDAG, *s.v.* ἕνεκεν, p. 334. Cf. LSJ, *s.v.* ἕνεκεν, p. 563; Robertson, pp. 641, 1073; Smyth §1700; Brooks and Winbery, *Syntax*, pp. 29, 30; Porter, *Idioms*, 179; Moule, *Idiom Book*, p. 83.

55. BDF, §216(1): 'The meaning of ἕνεκεν is almost always *propter* (hardly distinguished from διά with the acc.), less frequently *causa*'. Cf. Ludwig Radermacher, *Neutestamentliche Grammatik: Das Griechisch des Neuen Testaments im Zusammenhang mit der Volkssprache* (Handbuch zum Neuen Testament; Tübingen: J.C.B. Mohr, 1925), p. 138: 'Auf attischen Inschriften weicht, wie Meisterhans feststellte, ἕνεκα allmählich vor διά cum acc. zurück; in der Koine ist ἕνεκεν die geläufige Form (obwohl Epiktet anscheinend immer ἕνεκα hat)'.

sense of "for the sake of"—"on account of, because of" ',[56] or conversely, 'a marker of purpose, with the frequent implication of some underlying reason —"in order that, for the sake of, for" '.[57] The result is that both *cause* and *purpose* emerge as legitimate interpretations of ἕνεκεν in any given text. The translation will depend upon which aspect (*cause* or *purpose*) is being emphasized in the context.

This dual sense of ἕνεκεν comes through in the three uses of ἕνεκεν in 2 Cor. 7.12, ἄρα εἰ καὶ ἔγραψα ὑμῖν, οὐχ ἕνεκεν τοῦ ἀδικήσαντος οὐδὲ ἕνεκεν τοῦ ἀδικηθέντος ἀλλ᾽ ἕνεκεν τοῦ φανερωθῆναι τὴν σπουδὴν ὑμῶν τὴν ὑπὲρ ἡμῶν πρὸς ὑμας ἐνώπιον τοῦ θεοῦ ('Therefore, even though I wrote to you, [I did it] not for the sake of the one who offended nor for the sake of the one who was offended but for the sake of [having] your earnestness on my behalf revealed to you before God'). The first two uses of ἕνεκεν probably emphasize cause, even though the idea of purpose is clearly implied. The third use of ἕνεκεν clearly denotes purpose, even though the idea of cause is clearly implied. In all three instances, the ablatival genitive idea of *separation* fits.[58] A recognition of this two-fold sense is the only interpretation that follows a consistent understanding of the preposition. To simply say that the first two uses are causal and the third purpose misses the underlying duality of ἕνεκεν.[59]

(6) *Genitive articular infinitive following* ἐκ. As was noted above, in Hellenistic Greek ἀπό and ἐκ are increasingly being employed with the genitive case to denote the ablative idea. The 'local' meaning of ἐκ can be identified by contrasting it with its synonym ἀπό. Murray J. Harris writes, '*apo* generally denotes motion from the edge or surface of an object; *ek*, motion from within'.[60] He elaborates: 'Originally *ek* signified an exit "from within" something with which there had earlier been a close connexion. Therefore it naturally came to be used to denote origin, source, derivation or separation.'[61] In 2 Cor. 8.11, the idea of separation is expressed in terms of *source*: νυνὶ δὲ καὶ τὸ ποιῆσαι ἐπιτελέσατε, ὅπως καθάπερ ἡ προθυμία τοῦ θέλειν, οὕτως καὶ τὸ ἐπιτελέσαι ἐκ τοῦ ἔχειν ('But now also finish doing

56. L&N, *s.v.* ἕνεκεν, I, p. 781.

57. L&N, *s.v.* ἕνεκεν, I, p. 785.

58. Robertson mistakenly assigns the articular infinitive a pure genitive function: 'The case is, of course, the genitive' (Robertson, p. 1073). *Contra* Brooks and Winbery who label it an ablative of purpose (*Syntax*, p. 30).

59. This use is the semantic equivalent of the genitive infinitive of *purpose* discussed in Chapter 3.

60. Harris, 'Prepositions and Theology', p. 1180: 'However the fact that *apo* is regularly used with *exerchomai* in Luke (13 times) shows that even the broad distinction is not everywhere applicable'.

61. Harris, 'Prepositions and Theology', p. 1188.

it so that just as there was the eagerness to desire it, so there may be also the completion of it *out of your having* [i.e. *out of what you have*]'). Brooks and Winbery write that 'it is admittedly a fine line which distinguishes separation and source'.[62] How does the idea of *source* derive from the ablatival notion of *separation*?[63] Normally, the ablatival genitive of separation denotes that from which something is separated; after ἐκ, the ablatival genitive denotes that from which something is sourced. Clearly the source of the Corinthians' financial support is what is emphasized in 2 Cor. 8.11. The source of the support was their 'having', an idiomatic way of referring to their possessions.

3. *Dative Articular Infinitives Following Prepositions*

a. *Semantics of the Construction*
Following Porter (and Louw to some extent) in the previous chapter, we discovered that the dative case-form encodes the singular idea of *relation*, with the *instrumental* and *locative* uses being specific contextualizations of *relation*. The preposition ἐν in its most basic sense designates the *local* idea of 'the sphere within which some action occurs or the element or reality in which something is contained or consists'.[64] Because the preposition ἐν has this meaning, it is best suited to bring out the semantic notion of *togetherness* inherent in the *locative* or *instrumental* dative. And this is precisely how the two ideas (ἐν + dative) function in the Greek of the New Testament. There is no question but that the authors of the New Testament employ ἐν plus the dative articular infinitive in order to specify this *locative* meaning.[65] This locative notion denotes literally a *place*, but that 'location' can function figuratively as a *temporal* 'location',[66] or a *circumstantial* 'location'.[67]

---

62.   Brooks and Winbery, *Syntax*, p. 23.

63.   Robertson says of this prepositional phrase, 'the case is ablative' (Robertson, p. 1073). While I do not agree with his definition of *case*, he certainly has correctly identified the function of this form.

64.   Harris, 'Prepositions and Theology', p. 1191.

65.   Robertson assumes the case (which he defines in terms of function, not form) is locative: 'No other preposition occurs in the N.T. with the inf. in the locative case' (Robertson, p. 1073). Further: 'The Greek uses the instrumental with only two prepositions ἅμα and σύν, both with the comitative idea' (Robertson, p. 534).

66.   Louw contends that even more specific ideas such as *time* and *instrument* grow out of the one fundamental idea of *togetherness*: 'Constructions expressing time also clearly illustrate the Greek dative (as locative or instrumental) *versus* the accusative. The locative denotes time *at which*, i.e., point of time at which: τῇ δὲ ὑστεραίᾳ—a particular point of time of the following day. The instrumental denotes the amount of time used, i.e., how much time anything takes: ἐν τρισὶν ἡμέραις—it lasted three days' (Louw, 'Linguistic Theory and the Greek Case System', p. 83).

b. *Discussion of Texts*

There are 56 dative articular infinitives following prepositions in the New Testament. The only preposition represented among the 56 is ἐν.[68] To reiterate, my thesis concerning the meaning of the article with the infinitive is that the article is a function word, appearing for one of two reasons: (1) to mark the case of the infinitive or (2) to mark some other syntactical relation that can only be made explicit by the presence of the article. Every instance of the articular infinitive is grammatically motivated in one or both of these ways. With respect to the dative articular infinitive after prepositions, the article has two functions: (1) to mark the case of the infinitive and (2) to mark the infinitive as object of the preposition. With respect to the former, regardless of the alleged influence or non-influence of Hebrew on this construction,[69] the dative articular infinitive comprises the normal semantic notions associated with its case. With regard to the latter, the dative article marks the infinitive as object of the preposition. This latter aspect is crucial to observe because the preposition ἐν is used so frequently in composition with verbs.

67. BDAG, *s.v.* ἐν, p. 329 (7): 'Somet. the circumstantial and temporal (s. 7 and 10) uses are so intermingled that it is difficult to decide between them'. Sometimes the specific nuance is difficult to nail down. For this reason, BDF has ἐν τῷ plus the infinitive as 'mostly temporal', but 'occasionally…in a sense not purely temporal' (BDF §404.1 and 3; cf. Robertson, p. 1073).

68. The papyri show three additional prepositions being used before the dative articular infinitive: ἅμα, ἐπί, and πρός (Mayser, *Grammatik*, II.1, pp. 328-29, 332-33). All four prepositions are being used with the dative articular infinitive as early as the third century BCE.

69. Many of the older grammars attribute the usage of ἐν τῷ with the infinitive in Luke's writings to the influence of Hebrew on the Greek language. Lawrence O. Grant frames the question clearly: 'With the Septuagint being Luke's Bible, does its use of ἐν τῷ with the infinitive influence the Lukan usage? If so, the Lukan usage becomes a Hebraism' ('The History of ἐν τῷ with the Infinitive and its Bearing on Luke's Writings' [PhD dissertation, The Southern Baptist Theological Seminary, 1945], pp. 3-4). So Gustaf Dalman, *The Words of Jesus Considered in the Light of Post-Biblical Jewish Writings and the Aramaic Language* (trans. D.M. Kay; Edinburgh: T. & T. Clark, 1902), p. 33: 'This construction…has been formed by the LXX, after the model of the Hebrew בְּ with the infinitive; see, e.g., Gen. 38.28 בְּלִדְתָּהּ; LXX ἐν τῷ τίκτειν αὐτήν'. So also Robertson, p. 1072: 'The Semitic influence is undoubted in the O.T. and seems clear in Luke, due probably to his reading the LXX or to his Aramaic sources'. John H. Winstead, 'The Greek Infinitive in Luke's Gospel' (PhD dissertation, The Southern Baptist Theological Seminary, 1930), p. 36: 'There is no question as to the Semitic influence in the Old Testament and the same seems clear in Luke'.

Grant has shown that this construction has precedent in other Greek writers and should not be thought of as mere Hebraism. Grant concludes: 'The Semitic influence is at a minimum in the writings of Luke… Deissmann and Moulton have reduced the majority of the so-called Semiticisms [*sic*] with parallels from contemporary vernacular Greek papyri documents' ('The History of ἐν τῷ with the Infinitive', p. 99).

Table 8. *Dative Articular Infinitives Governed by a Preposition*

	ἐν τῷ	Total
Matthew	13.4, 25; 27.12	3
Mark	4.4; 6.48	2
Luke	1.8, 21; 2.6, 27, 43; 3.21; 5.1 (×2), 12; 8.5, 40, 42; 9.18, 29, 33, 34, 36, 51; 10.35, 38; 11.1, 27, 37; 12.15; 14.1; 17.11, 14; 18.35; 19.15; 24.4, 15 (×2), 30, 51	34
Acts	2.1; 3.26; 4.30 (×2); 8.6 (×2); 9.3; 11.15; 19.1	9
Romans	3.4; 15.13	2
1 Corinthians	11.21	1
Galatians	4.18	1
Hebrews	2.8; 3.12, 15; 8.13	4
Total	56	56

Table 9. *Temporal Uses of ἐν τῷ Plus the Infinitive in the New Testament*[70]

	Present Infinitives		Aorist Infinitives	
	With ἐγένετο	Without ἐγένετο	With ἐγένετο	Without ἐγένετο
Matthew		13.4, 25; 27.12		
Mark	4.4			
Luke	1.8; 2.6; 5.1 (×2); 9.18, 29, 33, 51; 11.1, 27; 17.11, 14; 18.35; 24.4, 15, 51	2.43; 8.5, 40*, 42; 10.35, 38; 12.15*	3.21; 14.1; 19.15; 24.30	2.27; 9.34*, 36; 11.37
Acts		2.1; 8.6; 9.3		11.15
Romans		3.4		
1 Corinthians				11.21
Galatians		4.18		
Hebrews		3.15		

c. *Temporal Use of ἐν τῷ Plus the Infinitive*

The majority of the temporal uses of ἐν τῷ plus the infinitive are concentrated in Luke's writings. The characteristic Lukan pattern is to employ ἐν τῷ plus the infinitive in conjunction with ἐγένετο to express the idea 'it came to pass when…' The only use of this combination outside of Luke's writings is in Mk 4.4 where we read, καὶ ἐγένετο ἐν τῷ σπείρειν ὃ μὲν

---

70. Mt. 13.4, 25; 27.12; Mk 4.4; Lk. 1.8; 2.6, 27, 43; 3.21; 5.1 (×2), 12; 8.5, 40*; 8.42; 9.18, 29, 33, 34*, 36, 51; 10.35, 38; 11.1, 27, 37; 12.15*; 14.1; 17.11, 14; 18.35; 19.15; 24.4, 15 (×2), 30, 51; Acts 2.1; 8.6 (×2); 9.3; 11.15; 19.1; Rom. 3.4; 1 Cor. 11.21; Gal. 4.18; Heb. 3.15. The asterisks indicate those texts which could plausibly fit in either category, temporal or circumstantial.

ἔπεσεν παρὰ τὴν ὁδόν, καὶ ἦλθεν τὰ πετεινὰ καὶ κατέφαγεν αὐτό ('And it came about that as he was sowing, some fell beside the road, and the birds came and devoured it'). This prepositional phrase ἐν τῷ σπείρειν appears in the triple tradition (cf. Mt. 13.4; Lk. 8.5), yet the ἐγένετο which is so characteristic of Luke appears only in Mark.[71] Whatever the reason for this anomaly, we can observe that every use of ἐγένετο in combination with ἐν τῷ plus the infinitive denotes a temporal meaning. It is important to remember, however, that ἐν τῷ plus the infinitive does not need ἐγένετο in order to be temporal (as is indicated in Table 9).

BDF suggests that the ἐν τῷ plus the present infinitive denotes contemporaneous time while ἐν τῷ plus the aorist infinitive denotes antecedent time. BDF goes so far as to suggest that ἐν τῷ plus the aorist infinitive has a temporal meaning that is equal to the aorist participle.[72] Some texts seem to bear out this observation, such as Lk. 11.37, Ἐν δὲ τῷ λαλῆσαι ἐρωτᾷ αὐτὸν Φαρισαῖος ὅπως ἀριστήσῃ παρ' αὐτῷ ('Now when he had spoken, a Pharisee asked him to eat a meal with him'). The context clearly indicates that the 'asking' comes after Jesus' 'speaking'. Similar contextual indicators appear in other Lukan uses of ἐν τῷ plus the aorist infinitive (see Lk. 2.27; 19.15; 24.30; Acts 11.15).

Nevertheless, Ernest Burton has rightly rejected this view of the aorist tense in ἐν τῷ plus the infinitive. For Burton, ἐν τῷ plus the aorist infinitive does not denote antecedent time like the aorist participle: 'In 1 Cor. 11.21 and Heb. 3.12 the action of the Infinitive cannot be antecedent to that of the principal verb... In Lk. 9.34 such a relation is very difficult, and in Lk. 14.1 improbable in view of the Imperfect tense following'.[73] Burton anticipates what is the settled judgment of grammarians today. Simply put, the infinitive uses tense morphemes not to grammaticalize time, but verbal aspect.[74] Furthermore, the temporal value of the tense of the infinitive does not necessarily relate to the time of the main verb (as in the participle).

This understanding of the tense of the infinitive comports well with inherent locative notion of ἐν τῷ plus the infinitive. As Burton argues, 'The preposition in this sense does not seem necessarily to denote exact coincidence,

71. This is of course rather strange if one supposes that Luke depended upon a written version of Mark's Gospel. Why would Luke omit an idiom that he is so accustomed to using?

72. BDF §404(2).

73. Burton, *Moods and Tenses*, p. 50. Cf. Robertson, p. 1073: 'It is more correctly just the simple action of the verb which is thus presented, leaving the precise relation to be defined by the context, like the aorist participle of simultaneous action'. Wallace advises the following in translating ἐν τῷ plus the infinitive: 'It should be translated *while* (for present infinitives) or *as*, *when* (for aorist infinitives) plus an appropriate *finite* verb' (*Greek Grammar*, 595).

74. E.g. Porter, *Idioms*, p. 194.

but in no case expresses antecedence'.[75] Burton's point is simply that the preposition ἐν does not allow the notion of antecedent time, but concurrent time: 'The Aorist Infinitive after ἐν may be compared to the Aorist Indicative after ὅτε, which simply marks in general the time of the event denoted by the principal verb, leaving it to the context to indicate the precise nature of the chronological relation'.[76] While Burton's argument may not be sustained in all its details, one aspect of his analogy is very insightful. The preposition ἐν functions as a temporal locator in precisely the same way that ὅτε does. Thus, this use of the dative articular infinitive is very much a function of its case, which is made explicit by the presence of the article. The articular infinitive emphasizes the *locative* use of the dative case.

d. *Circumstantial Use of ἐν τῷ Plus the Infinitive*
The circumstantial use of ἐν τῷ plus the infinitive occurs primarily in modifying verbs that imply emotion.

Table 10. *Circumstantial Uses of ἐν τῷ*
Plus the Infinitive in the New Testament[77]

	Present Infinitives		Aorist Infinitives	
	With ἐγένετο	Without ἐγένετο	With ἐγένετο	Without ἐγένετο
Mark		6.48		
Luke		1.21; 8.40*		9.34*; 12.15*
Acts		3.26; 4.30 (×2)		
Romans		15.13		
Hebrews		8.13		2.8; 3.12

In the *circumstance* of doing something, an emotion is aroused. We see this, for example, in Mk 6.48: καὶ ἰδὼν αὐτοὺς βασανιζομένους ἐν τῷ ἐλαύνειν ('And seeing them being tormented in their rowing [idiomatically, "straining at the oars"]'). The idiom pictures one being 'tormented' in the circumstance of 'rowing'. This circumstance thus becomes the reason for the torment, thereby indicating an instrumental use of ἐν τῷ plus the infinitive (cf. Lk. 1.21). Sometimes, no emotion is implied, and the meaning intends only to emphasize the circumstance in which something else is done. In either case, the resultant meaning of ἐν τῷ plus the infinitive approaches the *instrumental* or *causal* idea. The preposition ἐν gives the *locative* dative a 'circumstantial' location that then becomes the instrument of the action of

75. Burton, *Moods and Tenses*, p. 50.
76. Burton, *Moods and Tenses*, p. 51.
77. Mk 6.48; Lk. 1.21; 8.40*; 9.34*; 12.15*; Acts 3.26; 4.30 (×2); Rom. 15.13; Heb. 2.8; 3.12; 8.13. The asterisks indicate those texts which could plausibly fit in either category, temporal or circumstantial.

the main verb. Thus, this use of the dative articular is also very much a function of its case, which is made explicit by the presence of the article.

4. *Accusative Articular Infinitives Following Prepositions*

a. *Semantics of the Construction*

As noted in the previous chapter, the accusative case does not bear a heavy semantic load but resembles the nominative case in that it primarily encodes a syntactic function.[78] Some grammarians have argued that the accusative case encodes the semantic idea of 'motion towards' or 'extension'.[79] But, as Louw points out, this idea is certainly mistaken: 'The accusative *on its own* does not denote (as is often said) "motion towards"... The accusative, however, is the most frequent case with verbs of motion, but this is so simply because it is usually not necessary to add detail or specification to illustrate the relationship more fully.'[80] Thus, unlike the genitive and dative, the accusative case does not contribute much to the meaning of the accusative prepositional phrase since the accusative is by nature 'non-defining'.[81] With respect to the accusative articular infinitive, therefore, the accusative article appears merely to mark the infinitive as the object of the preposition, with the primary semantic component being encoded in the preposition (e.g. telic εἰς τό, causal διὰ τό, temporal μετὰ τό, purpose πρὸς τό).

b. *Discussion of Texts*

There are 132 accusative articular infinitives following prepositions in the New Testament, by far the most frequently used case in this construction. There are only four prepositions represented among the 132: εἰς, διά, μετά, and πρός.[82] In all of these texts we find that the prepositional phrase derives its primary semantic component from the preposition while the accusative case merely marks the infinitive as the object of the preposition.

---

78.   It is probably for this reason that Robertson notes that Brugmann cannot give a good semantic description of the accusative case: 'The real ground-idea of the accusative case is unknown, though the relation between noun and verb is expressed by it' (Robertson, p. 467). Yet even in this statement, we can clearly see that Robertson recognizes the syntactic value of the accusative case. This observation only confirms my statement in Chapter 3 that the accusative is a syntactic case.

79.   Robertson, p. 468.

80.   Louw, 'Linguistic Theory and the Greek Case System', p. 81 and n. 55.

81.   Louw, 'Linguistic Theory and the Greek Case System', p. 80.

82.   These four appear with accusative articular infinitives in the papyri as well as with παρά (Mayser, *Grammatik*, II.1, pp. 329-33). All five begin showing up as early as the third century BCE.

Table 11. *Accusative Articular Infinitives Governed by a Preposition*

	εἰς τό	διὰ τό	μετὰ τό	πρὸς τό	*Total*
Matthew	20.19 (×3); 26.2; 27.31	13.5, 6; 24.12	26.32	5.28; 6.1; 13.30; 23.5; 26.12	14
Mark	14.55	4.5, 6; 5.4 (×3)	1.14; 14.28; 16.19	13.22	10
Luke	5.17	2.4; 6.48; 8.6; 9.7; 11.8; 18.5; 19.11 (×2); 23.8	12.5; 22.20	18.1	13
John		2.24			1
Acts	3.19; 7.19	4.2 (×2); 8.11; 12.20; 18.2, 3; 27.4, 9; 28.18	1.3; 7.4; 10.41; 15.13; 19.21; 20.1		17
Romans	1.11, 20; 3.26; 4.11 (×2), 16, 18; 6.12; 7.4, 5; 8.29; 11.11; 12.2, 3; 15.8, 13, 16				17
1 Corinthians	8.10; 9.18; 10.6; 11.22 (×2), 33		11.25		7
2 Corinthians	1.4; 4.4; 7.3 (×2); 8.6			3.13	6
Galatians	3.17				1
Ephesians	1.12, 18			6.11	3
Philippians	1.10, 23 (×2)	1.7			4
1 Thessalonians	2.12, 16; 3.2 (×2), 3, 5, 10 (×2), 13; 4.9			2.9	11
2 Thessalonians	1.5; 2.2 (×2), 6, 10, 11; 3.9			3.8	8
Hebrews	2.17; 7.25; 8.3; 9.14, 28; 11.3; 12.10; 13.21	7.23, 24; 10.2	10.15, 26		13
James	1.18, 19 (×2); 3.3	4.2			5
1 Peter	3.7; 4.2				2
Total	74	32	15	11	132

(1) *Accusative infinitives following* εἰς. There are 74 instances of accusative articular infinitives following the preposition εἰς in the New Testament. The fundamental *local* idea encoded in εἰς indicates *motion into*.[83] This is in fact the underlying definition given in BDAG: 'prep. w. acc. ...indicating motion into a thing or into its immediate vicinity or relation to something'.[84] The point is that the various semantic nuances of εἰς, both literal and figurative, grow out of this idea of *motion into*. All of the uses of εἰς with the accusative infinitive take on the figurative sense of *motion into* or *motion towards* in that the construction often indicates *goal*, *end*, or *purpose*. In the past, Greek scholars have debated whether or not there is an *ecbatic* use (pure result) of this construction in the New Testament.[85] Yet the *ecbatic* use is generally recognized today.[86]

In a thorough article in the *Journal of Biblical Literature*, I.T. Beckwith compares the usage of εἰς τό plus the infinitive in the New Testament with examples of this construction in extra-biblical Greek. He concludes that in extra-biblical Greek there are at least six distinguishable semantic nuances evident in the varied usage of this construction, five of which nuances are represented in the New Testament.[87] By far the most frequent use in the New Testament is that of purpose. Sometimes εἰς τό plus the infinitive is joined so closely with a noun or verb that it forms a single phrase.[88] For instance, in Mt. 20.19 we read, καὶ παραδώσουσιν αὐτὸν τοῖς ἔθνεσιν εἰς τὸ ἐμπαῖ-ξαι καὶ μαστιγῶσαι καὶ σταυρῶσαι ('And they will deliver him to the Gentiles to mock and scourge and crucify him'). At other times, this construction denotes purpose in such a way that it forms a separate final clause that is roughly equivalent to a ἵνα or ὅπως clause.[89] For example, consider Rom. 1.11: ἐπιποθῶ γὰρ ἰδεῖν ὑμᾶς, ἵνα τι μεταδῶ χάρισμα ὑμῖν πνευ-ματικὸν εἰς τὸ στηριχθῆναι ὑμᾶς ('For I long to see you in order that I may impart some spiritual gift to you, in order that you may be established'). Notice that in Rom. 1.11 the articular infinitive takes its own subject that is distinct from that of the main verb. Whether or not Beckwith's distinction between types of purpose clauses is legitimate is not really my concern here. The point is that εἰς τό plus the infinitive often denotes purpose.[90] This is

83. Harris, 'Prepositions and Theology', p. 1172.

84. BDAG, *s.v.* 'εἰς', p. 288.

85. Beckwith, 'The Articular Infinitive with εἰς', pp. 155-56, surveys the debate up to his day.

86. Harris, 'Prepositions and Theology', p. 1187; Moule, *Idiom Book*, p. 70; BDAG, *s.v.* 'εἰς', p. 290: 'Marker of goals...w. the result of an action or condition indicated'.

87. Beckwith, 'The Articular Infinitive with εἰς', pp. 157-63.

88. Beckwith, 'The Articular Infinitive with εἰς', p. 158.

89. Beckwith, 'The Articular Infinitive with εἰς', p. 158.

90. See also Mt. 20.19 (×3); 27.31; Mk 14.55; Acts 3.19; Rom. 1.11; 4.11 (×2), 16, 18; 7.4; 8.29; 11.11; 15.8, 13, 16; 1 Cor. 10.6; 11.22 (×2), 33; Eph. 1.12, 18; 1 Thess.

not a disputed category of meaning and does not require further comment except to say that it is important to notice that the semantic nuance of purpose grows out of the preposition, not the accusative case.

Beckwith claims that sometimes εἰς τό plus the infinitive is joined with other words to denote the respect in which the modified word is to be understood.[91] For instance, in Jas 1.19 we read, ἔστω δὲ πᾶς ἄνθρωπος ταχὺς εἰς τὸ ἀκοῦσαι, βραδὺς εἰς τὸ λαλῆσαι, βραδὺς εἰς ὀργήν ('But let everyone be quick with respect to hearing, slow with respect to speaking, slow with respect to wrath'). Antonius N. Jannaris gives a different analysis of the situation with respect to Jas 1.19 by pointing out the general tendency in late Greek for simple complementary infinitives to be replaced by εἰς τό plus the infinitive.[92] In either case, the original *local* sense of εἰς is discernable in a figurative way in Jas 1.19: 'Let everyone be quick *in their movement toward* hearing, slow *in their movement toward* speaking, slow *in their movement toward* wrath' (my translation). In this instance, the author employs εἰς to denote what Murray J. Harris has called 'metaphorical direction'.[93]

Beckwith argues that the construction εἰς τό plus the infinitive is also employed like an object-infinitive with a large class of words (including verbs, nouns, and adjectives) that signify to *encourage, impel, admonish, influence, effect,* and so forth. and with words implying *ability, fitness, readiness,* etc.[94] Moulton agrees that this usage as pure object appears in certain New Testament passages.[95] Beckwith suggests that this sense is perhaps discernible in the following texts:

> Lk. 5.17:
> καὶ δύναμις κυρίου ἦν εἰς τὸ ἰᾶσθαι αὐτόν.
>
> And the power of the Lord was there for him to perform healing.
>
> Phil. 1.23:
> συνέχομαι δὲ ἐκ τῶν δύο, τὴν ἐπιθυμίαν ἔχων εἰς τὸ ἀναλῦσαι καὶ σὺν Χριστῷ εἶναι.
>
> But I am distressed by the two options, having the desire to depart and to be with Christ.

2.16; 3.2 (×2), 3, 5, 13; 2 Thess. 2.6, 10; 3.9; Heb. 7.25; 8.3; 9.14, 28; 12.10; 13.21; Jas 1.18; 1 Pet. 3.7.
    91. Beckwith, 'The Articular Infinitive with εἰς', p. 159.
    92. Jannaris, *An Historical Greek Grammar*, §§2090-91.
    93. Harris, 'Prepositions and Theology', p. 1186.
    94. Beckwith, 'The Articular Infinitive with εἰς', p. 159.
    95. Moulton, *Prolegomena*, p. 219.

1 Thess. 2.12:

παρακαλοῦντες ὑμᾶς καὶ παραμυθούμενοι καὶ μαρτυρόμενοι εἰς τὸ περιπατεῖν ὑμᾶς ἀξίως τοῦ θεοῦ τοῦ καλοῦντος ὑμᾶς εἰς τὴν ἑαυτοῦ βασιλείαν καὶ δόξαν.

Exhorting you and encouraging and imploring so that you may walk in a manner worthy of the God who calls you into his own kingdom and glory.

1 Thess. 3.10:

νυκτὸς καὶ ἡμέρας ὑπερεκπερισσοῦ δεόμενοι εἰς τὸ ἰδεῖν ὑμῶν τὸ πρόσωπον καὶ καταρτίσαι τὰ ὑστερήματα τῆς πίστεως ὑμῶν.

Night and day praying most earnestly that we may see your face, and may complete what is lacking in your faith.

1 Thess. 4.9:

Περὶ δὲ τῆς φιλαδελφίας οὐ χρείαν ἔχετε γράφειν ὑμῖν, αὐτοὶ γὰρ ὑμεῖς θεοδίδακτοί ἐστε εἰς τὸ ἀγαπᾶν ἀλλήλους.

Now concerning the love of the brethren, you do not have need for anyone to write to you, for you yourselves are taught by God that you might love one another.

2 Thess. 2.1-2:

Ἐρωτῶμεν δὲ ὑμᾶς…εἰς τὸ μὴ ταχέως σαλευθῆναι ὑμᾶς ἀπὸ τοῦ νοὸς μηδὲ θροεῖσθαι.

Now we request you…that you may not be quickly shaken from your composure or be disturbed.

In classifying these examples as object-infinitives, Beckwith suppresses the semantic value of the preposition εἰς. This suppression is most conspicuous in the examples involving words implying *encourage, impel, admonish*, and so on. In 1 Thess. 2.12, for instance, if we were to interpret εἰς τὸ περιπατεῖν ὑμᾶς as an object-infinitive, the focus would be solely on the *content* of Paul's exhorting (παρακαλοῦντες, παραμυθούμενοι, μαρτυρόμενοι). But the preposition εἰς cannot be reduced in this way. In this text, Paul is not just focusing on the *content* of his exhortation but also on its *purpose*. Granted, there is a semantic overlap between these two categories. In this case, the *content* and the *purpose* of the exhortation are one.[96] Nonetheless, there is not a philologically sound basis for suppressing the *telic* notion inherent in εἰς.[97] We must assume that Paul selects the prepositional phrase

96.   Commenting on the same construction in 1 Thess. 3.10, Bruce notes this semantic overlap: 'The simple infinitive is sufficient after a verb of praying; the construction εἰς τὸ ἰδεῖν (equivalent of ἵνα ἴδωμεν) expresses purpose (cf. 2.12; 4.9). To see the Thessalonians was both the content and the purpose of their prayer to God' (Bruce, *1 and 2 Thessalonians*, p. 69).

97.   Charles A. Wanamaker, *The Epistles to the Thessalonians: A Commentary on the Greek Text* (NIGTC; Grand Rapids: Eerdmans, 1990), p. 107: 'The εἰς τό construction

over the bare accusative infinitive for a reason. The use of εἰς is not incidental, but purposeful. Leon Morris agrees with the interpretation taken here:

> Some idea of purpose does seem to be expressed here by εἰς τό, though Moulton says, 'Purpose is so remote here as to be practically evanescent'… But this is to make the exhortation purposeless, which is not Paul's meaning. Nor is he simply giving the content of the exhortation, but exhorting with a view to a certain result in the lives of the Thessalonians.[98]

For this reason, Beckwith should not have distinguished these texts semantically from the texts already cited that clearly employ εἰς τό plus the infinitive to denote purpose.

Beckwith distinguishes another semantic nuance of this construction, arguing that 'As εἰς is used with the noun proper to denote measure or degree…so also it stands with the articular infin. in the same relation'.[99] He includes the following New Testament texts under this category of usage:

> Rom. 6.12:
> Μὴ οὖν βασιλευέτω ἡ ἁμαρτία ἐν τῷ θνητῷ ὑμῶν σώματι εἰς τὸ ὑπακούειν ταῖς ἐπιθυμίαις αὐτοῦ.
>
> Therefore do not let sin reign in your mortal body that you should obey its lusts.
>
> Rom. 12.3:
> Λέγω γὰρ διὰ τῆς χάριτος τῆς δοθείσης μοι παντὶ τῷ ὄντι ἐν ὑμῖν μὴ ὑπερφρονεῖν παρ' ὃ δεῖ φρονεῖν ἀλλὰ φρονεῖν εἰς τὸ σωφρονεῖν, ἑκάστῳ ὡς ὁ θεὸς ἐμέρισεν μέτρον πίστεως.
>
> For through the grace given to me I say to every one among you not to think more highly of oneself than one ought to think; but to think so as to have sound judgment, as God has allotted to each a measure of faith.
>
> 1 Cor. 8.10:
> ἐὰν γάρ τις ἴδῃ σὲ τὸν ἔχοντα γνῶσιν ἐν εἰδωλείῳ κατακείμενον, οὐχὶ ἡ συνείδησις αὐτοῦ ἀσθενοῦς ὄντος οἰκοδομηθήσεται εἰς τὸ τὰ εἰδωλόθυτα ἐσθίειν;
>
> For if someone sees you, who have knowledge, dining in an idol's temple, will not his conscience, if he is weak, be strengthened to eat things sacrificed to idols?

indicates that this was the aim of the "exhorting, comforting, and insisting" that Paul and his coworkers had done'.

98. Leon Morris, *The First and Second Epistles to the Thessalonians* (NICNT; Grand Rapids: Eerdmans, rev. ed., 1991), p. 77 n. 56.

99. Beckwith, 'The Articular Infinitive with εἰς', p. 159.

2 Cor. 7.3:

πρὸς κατάκρισιν οὐ λέγω· προείρηκα γὰρ ὅτι ἐν ταῖς καρδίαις ἡμῶν ἐστε εἰς τὸ συναποθανεῖν καὶ συζῆν.

I do not speak to condemn you; for I have said before that you are in our hearts to die together and to live together.

Beckwith has wrongly distinguished these texts as representing a separate category of usage, a point which he concedes: 'This usage is so nearly allied to that of pure result…that some cases can be referred indifferently to either category'.[100] Once again, this category diminishes too much the force of εἰς. For this reason, we should understand these uses of εἰς τό plus the articular infinitive as *ecbatic* (result). In Rom. 6.12, it is not so much the *extent* of 'reigning sin' that Paul addresses as it is the *result*[101] of reigning sin—obedience to its lusts. This observation applies equally to all four of these texts. On Rom. 12.3, Turner has gone too far in saying that εἰς τό plus the infinitive almost always expresses purpose in Paul.[102] Moo is correct in saying that, 'The infinitive construction εἰς τὸ σωφρονεῖν does not indicate purpose…but modifies φρονεῖν, stating the way in which one is to "think"'.[103] Moo includes 1 Cor. 8.10 and 2 Cor. 7.3 among the nine instances of this construction in Paul that clearly should be interpreted as *result*.[104]

Finally, Beckwith argues that εἰς τό plus the articular infinitive can denote *result* (the so-called *ecbatic* use).[105] This was truly the sense that was controversial in his day but which has nonetheless received wide acceptance today among New Testament scholars. Along with the texts in the previous paragraph, we should make note of the following:

Rom. 1.20:
τὰ γὰρ ἀόρατα αὐτοῦ ἀπὸ κτίσεως κόσμου τοῖς ποιήμασιν νοούμενα καθορᾶται, ἥ τε ἀΐδιος αὐτοῦ δύναμις καὶ θειότης, εἰς τὸ εἶναι αὐτοὺς ἀναπολογήτους.

100.   Beckwith, 'The Articular Infinitive with εἰς', p. 159.

101.   This is precisely the way that Cranfield understands this construction: 'εἰς τὸ ὑπακούειν ταῖς ἐπιθυμίαις αὐτοῦ is added as a reminder of the consequences which would result from allowing sin to go on reigning unchallenged' (C.E.B. Cranfield, *A Critical and Exegetical Commentary on the Epistle to the Romans*. I. *Introduction and Commentary on Romans I–VIII* [ICC; Edinburgh: T. & T. Clark, 1975], p. 317). So also Thomas R. Schreiner, *Romans* (BECNT; Grand Rapids: Baker Book House, 1998), p. 323 n. 22; Douglas J. Moo, *The Epistle to the Romans* (NICNT; Grand Rapids: Eerdmans, 1996), p. 383. Moo shows some acquaintance with Beckwith's article and the dispute over the precise significance of this construction in Paul (pp. 105-106 n. 66).

102.   Turner, *Syntax*, p. 143.

103.   Moo, *Romans*, p. 760 n. 12.

104.   Moo, *Romans*, p. 105 n. 66.

105.   Beckwith, 'The Articular Infinitive with εἰς', p. 159.

For since the creation of the world his invisible attributes, his eternal power and divine nature, have been clearly seen, being understood through what has been made, so that they are without excuse.

Rom. 7.5:
ὅτε γὰρ ἦμεν ἐν τῇ σαρκί, τὰ παθήματα τῶν ἁμαρτιῶν τὰ διὰ τοῦ νόμου ἐνηργεῖτο ἐν τοῖς μέλεσιν ἡμῶν, εἰς τὸ καρποφορῆσαι τῷ θανάτῳ.

For while we were in the flesh, the sinful passions, which were [aroused] by the Law, were at work in the members of our body to bear fruit for death.

Rom. 12.2:
καὶ μὴ συσχηματίζεσθε τῷ αἰῶνι τούτῳ, ἀλλὰ μεταμορφοῦσθε τῇ ἀνακαινώσει τοῦ νοὸς εἰς τὸ δοκιμάζειν ὑμᾶς τί τὸ θέλημα τοῦ θεοῦ, τὸ ἀγαθὸν καὶ εὐάρεστον καὶ τέλειον.

And do not be conformed to this world, but be transformed by the renewing of your mind, that you may prove what the will of God is, that which is good and acceptable and perfect.

2 Cor. 8.5-6:
ἀλλὰ ἑαυτοὺς ἔδωκαν πρῶτον τῷ κυρίῳ καὶ ἡμῖν διὰ θελήματος θεοῦ εἰς τὸ παρακαλέσαι ἡμᾶς Τίτον, ἵνα καθὼς προενήρξατο οὕτως καὶ ἐπιτελέσῃ εἰς ὑμᾶς καὶ τὴν χάριν ταύτην.

But they first gave themselves to the Lord and to us by the will of God with the result that we urged Titus that, as he had previously made a beginning, so he would also complete in you this gracious work as well.

Gal. 3.17:
τοῦτο δὲ λέγω· διαθήκην προκεκυρωμένην ὑπὸ τοῦ θεοῦ ὁ μετὰ τετρακόσια καὶ τριάκοντα ἔτη γεγονὼς νόμος οὐκ ἀκυροῖ εἰς τὸ καταργῆσαι τὴν ἐπαγγελίαν.

What I am saying is this: the Law, which came four hundred and thirty years later, does not invalidate a covenant previously ratified by God, with the result that [the law] nullifies the promise.

Phil. 1.9-10:
Καὶ τοῦτο προσεύχομαι, ἵνα ἡ ἀγάπη ὑμῶν ἔτι μᾶλλον καὶ μᾶλλον περισσεύῃ ἐν ἐπιγνώσει καὶ πάσῃ αἰσθήσει εἰς τὸ δοκιμάζειν ὑμᾶς τὰ διαφέροντα.

And this I pray, that your love may abound still more and more in real knowledge and all discernment, so that you may approve the things that are excellent.

Heb. 11.3:
Πίστει νοοῦμεν κατηρτίσθαι τοὺς αἰῶνας ῥήματι θεοῦ, εἰς τὸ μὴ ἐκ φαινομένων τὸ βλεπόμενον γεγονέναι.

By faith we understand that the worlds were prepared by the word of God, so that what is seen was not made out of things which are visible.

Jas 3.3:

εἰ δὲ τῶν ἵππων τοὺς χαλινοὺς εἰς τὰ στόματα βάλλομεν εἰς τὸ πεί-
θεσθαι αὐτοὺς ἡμῖν, καὶ ὅλον τὸ σῶμα αὐτῶν μετάγομεν.

Now if we put the bits into the horses' mouths so that they may obey us, we
direct their entire body as well.

Certainly, it is possible for some of these examples to be understood as *telic*
(e.g. Rom. 1.20; 12.2), but the *ecbatic* sense is clearly seen in at least some
of these texts, if not all of them. If the context indicates that the *end* is
intended and not yet realized, then the construction indicates purpose. If the
context indicates that the *end* is not intended and has been realized, then the
construction indicates result. What is clear is that εἰς τό combines with the
infinitive to indicate that a certain *end* is in mind on the part of the speaker
and that εἰς figuratively denotes *movement toward* that end.

(2) *Accusative infinitives following* διά. There are 32 infinitives in this
construction in the New Testament. The local sense of διά is 'passing
through and out from'.[106] The *instrumental* notion grew naturally out of this
fundamental local idea by marking the medium *through* which an action
passes before its accomplishment.[107] In the preceding chapter, I noted with
respect to the dative articular infinitive that *instrumentality* and *cause* are
overlapping semantic concepts. We see the same semantic overlap in the use
of διά plus the accusative infinitive. Yet in many of the examples the *instrumental* idea has succumbed completely to the *causal* notion. Over half of the
instances of this construction occur in Luke's writings where it clearly bears
a causal meaning.[108] In Lk. 2.4 for instance, we read, ᾽Ανέβη δὲ καὶ
᾽Ιωσὴφ...εἰς πόλιν Δαυὶδ...διὰ τὸ εἶναι αὐτὸν ἐξ οἴκου καὶ πατριᾶς
Δαυίδ ('And Joseph also went up...into the city of David...*because* he was
from the house and lineage of David'). The construction appears likewise in
other narrative literature[109] as well as in three of the Epistles.[110] The semantics of this construction are not disputed in the literature; there is wide
agreement that it denotes causality.[111] So we need not belabor the point here.

106. Harris, 'Prepositions and Theology', p. 1181. This is the routine use of διά that
appears, for instance, in 1 Cor. 3.15: αὐτὸς δὲ σωθήσεται, οὕτως δὲ ὡς διὰ πυρός
('but he himself shall be saved, yet so as through fire').

107. Harris, 'Prepositions and Theology', p. 1182.

108. Lk. 2.4; 6.48; 8.6; 9.7; 11.8; 18.5; 19.11 (×2); 23.8; Acts 4.2 (×2); 8.11; 12.20;
18.2, 3; 27.4, 9; 28.18.

109. Mt. 13.5, 6; 24.12; Mk 4.5, 6; 5.4 (×3); Jn 2.24.

110. Phil. 1.7; Heb. 7.23, 24; 10.2; Jas 4.2.

111. BDF §402(1); Burton, *Moods and Tenses*, §408; Porter, *Idioms*, p. 201; Turner,
Syntax, p. 142. Yet Burton does note that in at least one instance, 'The Infinitive expresses
the evidence rather than the cause strictly so called' (Burton, *Moods and Tenses*, §408).

Robertson's expresses his certitude on the matter by saying, 'It is always the cause that is given by διὰ τό'.[112]

(3) *Accusative infinitives following* μετά. There are 15 accusative infinitives following the preposition μετά in the New Testament. The basic idea of μετά is 'in the vicinity of', and for this reason it is a close synonym of σύν in Koine literature.[113] Yet in the Koine dialect, when μετά is followed by the accusative case, it is a marker of a position that is behind something. Thus when the construction is used with respect to time, it marks a time that occurs after another point of time, 'after'.[114] All of the accusative articular infinitives following μετά in the New Testament are to be taken in this temporal sense.[115] Thus the NASB's rendering of Mk 16.19[116] probably misses the mark: Ὁ μὲν οὖν κύριος Ἰησοῦς μετὰ τὸ λαλῆσαι αὐτοῖς ἀνελήμφθη εἰς τὸν οὐρανόν ('So then, when the Lord Jesus had spoken to them, He was received up into heaven' [NASB]). The preposition 'after' better expresses the author's meaning than 'when'. The important thing to note in these examples is that the article appears to mark the infinitive as the object of the preposition. In 1 Cor. 11.25, we read, ὡσαύτως καὶ τὸ ποτήριον μετὰ τὸ δειπνῆσαι λέγων... ('Likewise also [he took] the cup after eating, saying...').[117] If the article were absent here, the infinitive might be mistaken

That one instance is Mk 5.4 and has three infinitives governed by one διὰ τό: καὶ οὐδὲ ἁλύσει οὐκέτι οὐδεὶς ἐδύνατο αὐτὸν δῆσαι διὰ τὸ αὐτὸν πολλάκις πέδαις καὶ ἁλύσεσιν δεδέσθαι καὶ διεσπάσθαι ὑπ' αὐτοῦ τὰς ἁλύσεις καὶ τὰς πέδας συντετρῖφθαι ('And no one was able to bind him anymore, even with a chain; because he had often been bound with shackles and chains, and the chains had been torn apart by him, and the shackles broken in pieces' [NASB]).

112.   Robertson, p. 1071.
113.   BDAG, *s.v.* μετά, p. 636.
114.   BDAG, *s.v.* μετά, p. 637.
115.   See Table 17 in the Appendix for a complete listing.
116.   I agree with Craig Evan's and the majority of modern scholarship that this verse is not Markan: Craig A. Evans, *Mark 8.27–16.20* (WBC, 34B; Nashville: Thomas Nelson, 2001), p. 547. Nevertheless, I include this text in my analysis as a typical example of Koine usage.
117.   I take the prepositional phrase to be adverbial modifying an elliptical ἔλαβεν. My reading is in line with Hofius's conclusion that we should not construe this prepositional phrase as an attributive to the noun τὸ ποτήριον, thereby excluding the possibility that this phrase is a reference to the 'after dinner cup' (i.e. the third cup in the Passover meal). However, Hofius has overstated his linguistic argument because attributive prepositional phrases are used a number of times in the New Testament without the attributive article (e.g. Rom. 6.4; Lk. 16.10). Otfried Hofius, 'The Lord's Supper and the Lord's Supper Tradition: Reflections on 1 Corinthians 11.23b-25', in Ben F. Meyer (ed.), *One Loaf, One Cup: Ecumenical Studies of 1 Cor 11 and Other Eucharistic Texts. The Cambridge Conference on the Eucharist, August 1988* (New Gospel Studies, 6; Macon,

as the compound μεταδειπνέω, a verb that is attested outside of the New Testament literature.[118]

(4) *Accusative infinitives following* πρός. There are eleven accusative infinitives following the preposition πρός in the New Testament. Seven of the eleven instances occur in narrative literature[119] and four in epistolary literature.[120] In Classical Greek πρός was regularly followed by all three oblique cases, but in the New Testament the accusative predominates.[121] Murray J. Harris explains how the various nuances of this preposition grew out of its fundamental local sense. He is worth quoting at length:

> In its basic spatial sense *pros* denotes actual motion or literal direction…but the developed sense of mental direction or tendency followed naturally, referring to relationships that are friendly…or hostile… In turn, this notion of psychological orientation let to the use of *pros* to express the ideas of estimation, 'in view of' (Matt. 19.8), purpose, 'with a view to' (1 Cor. 10.11), conformity, 'in accordance with' (Lk. 12.47; 2 Cor. 5.10; Eph. 4.14) and reference (Lk. 18.1; Gal. 2.14; Heb. 1.7).[122]

In Harris's description, πρός plus the accusative encodes the general idea of 'mental direction'. It is not difficult to see how the notions of purpose and result grow out of this fundamental sense. *Purpose* refers to intended direction towards a specified end, and *result* refers to unintended direction towards a specified end. Thus πρός plus the accusative is well-suited to express both of these notions.

On the final sense of this construction, Zerwick writes, 'Πρὸς τό with the infinitive usually has final sense, but the preposition itself merely indicates direction without specifying whether the direction is intended or not'.[123] Thus context must decide in any given text which notion is intended: *purpose* or *result*. It is generally agreed that Paul's four uses of πρός plus the infinitive indicate *purpose*:

GA: Mercer University Press, 1993), p. 83: 'The conclusion to be drawn from these linguistic considerations: It is certain that the words μετὰ τὸ δειπνῆσαι do not belong adjectivally—i.e., as prepositional attributive—to το ποτηριον; rather, they belong adverbially to ἔλαβεν εὐχαριστήσας, to which ὡσαύτως relates as complementary predicate'.

118.   LSJ, *s.v.* μεταδειπνέω, p. 1111.

119.   Mt. 5.28; 6.1; 13.30; 23.5; 26.12; Mk 13.22; Lk. 18.1.

120.   2 Cor. 3.13; Eph. 6.11; 1 Thess. 2.9; 2 Thess. 3.8.

121.   One instance of the genitive (Acts 27.34), 6 with the dative, and 679 with the accusative (Harris, 'Prepositions and Theology', p. 1204).

122.   Harris, 'Prepositions and Theology', p. 1204.

123.   Zerwick, §391.

2 Cor. 3.8:

Μωϋσῆς ἐτίθει κάλυμμα ἐπὶ τὸ πρόσωπον αὐτοῦ πρὸς τὸ μὴ ἀτενίσαι τοὺς υἱοὺς 'Ισραὴλ εἰς τὸ τέλος τοῦ καταργουμένου.

Moses put a veil over his face so that the sons of Israel might not gaze into the end of what was fading away.

Eph. 6.11:

ἐνδύσασθε τὴν πανοπλίαν τοῦ θεοῦ πρὸς τὸ δύνασθαι ὑμᾶς στῆναι πρὸς τὰς μεθοδείας τοῦ διαβόλου.

Put on the armor of God so that you might be able to stand against the tricks of the devil.

1 Thess. 2.9:

νυκτὸς καὶ ἡμέρας ἐργαζόμενοι πρὸς τὸ μὴ ἐπιβαρῆσαί τινα ὑμῶν.

Night and day [we were] working so that we would not burden any of you.

2 Thess. 3.8:

νυκτὸς καὶ ἡμέρας ἐργαζόμενοι πρὸς τὸ μὴ ἐπιβαρῆσαί τινα ὑμῶν.

Night and day [we were] working so that we would not burden any of you.

Robertson regards these four texts as clearly denoting purpose, 'Paul's four examples...all give the "subjective purpose"'.[124]

There is some question as to the meaning of this construction in the Synoptic Gospels. The range of interpretation on these seven texts ranges from *purpose* to *result* to *reference* (with no trace of the *telic* sense in the latter). Scholars dispute whether or not πρὸς τό with infinitive appears without any trace of the consecutive sense. The dispute centers on whether or not the construction is a 'servile rendering' of the Hebrew infinitive construct (ל + infinitive), a construction which can occur without any connotation of *purpose* or *result*.[125] The classic example of this construction in Hebrew is לֵאמֹר which is used to introduce direct speech.[126] Nigel Turner argues, 'No doubt the obvious correspondence with the Heb. ל c. inf. assisted in the weakening of this expression in Bibl. Greek, till it means simply *in — ing* or is merely like a simple ptc, as in לֵאמֹר.'[127]

Those who see πρὸς τό with infinitive as a Semitism are inclined to render the construction as *reference*, with no notion of *purpose* or *consequence*

---

124.   Robertson, p. 1075, quoting Winer–Moulton.
125.   Zerwick, §391. Cf. 'The weakened participle-like Hebr. inf. preceded by ל...also contributed to this construction' (BDF §402[5]). See also Bruce K. Waltke and M. O'Connor, *An Introduction to Biblical Hebrew Syntax* (Winona Lake, IN: Eisenbrauns, 1990), p. 608; Wilhelm Gesenius, *Gesenius' Hebrew Grammar* (ed. A.E. Cowley and E. Kautzsch; Oxford: Clarendon Press, 2nd Eng. edn, 1910), p. 351.
126.   Zerwick, §391.
127.   Turner, *Syntax*, p. 144.

whatsoever. For example, many interpreters include Lk. 18.1 in this category:[128] Ἔλεγεν δὲ παραβολὴν αὐτοῖς πρὸς τὸ δεῖν πάντοτε προσεύχεσθαι αὐτοὺς καὶ μὴ ἐγκακεῖν ('Now he was telling them a parable *with regard to* showing that at all times they ought to pray and not to lose heart'). Concerning Mt. 5.28, Turner argues that 'there is hardly any telic force, but simple accompaniment'.[129] Thus Turner would render the sentence as follows: πᾶς ὁ βλέπων γυναῖκα πρὸς τὸ ἐπιθυμῆσαι αὐτὴν ('everyone who looks at a woman *and* lusts after her'). With respect to Mt. 5.28, Moulton and Robertson suggest that the idea of the construction is *explanatory*.[130] A profound difference of application occurs depending on how one understands the semantics of this construction.[131] For our purposes, we need to note that in both of these texts interpreters have allowed the possibility that the meaning of the preposition ('direction towards') has more or less faded from view and that the only reason the preposition is used is to imitate the Hebrew dialect.

5. *Conclusion*

At the beginning of this chapter, I hypothesized that prepositions always require the articular infinitive (as opposed to the anarthrous infinitive) in order to clear away two potential ambiguities. The first ambiguity is semantic, and the second syntactic. The semantic ambiguity stems from the observation that the proper method for studying prepositions involves first identifying the case of the object and second observing how the preposition clarifies the case usage. The meaning of any given prepositional phrase would not be clear if the case were not made explicit by the presence of the article. In order to illustrate how the article diffuses the first ambiguity, I have set forth how prepositions combine with cases (articular infinitives) to encode various semantic ideas. Thus we have found that the article's status as a case-identifier is crucial in the interpretation of articular infinitives that follow prepositions. This explanation of the semantic roles of cases in

128.   'With reference to' (BDF §402[5]; Burton, *Moods and Tenses*, §414; Moulton, *Prolegomena*, p. 218); 'With regard to' (Turner, *Syntax*, p. 144).

129.   Turner, *Syntax*, p. 144. BDF §402[5] renders the construction in Mt. 5.28, 'With reference to'.

130.   Moulton, *Prolegomena*, p. 218; Robertson, p. 1075.

131.   Davies and Allison take this construction as *result*, but offer no grammatical justification for their interpretation, even though they acknowledge the possible presence of a Semitism (W.D. Davies and Dale C. Allison, Jr, *A Critical and Exegetical Commentary on the Gospel according to Saint Matthew*. I. *Introduction and Commentary on Matthew I–VII* [ICC; Edinburgh: T. & T. Clark, 1988], p. 523). Hagner translates the phrase as *purpose* (Donald A. Hagner, *Matthew 1–13* [WBC, 33A; Dallas, TX: Word Books, 1993], p. 120).

combination with prepositions has taken up the majority of the preceding discussion.

The syntactic ambiguity consists in the fact that the structural relation of the infinitive to the preposition would be unclear without the article. I argued at the beginning of the chapter that the article is necessary in order to mark the infinitive as the object of the preposition. If the article were not regularly used as a function word with infinitives following prepositions, then it would be impossible to distinguish compound infinitives from infinitives functioning as object of a preposition. This latter point is strengthened by the observation that many of the uses of the articular infinitive after prepositions reflect a Semitizing influence on the language of Biblical Greek. In its temporal sense, Luke's frequent ἐν τῷ plus the infinitive is widely regarded as an imitation of the Hebrew. Ἐν τῷ plus the infinitive is decidedly non-Classical but is the usual LXX rendering of בְּ plus the Hebrew infinitive.[132] Likewise, we have seen that πρὸς τό with the infinitive most likely derives from an imitation of לְ plus the Hebrew infinitive. If these two constructions really are imitations of the Hebrew, then we have to ask ourselves why an author writing in Greek would insert an article where there is no article in the Hebrew that he is imitating. It is obvious that the Greek article is not employed with its normal semantic force as a determiner because there is no such determiner in the Hebrew original.[133] Therefore, the only logical conclusion of the matter is that the article serves some other purpose. Whereas Hebrew does not require an article to mark the infinitive as prepositional object, Greek does. The Greek article marks the infinitive as object so that it will not be construed as forming a compound with the preposition. The conclusion of the matter is that the article is grammatically obligatory as a case-identifier and as a syntactical marker and is not a definitizing determiner. The following chapter will test this conclusion against the evidence contained in the LXX.

---

132.   Aalto, *Studien zur Geschichte des Infinitivs im Griechischen*, p. 45: 'Der Dativ mit ἐν gibt einen hebr. Infinitiv mit *be*'. See also Turner, *Synatx*, p. 144. Cf. BDF §404 (1): 'Attic does not use ἐν τῷ in this way, but Hebrew does so use בְּ with the infinitive…for which the LXX has ἐν τῷ'. Robertson writes, 'The Semitic influence is undoubted in the O.T. and seems clear in Luke, due probably to his reading the LXX or to his Aramaic sources' (Robertson, p. 1072).

133.   Votaw, *The Infinitive in Biblical Greek*, p. 54: 'In Hebrew the article is not used with the infinitive. The conspicuous frequency of the articular infinitive in the O.T. is not therefore an imitation of the Hebrew.'

5

ARTICULAR INFINITIVES IN THE SEPTUAGINT

1. *Introduction*

I have argued thus far that in the New Testament the Greek article does not bear its normal semantic weight as a determiner when used with the infinitive. While its usual semantic role is to determine nominals as definite, in Chapter 2 I showed various syntactical situations in which the article appears to have no definitizing effect. In such contexts, the article emerges as a pure function word marking a variety of grammatical relationships. In Chapters 3 and 4 I argued that the article has such a force when used in connection with the infinitive. I demonstrated the article's necessity as a case-identifier and as a structural marker in the articular infinitive (i.e. as a function word). Because the use of the article with the infinitive thus appears to be a function marker, I concluded that the article does not have its usual definitizing effect. This thesis was tested against each occurrence of the articular infinitive in the New Testament and was found to be an adequate explanation of the data contained therein.

Yet even though the evidence of the New Testament accords with my theory, the scientific approach that I advocate in my section on methodology requires that the theory be scrutinized even further. As Ruth Kempson argues, 'Scientific endeavour is not concerned with evidence which seems to show theories to be correct but only with evidence which might show them to be false'.[1] As I stated in Chapter 1, textual data must be used primarily to form hypotheses and to falsify theories. We have thus far used the data to form the hypothesis; now we must determine if there are any data that would falsify the hypothesis. We have seen that there are no such data in the New Testament. So we must look elsewhere in the body of extant Koine literature to see if such data exist. The crucial question that we must bring to this study is not merely whether there is textual evidence to support my thesis in Koine literature, but whether there exists any evidence that contradicts my thesis.

---

1. Kempson, *Semantic Theory*, p. 1.

The purpose of this chapter is to test my thesis by the data as they stand in a related body of Koine literature, the LXX. I have already made some comparisons of New Testament usage to broader Koine usage in Chapter 4. Mayser's grammar of the Greek papyri reveals that the use of the articular infinitive in the New Testament is basically consistent with the use of the articular infinitive in other Koine literature.[2] I have selected the LXX as a control for a few reasons. First, the LXX is a good representation of the Koine dialect. As Henry Thackeray has noted in his important grammar on the LXX, 'The Septuagint, considered as a whole, is the most extensive work which we possess written in the vernacular of the κοινή or Hellenistic language, and is therefore of primary importance for a study of later Greek'.[3] In this chapter, I will briefly set forth a comparison of the usage of the articular infinitive in the LXX and that of the New Testament. Afterward, I will focus attention on those instances from the LXX which might be construed as inconsistent with my thesis and give an explanation for their apparent exceptional nature. My argument will be that the article appears with the infinitive in the LXX as a pure function word, just as it does in the New Testament.

2. *Comparison of Septuagint and New Testament Usage*

The usage of the articular infinitive in the LXX is by and large the same as we find it in the New Testament. A brief perusal of any advanced grammar of Koine Greek confirms this observation simply by the fact that New Testament usage is often explained by citing parallel texts in the LXX. In Blass's grammar, for example, each of the major subsections covering the articular infinitive shows the parallel usage in the LXX.[4] Clyde Votaw's monograph on the infinitive in biblical Greek,[5] provides another example of this comparison. In his careful tabulation of articular infinitive usage in the LXX and the New Testament, Votaw identifies at least 15 categories of usage of the articular infinitive and concludes that 'of the 15 articular uses the O.T.

---

2.   In Chapter 4 I pointed out the prepositions that were used with each case in the New Testament and compared this with the usage in the broader Koine literature. In the New Testament, ten prepositions are used with articular infinitives (εἰς, διά, μετά, πρός, πρό, ἕως, ἕνεκεν, ἐκ, ἀντί, ἐν). Mayser shows nine additional prepositions appearing in the papyri (ἄνευ, μέχρι, περί, πλήν, ὑπέρ, χάριν, ἅμα, ἐπί, παρά). Mayser's statistics show that the use of the articular infinitive as the object of the preposition is characteristic of the Koine literature (Mayser, *Grammatik*, II.1, pp. 332-33).

3.   Henry St John Thackeray, *A Grammar of the Old Testament in Greek according to the Septuagint* (Cambridge: Cambridge University Press, 1909), p. 16.

4.   BDF §398-404. The only exception to this is §401: 'The articular infinitive in the dative (not dependent on a preposition)'. For whatever reason, BDF did not cite the instances of this construction in the LXX: Judg. 10.3; 2 Chron. 28.22; Eccl. 1.16.

5.   By 'Biblical Greek', Votaw means the LXX and the New Testament.

has every one, the Apoc. and the N.T. have all but one'.[6] In other words, Votaw shows that there is only one particular use of the articular infinitive in the LXX that does not appear in the New Testament. This one use is not even a formal difference but a semantic one.[7] In terms of formal differences, Votaw observes none.

a. *Articular Infinitives Not Governed by Prepositions*
In the LXX, the article appears with the infinitive for one of two reasons: (1) to mark the case of the infinitive, and thereby a semantic idea associated with a given case, and/or (2) to mark a structural relation that could best be made explicit by the presence of the article. In the articular infinitives of the LXX, the nominative and accusative are syntactic, not content cases. Thus the nominative case encodes infinitives as syntactical subjects in the LXX. Psalm 72.28 is typical: ἐμοὶ δὲ τὸ προσκολλᾶσθαι τῷ θεῷ ἀγαθόν ('To be near to God is good for me').[8] Likewise, the accusative articular infinitive has the primarily syntactic function of encoding the verbal object. For example, τὸ δὲ καλῶς ποιῆσαι οὐκ ἐπέγνωσαν ('And they knew not to do well').[9] Though there are not very many nominative and accusative examples in the LXX, the usage in the LXX is consistent with what we find in the New Testament.[10]

The use of genitive articular infinitives in the LXX also mirrors that of the New Testament, though the LXX idiom often reflects the Semitizing influence of translating from the Hebrew original. One of the ways that the LXX renders לְ plus the Hebrew infinitive is by τοῦ plus the Greek infinitive. Votaw seems uneasy in the observation that no single Greek construction is used to translate this Hebrew infinitive construct:

> Especially is it noticeable that there is no exact reproduction of that everywhere present Hebrew idiom, the infinitive with *lᵉ*; this phrase is rendered into Greek by the anarthrous infinitive alone, by the articular (τοῦ) infinitive

6. Votaw, *The Infinitive in Biblical Greek*, p. 51.
7. Votaw sees a particular semantic nuance of τοῦ plus the infinitive that is present in the LXX but not in the New Testament (Votaw, *The Infinitive in Biblical Greek*, p. 22). The important thing to note here is that τοῦ plus the infinitive appears in both the LXX and in the New Testament.
8. Cf. 1 Sam. 15.22; 2 Macc. 2.32; *4 Macc.* 5.8, 20; Prov. 9.10; 16.7; Eccl. 5.4; Job 28.28; Wis. 11.21; 12.18; 15.3; Sir. 46.10; Jdt. 12.18; Tob. 12.6; Jon. 4.3; Jer. 2.19. Votaw notes that this use of the articular infinitive is found least often in the LXX compared to the usage in the New Testament (Votaw, *The Infinitive in Biblical Greek*, p. 28).
9. Jer. 4.22; cf. Tob. 8.1; 2 Macc. 2.28; 3.31, 33, 35; *3 Macc.* 2.23; 5.32; 7.6; *4 Macc.* 7.20; Isa. 21.3; Jer. 2.17; Ezek. 18.23; 33.11. Some of these are in apposition to the accusative object.
10. There are not very many uses of the nominative and accusative articular infinitives in the LXX. I have counted only 16 nominative and 13 accusative.

alone, by the articular infinitive with the preposition εἰς or πρός, and less frequently in other ways, but not by preposition with an anarthrous infinitive except perhaps in the four εἰς instances.[11]

Votaw finds this variety of renderings inexplicable. But my thesis provides a ready explanation. The semantic range of the Hebrew infinitive construct is not adequately covered by any one Greek construction. Therefore, the translators of the LXX used a variety of infinitive phrases to reproduce the sense of the Hebrew.

As I noted in Chapter 3, the genitive case is uniquely suited to encoding the ideas of *restriction* and *separation*, and these notions are bound up in many of the adverbial uses of the genitive infinitive in the LXX. In Judg. 1.1, the LXX renders the Niphal infinitive construct לְהִלָּחֶם with the genitive articular infinitive in order to denote purpose: τίς ἀναβήσεται ἡμῖν πρὸς τὸν Χαναναῖον ἀφηγούμενος τοῦ πολεμῆσαι ἐν αὐτῷ; ('Who shall lead and go up for us to the Canaanite in order to fight against him?'). The genitive articular infinitive is also used to render the Hebrew infinitive absolute in order to indicate purpose, καὶ ἀπέστειλεν τὸν κόρακα τοῦ ἰδεῖν εἰ κεκόπακεν τὸ ὕδωρ ('And he sent out the raven in order to see if the water had ceased', Gen. 8.7). The genitive articular infinitive is routinely used in this manner to denote purpose and result,[12] and this usage corresponds to the use of this construction in the New Testament (which was discussed at length in Chapter 3).[13]

The use of the genitive articular infinitive in the LXX also resembles New Testament usage in appearing as the object of finite verbs. There are a number of verbs in the LXX that take genitive objects, and we therefore find the genitive infinitive appearing after such verbs. Exodus 2.18 shows this usage: τί ὅτι ἐταχύνατε τοῦ παραγενέσθαι σήμερον; ('Why have you hurried to be present today?'). The genitive case is preferred often with verbs of hindering, as in 1 Esd. 2.23: νῦν οὖν ἐπέταξα ἀποκωλῦσαι τοὺς ἀνθρώπους ἐκείνους τοῦ οἰκοδομῆσαι τὴν πόλιν ('Therefore, I have now ordered to prevent those men *from* building the city'). In this text and others like it, the ablatival notion of *separation* from some activity is clear.

Adnominal uses of the genitive also abound in the LXX. The genitive infinitive in Judg. 8.33 modifies the noun διαθήκην: ἔθεντο αὐτοῖς τὸν Βααλβεριθ εἰς διαθήκην τοῦ εἶναι αὐτοῖς αὐτὸν εἰς θεόν ('They set to themselves Baal-berith unto a covenant, [a covenant saying that] he should

---

11. Votaw, *The Infinitive in Biblical Greek*, p. 56.

12. As I noted in Chapter 3, purpose and result are closely related semantically. I direct the reader to the lengthy list of examples that Votaw has gathered from the LXX (Votaw, *The Infinitive in Biblical Greek*, pp. 21-22, 25).

13. I specifically discussed how the notion of *purpose* grew out the ablative notion of *separation*.

be as a God to them'). Another interesting example occurs in Sir. 9.13, μακρὰν ἄπεχε ἀπὸ ἀνθρώπου ὃς ἔχει ἐξουσίαν τοῦ φονεύειν ('Keep far away from a person who has the power of murdering'). In this text, the genitive *restricts* the meaning of ἐξουσίαν by telling what kind of 'power' is being spoken of. The LXX even has examples of the genitive infinitive modifying an adjective, as in 1 Sam. 13.21: καὶ ἦν ὁ τρυγητὸς ἕτοιμος τοῦ θερίζειν ('And the harvest was ready to reap'). As in the New Testament, there are many such uses in the LXX.[14]

As in the New Testament, the dative articular infinitive is sparsely used. Votaw finds only six in the entire LXX, and significant textual problems are attached to the last four of the six: 2 Chron. 28.22; Eccl. 1.16; Isa. 56.6; *4 Macc.* 17.20-21 (three infinitives to one article).[15] Because of the textual problems, Votaw is unsure about the usefulness of these examples that he finds in the Swete text, even though they may very well be the more difficult original readings. In any case, at least the first two appear in the Rahlfs text also:

> 2 Chron. 28.21-22:
> οὐκ εἰς βοήθειαν αὐτῷ ἦν, ἀλλ᾽ ἢ τῷ θλιβῆναι αὐτὸν
>
> He was no help to him, but rather was with affliction [to him].
>
> Eccl. 1.16:
> ἐλάλησα ἐγὼ ἐν καρδίᾳ μου τῷ λέγειν ᾽Εγὼ ἰδοὺ ἐμεγαλύνθην
>
> I spoke in my heart by saying, 'Behold, I am increased'.

In both of these texts, the dative case is used to convey the manner in which or the means by which something is done. Thus the dative encodes the idea of *togetherness* that is observed in the lone instance of this construction in the New Testament, 2 Cor. 2.13.

This brief sketch of the use of the nominative, genitive, dative, and accusative articular infinitives in the LXX demonstrates the similarity of usage with that of the New Testament. Many more texts could be adduced as there are about 1495 examples of the articular infinitive not following a preposition in the LXX.[16] The important thing to note is that there is ample amount of evidence to support the hypothesis as set forth in Chapter 3, and this hypothesis can be confirmed by a survey of other grammars that cover the LXX.

---

14. Cf. modifying a noun: Gen. 2.9; 16.3; Deut. 8.18; 1 Kgs 3.9; 2 Chron. 22.3; Pss. 67.21; 101.14; Jer. 13.25; Amos 8.11; 1 Macc. 9.45; 10.73; 12.25, 40; *4 Macc.* 5.15. modifying an adjective: Gen. 3.6; 2 Kgs 4.8; Jer. 4.22; 47.5; Ezek. 21.11; Mic. 6.8; 1 Macc. 3.58; 5.39; 10.19; 13.37; Jdt. 12.16.

15. Votaw, *The Infinitive in Biblical Greek*, p. 29.

16. This is Votaw's count (Votaw, *The Infinitive in Biblical Greek*, pp. 43, 45).

b. *Articular Infinitives Governed by Prepositions*
The closest thing we find to a formal difference between LXX and New Testament usage is that there are a greater variety of prepositions that occur with the articular infinitive in the LXX than with the articular infinitive in the New Testament.[17] Table 12 illustrates this variation. The numbers in parentheses represent the number of times a particular preposition is used in connection with the articular infinitive.[18] Pentti Aalto's important study of the articular infinitive tabulates this usage by book in both the LXX and the New Testament.[19] Aalto's statistics confirm what I have already stated. The use of the articular infinitive as prepositional object in the LXX is basically consistent with what we find in the New Testament, even though the LXX utilizes a wider variety of prepositions. As was the case in the New Testament, in the LXX the article appears with the infinitive in prepositional phrases in order to mark the case and function of the infinitive. As I argued in the previous chapter with respect to the New Testament, in the LXX the primary reason for the presence of the article is to distinguish infinitives functioning as prepositional object from those that are being used in composition. Because of the absence of spaces between words, the article is needed in order to show that the infinitive is the prepositional object.

It is worthy of note here that the variety of prepositions used in this construction is greater than that found not only in the New Testament, but also in the papyri in general. In the New Testament, ten prepositions are used with articular infinitives (εἰς, διά, μετά, πρός, πρό, ἕως, ἕνεκεν, ἐκ, ἀντί, ἐν). Mayser shows nine prepositions appearing in the papyri that are not used in the New Testament (ἄνευ, μέχρι, περί, πλήν, ὑπέρ, χάριν, ἅμα, ἐπί, παρά).[20] At least two additional prepositions are used in the LXX that are not found in either the New Testament or the papyri: ἔμπροσθεν and ἐπέκεινα.

17. It is worth noting that the LXX shows a greater variety of prepositions than is found in non-biblical Koine Greek. In Mayser's grammar of the Greek papyri, he catalogues 18 prepositions that are used with the articular infinitive (Mayser, *Grammatik*, II.1, pp. 332-33), while we find at least 21 in the LXX. Πλήν and ἐπί are the only prepositions used in the papyri that are not found in the LXX. Ἀπό, ἐγγύς, ἔμπροσθεν, and ἐπέκεινα are all used in the LXX, but not in the papyri.
18. I used GRAMCORD's database to arrive at these statistics for the LXX. I created three different search queries to account for postpositive conjunctions that often break up prepositional phrases. Thus, I searched the following three combinations: (1) prep + art + inf, (2) prep + conj + art + inf, (3) prep + art + conj + inf.
19. Aalto, *Studien zur Geschichte des Infinitivs im Griechischen*, pp. 44-65 (LXX); pp. 65-71 (New Testament); p. 65: 'Der neutestamentliche Gebrauch weicht, wie der in LXX, von demjenigen in den Papyri ab. Die Semitismenfrage begegnet uns auch im New Testament, weil die Muttersprache einiger Verfasser offenbar eine andere war, als die von ihnen hier benutzte.'
20. Mayser, *Grammatik*, II.1, pp. 332-33.

Table 12. *Comparison of Articular Infinitives as Prepositional Objects*

Prepositions with Genitive Infinitives		Prepositions with Dative Infinitives		Prepositions with Accusative Infinitives	
LXX	*New Testament*	*LXX*	*New Testament*	*LXX*	*New Testament*
		ἅμα (12)			
ἀπό (4)					
ἄνευ (1)					
ἀντί (5)	ἀντί (1)				
	διά (1)			διά (30)	διά (32)
ἐγγύς (2)					
				εἰς (45)	εἰς (74)
		ἐν (524)	ἐν (56)		
ἔνεκα (3)					
(ἔνεκεν) (5)	ἔνεκεν (1)				
(εἵνεκεν) (1)					
ἐκ (2)	ἐκ (1)				
ἔμπροσθεν (1)					
ἐπέκεινα (1)					
ἕως (1)	ἕως (1)				
				μετά (105)	μετά (15)
μέχρι (7)					
				παρά (4)	
περί (3)					
πρό (40)	πρό (9)				
πρός (1)		πρός (1)		πρός (11)	πρός (11)
ὑπέρ (4)				ὑπέρ (1)	
χάριν (3)					
Total: 84	Total: 14	Total: 537	Total: 56	Total: 196	Total: 132

Thus, nine prepositions are found with the articular infinitive in the LXX that are not found in the New Testament: ἄνευ, μέχρι, περί, ὑπέρ, χάριν, ἅμα, παρά, ἔμπροσθεν and ἐπέκεινα.

Genitive
Amos 3.5:
σχασθήσεται παγὶς ἐπὶ τῆς γῆς ἄνευ τοῦ συλλαβεῖν τι

Shall a snare spring up on the ground without catching something?

1 Esd. 6.6:
καὶ οὐκ ἐκωλύθησαν τῆς οἰκοδομῆς μέχρι τοῦ ὑποσημανθῆναι Δαρείῳ

And they were not prevented from the building until sending word to Darius.[21]

21.   Cf. 1 Esd. 1.54; 4.51; 6.6, 27; Tob. 2.10; 1 Macc. 4.46; Ps. 104.19.

4 Macc. 5.29:
οὔτε τοὺς ἱεροὺς τῶν προγόνων περὶ τοῦ φυλάξαι τὸν νόμον ὅρκους οὐ
παρήσω

Neither shall I neglect the sacred oaths of the ancestors concerning keeping
the law.[22]

Tob. 6.16:
οὐ μέμνησαι τῶν λόγων ὧν ἐνετείλατό σοι ὁ πατήρ σου ὑπὲρ τοῦ λαβεῖν
σε γυναῖκα ἐκ τοῦ γένους σου;

Do you not remember the words which your father commanded you concerning your taking a wife from your family?[23]

1 Macc. 11.11:
καὶ ἐψόγισεν αὐτὸν χάριν τοῦ ἐπιθυμῆσαι αὐτὸν τῆς βασιλείας αὐτοῦ

And he censured him because he coveted his kingdom.[24]

1 Kgdms 9.15:
καὶ κύριος ἀπεκάλυψεν τὸ ὠτίον Σαμουηλ ἡμέρᾳ μιᾷ ἔμπροσθεν τοῦ
ἐλθεῖν πρὸς αὐτὸν Σαουλ

And the Lord uncovered the ear of Samuel one day before Saul came to him.

1 Macc. 10.30:
ἀφίημι ἀπὸ τῆς σήμερον καὶ ἐπέκεινα τοῦ λαβεῖν ἀπὸ γῆς Ιουδα

I release from today and beyond taking from the land of Judah.

Dative
Judg. 3.21:
καὶ ἐγένετο ἅμα τῷ ἀναστῆναι αὐτὸν καὶ ἐξέτεινεν Αωδ τὴν χεῖρα τὴν
ἀριστερὰν αὐτοῦ

And it came about when he stood up, and Ehud stretched out his left hand.[25]

Accusative
Ps. 51.5:
ἠγάπησας κακίαν ὑπὲρ ἀγαθωσύνην ἀδικίαν ὑπὲρ τὸ λαλῆσαι δικαιο-
σύνην

You loved evil above goodness, unrighteousness above speaking righteous-
ness.

---

22.   Cf. *3 Macc.* 2.32; *4 Macc.* 4.22.
23.   Cf. 3 Kgdms 16.7; 1 Chron. 29.9; Est. 4.8.
24.   Cf. 2 Macc. 1.14; Dan. 2.13.
25.   Cf. Judg. 9.33; 19.25; 1 Esd. 8.68; *3 Macc.* 3.25; *4 Macc.* 8.29; Ps. 36.20; Jon.
4.8; Ezek. 17.10; 23.40; Dan. 3.15.

Deut. 7.8:

ἀλλὰ παρὰ τὸ ἀγαπᾶν κύριον ὑμᾶς καὶ διατηρῶν τὸν ὅρκον ὃν ὤμοσεν
τοῖς πατράσιν ὑμῶν ἐξήγαγεν κύριος ὑμᾶς ἐν χειρὶ κραταιᾷ

But because the Lord loved you, even maintaining the oath which he swore to
your fathers, the Lord led you out with a strong hand.[26]

In all of these examples we find prepositions that are not used with the
articular infinitive in the New Testament. Yet even in these, the prepositions
are always followed by the articular infinitive, not the anarthrous.

What is consistent in the New Testament, the LXX, and the papyri is that
the articular infinitive is used almost invariably as the prepositional object
rather than the anarthrous. What we shall have to address in the final section
of this chapter is why this usage is *almost* invariable.

3. *Apparent Exceptions to the Hypothesis*

a. *Anarthrous Infinitival Objects*

In this chapter we are not so much concerned with the existence of evidence
that supports our hypothesis in the LXX. As stated above, this evidence is in
ample supply in any of the major grammars of the Hellenistic Greek of the
New Testament. We are mainly concerned to deal with any evidence which
has the potential to falsify the theory advocated thus far.

Table 13. *Anarthrous Infinitives Following Prepositions*

	ἕως	εἰς	μέχρι(ς)	ἐγγύς	ἐκτός	*Total*
Genesis	10.19 (×2), 30; 13.10					4
Judges	6.4; 11.33; 19.8	6.11				4
Ruth	3.3					1
3 Kingdoms	2.35ᶜ; 4.31; 5.14					3
1 Esdras			1.54; 6.6			2
2 Esdras		22.24 (×2)				2
Judith		4.15				1
Tobit			11.1			1
1 Maccabees	16.9					1
Psalms	122.2					1
Wisdom				6.19		1
Sirach		38.27			1.5	2
Totals	13	5	3	1	1	23

The most significant challenge to my thesis lies in the handful of texts that
do not use the article with the infinitive when the infinitive is the object of
the preposition. In the LXX, there are at least 23 instances of anarthrous

---

26.   Cf. Gen. 29.20; Deut. 9.28; 2 Kgs 10.3.

infinitives following prepositions.[27] At first blush, these 23 examples appear to have the potential to undermine the thesis. But I will argue that they do not.

b. *Misidentified Prepositional Objects*

Five of the infinitive examples that are cited by Votaw and Robertson as anarthrous objects of prepositions are in fact not prepositional objects at all and do not present a challenge to the thesis as I have argued it:

> Ruth 3.3 (Rahlfs):
> σὺ δὲ λούσῃ καὶ ἀλείψῃ καὶ περιθήσεις τὸν ἱματισμόν σου ἐπὶ σεαυτῇ καὶ ἀναβήσῃ ἐπὶ τὸν ἅλω μὴ γνωρισθῇς τῷ ἀνδρὶ ἕως οὗ συντελέσαι αὐτὸν πιεῖν καὶ φαγεῖν

> 1 Esd. 1.54 (Swete):
> καὶ ἦσαν παῖδες αὐτῷ καὶ τοῖς υἱοῖς αὐτοῦ μέχρι οὗ βασιλεῦσαι Πέρσας, εἰς ἀναπλήρωσιν τοῦ ῥήματος τοῦ κυρίου ἐν στόματι Ἰερεμίου

> 1 Esd. 6.6 (Swete):
> καὶ οὐκ ἐκωλύθησαν τῆς οἰκοδομῆς μέχρις οὗ ἀποσημανθῆναι Δαρείῳ περὶ αὐτῶν καὶ προσφωνηθῆναι.

> Tob. 11.1 (Göttingen):
> Καὶ ἐπορεύετο μέχρις οὗ ἐγγίσαι αὐτοὺς εἰς Νινευή.

> Ps. 122.2 (Göttingen):
> ἰδοὺ ὡς ὀφθαλμοὶ δούλων εἰς χεῖρας τῶν κυρίων αὐτῶν, ὡς ὀφθαλμοὶ παιδίσκης εἰς χεῖρας τῆς κυρίας αὐτῆς, οὕτως οἱ ὀφθαλμοὶ ἡμῶν πρὸς κύριον τὸν θεὸν ἡμῶν ἕως οὗ οἰκτιρήσαι ἡμᾶς

As one can plainly see in each of these instances, it is not the infinitive that is the object of the preposition, but the relative pronoun ὅς. Votaw has misunderstood the semantics of this construction when he claims that the genitive of ὅς has 'lost its force' when following the prepositions ἕως and μέχρις,[28] as if the relative were not present at all. In actuality, the genitive οὗ serves both as the object of the preposition and as the antecedent of the entire infinitive phrase. Because the pronoun stands in for the infinitive

---

27.   I have used a variety of sources to come up with these 23 texts. Robertson's list of anarthrous infinitives following prepositions apparently follows Votaw, to whom he often refers (Robertson, pp. 1069-70). Using Swete's text, Votaw identifies all the anarthrous infinitives that serve as object of the preposition (Votaw, *The Infinitive in Biblical Greek*, pp. 17-18). I used Votaw and Robertson's lists, and compared them to my own electronic search of the Rahlfs text. I compared these results to the Göttingen text to come up with the final tally. For this study, it does not matter which text preserves the original reading. Whether a given example is original or the alteration of a later scribe is of little concern since both require grammatical explanation.

28.   Votaw, *The Infinitive in Biblical Greek*, p. 18.

phrase semantically, Votaw has mistakenly concluded that the infinitive phrase is the object. This fact is clearly seen if we diagram the construction. For example, observe the syntactical structure of Ruth 3.3 in Figure 5:

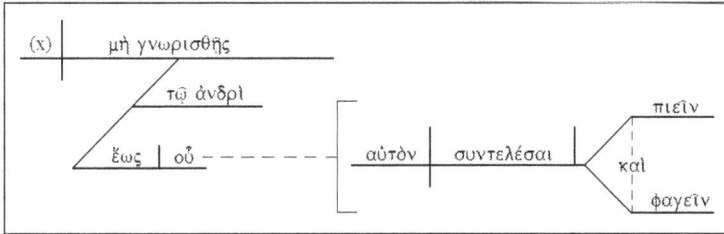

Figure 5. *Diagram of Ruth 3.3 (LXX)*

Here, it is clear that οὗ is the object of the preposition ἕως while the entire infinitive phrase is in fact the antecedent of the relative pronoun οὗ. A literal rendering would be as follows: 'Do not be known to the man *until which [time]* he finishes drinking and eating' (Ruth 3.3). The same structure also occurs with the preposition μέχρι in 1 Esd. 1.54. Notice in this instance also that οὗ is the object of the preposition μέχρι while the entire infinitive phrase is in fact the antecedent of the relative pronoun οὗ. A literal rendering of this phrase would be as follows: 'They were servants to him and to his sons *until which [time]* the Persians began to reign' (1 Esd. 1.54). See the construction in Figure 6:

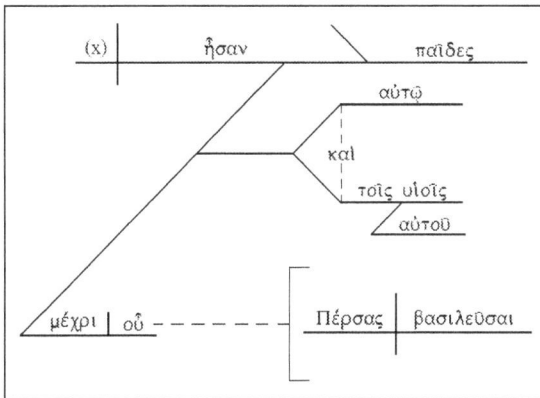

Figure 6. *Diagram of 1 Esdras 1.54 (LXX)*

In these two instances and in the other three, the prepositions ἕως and μέχρι combine with the genitive relative pronoun to denote the end of a period of time.[29] For our purposes, we simply need to note that the anarthrous

29. BDAG, *s.v.* ἕως, p. 423; *s.v.* μέχρι, p. 644.

infinitive is not in fact the prepositional object and therefore cannot stand as evidence against my thesis. Votaw and Robertson are therefore mistaken in including these texts as examples of anarthrous prepositional objects.[30]

c. *Anarthrous Infinitival Objects of Improper Prepositions*
Thirteen examples of the anarthrous infinitive indeed function as prepositional objects but nevertheless do remain consistent with my thesis.

> Gen. 10.19 (Göttingen):
> καὶ ἐγένοντο τὰ ὅρια τῶν Χαναναίων ἀπὸ Σιδῶνος ἕως ἐλθεῖν εἰς Γέραρα καὶ Γάζαν, ἕως ἐλθεῖν Σοδόμων καὶ Γομόρρας, Ἀδαμα καὶ Σεβωίμ ἕως Λασά.

> Gen. 10.30 (Göttingen):
> καὶ ἐγένετο ἡ κατοίκησις αὐτῶν ἀπὸ Μασση ἕως ἐλθεῖν εἰς Σωφηρα ὄρος ἀνατολῶν

> Gen. 13.10 (Göttingen):
> καὶ ἐπάρας Λὼτ τοὺς ὀφθαλμοὺς αὐτοῦ εἶδεν πᾶσαν τὴν περίχωρον τοῦ Ἰορδάνου ὅτι πᾶσα ἦν ποτιζομένη, πρὸ τοῦ καταστρέψαι τὸν θεὸν Σόδομα καὶ Γόμορρα, ὡς ὁ παράδεισος τοῦ θεοῦ καὶ ὡς ἡ γῆ Αἰγύπτου ἕως ἐλθεῖν εἰς Ζόγορα.

> Judg. 6.4 (Rahlfs):
> {καὶ παρενέβαλον εἰς αὐτοὺς καὶ κατέφθειραν τοὺς καρποὺς αὐτῶν ἕως ἐλθεῖν εἰς Γάζαν καὶ οὐ κατέλιπον ὑπόστασιν ζωῆς ἐν τῇ γῇ Ισραηλ οὐδὲ ἐν τοῖς ποιμνίοις ταῦρον καὶ ὄνον}

> Judg. 11.33 (Rahlfs):
> {καὶ ἐπάταξεν αὐτοὺς ἀπὸ Αροηρ ἕως ἐλθεῖν ἄχρις Αρνων ἐν ἀριθμῷ εἴκοσι πόλεις καὶ ἕως Εβελχαρμιν πληγὴν μεγάλην σφόδρα καὶ συνεστάλησαν οἱ υἱοὶ Αμμων ἀπὸ προσώπου υἱῶν Ισραηλ}

> Judg. 19.8 (Rahlfs):
> {καὶ ὤρθρισεν τὸ πρωὶ τῇ ἡμέρᾳ τῇ πέμπτῃ τοῦ πορευθῆναι καὶ εἶπεν ὁ πατὴρ τῆς νεάνιδος στήρισον δὴ τὴν καρδίαν σου καὶ στράτευσον ἕως κλῖναι τὴν ἡμέραν καὶ ἔφαγον οἱ δύο}

> 3 Kgdms 2.35ᶜ (Rahlfs):
> καὶ ἔλαβεν τὴν θυγατέρα Φαραω καὶ εἰσήγαγεν αὐτὴν εἰς τὴν πόλιν Δαυιδ ἕως συντελέσαι αὐτὸν τὸν οἶκον αὐτοῦ καὶ τὸν οἶκον κυρίου ἐν πρώτοις καὶ τὸ τεῖχος Ιερουσαλημ κυκλόθεν· ἐν ἑπτὰ ἔτεσιν ἐποίησεν καὶ συνετέλεσεν.

> 3 Kgdms 4.31 (Swete):
> Καὶ ἔλαβεν Σαλωμὼν τὴν θυγατέρα Φαραὼ ἑαυτῷ εἰς γυναῖκα, καὶ εἰσήγαγεν αὐτὴν εἰς τὴν πόλιν Δαυειδ ἕως συντελέσαι αὐτὸν τὸν οἶκον Κυρίου καὶ τὸν οἶκον ἑαυτοῦ καὶ τὸ τεῖχος Ἰερουσαλήμ.

---

30.   Robertson, pp. 1069-70; Votaw, *The Infinitive in Biblical Greek*, pp. 17-18.

3 Kgdms 5.14 (Rahlfs):
Καὶ ἔλαβεν Σαλωμων τὴν θυγατέρα Φαραω ἑαυτῷ εἰς γυναῖκα καὶ
εἰσήγαγεν αὐτὴν εἰς τὴν πόλιν Δαυιδ ἕως συντελέσαι αὐτὸν τὸν οἶκον
κυρίου καὶ τὸν οἶκον ἑαυτοῦ καὶ τὸ τεῖχος Ιερουσαλημ.

1 Macc. 16.9 (Swete):
τότε ἐτραυματίσθη ᾿Ιούδας ὁ ἀδελφὸς ᾿Ιωάννου· ᾿Ιωάννης δὲ κατεδίω-
ξεν αὐτοὺς ἕως ἐλθεῖν εἰς Κεδρών, ἣν οἰκοδόμησεν.

Wis. 6.18-19 (Göttingen):
φροντὶς δὲ παιδείας ἀγάπη, ἀγάπη δὲ τήρησις νόμων αὐτῆς, προσοχὴ δὲ
νόμων βεβαίωσις ἀφθαρσίας, ἀφθαρσία δὲ ἐγγὺς εἶναι ποιεῖ θεοῦ·

Sir. 1.5 (Göttingen):
ἀλλὰ καὶ τοῖς ἐκτὸς δύνασθαι τοὺς φιλομαθοῦντας χρησίμους εἶναι καὶ
λέγοντας καὶ γράφοντας

According to my thesis, the articular infinitive is used with prepositions
because of the lack of spaces between words and the subsequent need to
distinguish prepositional object-infinitives from those that are being used in
composition. Yet in all 13 of these instances, there is no such need for an
intervening word to show that the preposition is not forming a compound
with the infinitive. In contrast to prepositions such as ἐν, διά, and ἀπό, there
are at least 42 prepositions in the New Testament that are never used in
composition with verbs.[31] The three prepositions used in these texts are ἕως,
ἐγγύς, and ἐκτός, and they are all 'improper' prepositions. Ἕως, ἐγγύς,
and ἐκτός are among that group of prepositions 'that never came to be used
in composition with verbs'.[32]

This fact means that the native reader and speaker of Koine Greek would
not have needed an intervening word to distinguish the anarthrous infinitives
as prepositional objects. Because ἕως, ἐγγύς, and ἐκτός were never used in
composition in the first place, there would have been no confusion. I argued
in Chapter 4 that the case of the prepositional object infinitive needs to be
made explicit because cases govern the meaning of prepositions and not vice
versa. Yet, in these texts, the native reader and speaker would not necessarily have needed the case of the infinitive to be marked. The construction
in these 13 texts bears a semantic resemblance to the prepositional phrases
with indeclinable foreign loan-words as objects (to which I referred in the
previous chapter). Just as the case-function of Aramaic indeclinables can be
deduced from context, so can it be in these 13 texts. Because ἕως, ἐγγύς,
and ἐκτός are only used with the genitive case, it is clear even without the
article what case-function the infinitive performs.

31.   There is a convenient list of these in Robertson's table of contents (Robertson,
pp. xli-xlii).
32.   Robertson, p. 636.

d. Εἰς *with Anarthrous Infinitival Objects*

There are at least five instances in which the anarthrous infinitive follows the preposition εἰς:

Judg. 6.11 (Rahlfs [Vaticanus B]):
καὶ ἦλθεν ἄγγελος κυρίου καὶ ἐκάθισεν ὑπὸ τὴν τερέμινθον τὴν ἐν Εφραθα τὴν Ιωας πατρὸς τοῦ Εσδρι καὶ Γεδεων υἱὸς αὐτοῦ ῥαβδίζων σῖτον ἐν ληνῷ εἰς ἐκφυγεῖν ἀπὸ προσώπου τοῦ Μαδιαμ.

And the angel of the Lord came and sat by the terebinth tree that was in Ephrath, [the tree] that belonged to Joash whose father was Ezri, and Gideon his son was beating the grain in the wine-press in order that he might escape from the face of Midian.

2 Esd. 22.24 (Göttingen):
καὶ οἱ ἄρχοντες τῶν Λευιτῶν, ʽΑσαβιὰ καὶ Σαραβιὰ καὶ ᾽Ιησοὺ καὶ υἱοὶ Καδμιὴλ καὶ ἀδελφοὶ αὐτῶν κατεναντίον αὐτῶν εἰς ὑμνεῖν καὶ αἰνεῖν ἐν ἐντολῇ Δαυὶδ ἀνθρώπου τοῦ θεοῦ ἐφημερία πρὸς ἐφημερίαν.

And the leaders of the Levites: Hashabiah and Sherabiah and Joshua and the sons of Kadmiel and their brothers over against them, to sing and to praise in the commandment of David, the man of God, division by division.

Jdt. 4.15 (Göttingen):
καὶ ἦν σποδὸς ἐπὶ τὰς κιδάρεις αὐτῶν, καὶ ἐβόων πρὸς κύριον ἐκ πάσης δυνάμεως εἰς ἀγαθὸν ἐπισκέψασθαι πᾶν οἶκον ᾽Ισραήλ.

And ash was on their turbans, and they were crying to the Lord with all their might that he would look upon the whole house of Israel for good.

Sir. 38.27 (Göttingen):
οὕτως πᾶς τέκτων καὶ ἀρχιτέκτων, ὅστις νύκτωρ ὡς ἡμέρας διάγει. οἱ γλύφοντες γλύμματα σφραγίδων, καὶ ἡ ἐπιμονὴ αὐτοῦ ἀλλοιῶσαι ποικιλίαν· καρδία αὐτοῦ δώσει εἰς ὁμοιῶσαι ζωγραφίαν, καὶ ἡ ἀγρυπνία αὐτοῦ τελέσαι ἔργον.

Thus every carpenter and master-carpenter, who works by night as he does in the day, the ones who carve inscriptions of seals, and his steadfastness to make a great variety, he will set his heart so that he might make a life-like painting, and his watchfulness to complete a work.

Because εἰς is regularly used in composition with verbs, these five uses of the anarthrous infinitive present the biggest obstacle so far to my thesis. Yet even in these five texts, a ready explanation of their exceptional nature is at hand.

We should begin by noticing that Robertson and Votaw have misidentified Jdt. 4.15 as an example of an anarthrous infinitival object of a preposition.[33] This misidentification is probably due to a failure to recognize εἰς

33.   Robertson, p. 1070; Votaw, *The Infinitive in Biblical Greek*, p. 18.

ἀγαθὸν as a common LXX idiom and rendering of the Hebrew phrases לְטוֹבָה and לְטוֹב ('for good'). Thus the infinitive ἐπισκέψασθαι is not the object of the preposition εἰς, but the adjective ἀγαθόν is. This meaning is found in texts such as Jer. 24.6: καὶ στηριῶ τοὺς ὀφθαλμούς μου ἐπ' αὐτοὺς εἰς ἀγαθά ('I will set my eyes upon them for good').[34] For this reason, I have rendered Jdt. 4.15 with, 'they were crying to the Lord with all their might that he would look upon the whole house of Israel *for good* [εἰς ἀγαθόν]'. The example in Jdt. 4.15, therefore, offers no challenge to my thesis.

The other four instances of this construction reflect the influence of Ionic on the language of the Koine. Moulton points out that 'the articular infinitive is almost entirely a development of Attic literature, especially oratory, from which it passed into the daily speech of the least cultured people in the later Hellenistic world... The application of the articular infin. in New Testament Greek does not in principle go beyond what is found in Attic writers'.[35] Moulton's point is simply that the articular infinitive grew out of that dialect that came to be pre-eminent among Greek speakers of the day, the Attic. Other dialects (like Ionic) never came to use the articular infinitive as we find it in the Attic. Whereas the use of the articular infinitive in the Attic tongue is very similar to what we find in the Koine, the same is not true with respect to the Ionic. In that dialect, the anarthrous infinitive could be found as object of the preposition. The use of the articular infinitive in the Ionic did not exert a significant influence on Koine dialect. Nevertheless, traces of it emerge in some of the papyri. Moulton comments on this connection,

> we [readers of the New Testament] have nothing [in our literature] answering to the vernacular idiom by which the article may be omitted between preposition and infinitive. In family or business accounts among the papyri we find with significant frequency an item of so much εἰς πεῖν... There are three passages in Herodotus where ἀντί behaves thus...ἀντὶ εἶναι... In these three points we may possibly recognize Ionic influence.[36]

Moulton attributes this uncommon construction to an age gone by in the history of the Greek language. For whatever reason, this particular usage has hung on in a very small number of instances in the vernacular literature, and apparently in these four texts from the LXX.[37]

---

34. Compare the Hebrew with the LXX in the following texts: Gen. 50.20; Deut. 28.11; 30.9; 2 Chron. 10.7; 18.7; 2 Esd. 8.22; 12.18; 15.19; Jdt. 4.15; Pss. 85.17; 118.122; Sir. 2.9; 7.13; 11.12; 13.25; 39.27; Amos 9.4; Mic. 1.12; Jer. 14.11; 15.11; 21.10; 24.5, 6; 39.39; 46.16.

35. Moulton, *Prolegomena*, p. 215.

36. Moulton, *Prolegomena*, p. 81.

37. Mayser notes how uncommon this construction is in Classical Greek: 'Der in der klassischen Sprache überaus seltene Gebrauch einer Präposition oder eines Präpositionaladverbium mit dem artikellosen Infinitiv...Sicher steht der auch in Rechnungen

The example from Judg. 6.11 probably can be explained by this unusual influence from the Ionic, though it technically does not conflict with my thesis. The construction appears as follows, εἰς ἐκφυγεῖν ('in order to escape'). Notice that the preposition ἐκ, which is in composition with the verb φεύγω, intervenes between εἰς and the infinitive. The position of ἐκ makes it clear that εἰς is not being used in composition with φυγεῖν. Thus an article would not be needed in this instance to disambiguate the construction. Ἐκ does the job by itself.

The final three examples are from 2 Esd. 22.24 (εἰς ὑμνεῖν καὶ αἰνεῖν) and Sir. 38.27 (εἰς ὁμοιῶσαι). The question that we have to bring to these two texts is as follows: Why would an obscure Ionic idiom survive at all when the native reader would have needed an article or some other linguistic signal to mark the infinitives as objects of the preposition? There are three possible answers to this question: (1) my thesis is correct, even though these exceptions cannot be explained (they are the exceptions that prove the rule); (2) these three examples overturn my thesis, and the argument that I have made thus far is completely undermined; (3) these three exceptional instances can be reconciled with my thesis by arguing that no signal is needed in these particular instances to disambiguate the construction. I will argue for the third option. These two texts do not require an article or some other clarifying signal because the native speaker and reader of Koine Greek would have recognized that ὑμνέω, αἰνέω, and ὁμοιόω are never used in composition with εἰς and therefore would have been understood clearly as prepositional objects. Unlike other compounds formed with εἰς that appear very frequently in the Koine (e.g. εἰσβαίνω, εἰσακούω, εἰσέρχομαι, εἰσπορεύω, etc.), the compounds εἰσ-ὑμνέω, εἰσ-αἰνέω, and εἰσ-ὁμοιόω appear nowhere in Greek literature.[38] The native speakers would have recognized this fact intuitively and therefore would not have experienced any misunderstanding with the anarthrous infinitives in 2 Esd. 22.24 and Sir. 8.27.

4. *Conclusion*

I contend that in the New Testament the Greek article does not bear its normal semantic weight as a determiner when used with the infinitive. While its usual semantic role is to determine nominals as definite, I have showed that the article appears to have no definitizing effect when used in connection with the infinitive. In the New Testament literature, I have demonstrated the article's necessity as a case-identifier and as a structural marker in this construction. My thesis was found to be an adequate explanation of the data

nachchristlicher Jahrhunderte nicht seltene Ausdruck εἰς πιεῖν... Alle anderen in Betracht kommenden Fälle sind höchst zweifelhaft' (Mayser, *Grammatik*, 324).
   38.   LSJ, *s.v.* εἰσαγείρω-εἰσωθέω, pp. 492-98.

contained in the New Testament. In this chapter I have used the LXX as a control by which to test the thesis that I have formulated on the basis of the New Testament literature.

The LXX reveals a broad consistency of usage with that of its counterparts in the New Testament. The use of the article with the infinitive is identical to that found in the New Testament, with the exception that there are more prepositions used in the LXX in this construction than there are in the New Testament. We have seen 23 examples of the anarthrous infinitive that appear to reflect a usage not found in the New Testament—namely, the object of the preposition. Yet in each of these 23 examples, there are mitigating factors that show these examples to be consistent with my thesis.

6

CONCLUSION AND IMPLICATIONS

1. *Introduction*

We can summarize the conclusions of this study before considering some implications for the study of the New Testament. In Chapter 2, I argued that the article is a determiner and that determiners have the sole semantic function of marking substantives as definite. Of the three Greek determiners (ὁ-ἡ-τό/οὗτος/ἐκεῖνος), only the article appears on occasion without its normal semantic weight as a determiner. I drew attention to various contexts in the New Testament in which it is clear that the Greek article appears only as a syntactical marker. Following Haiim B. Rosén's work, I concluded that when the article is grammatically obligatory, one should not look for the additional semantic significance of determination. This conclusion set up my analysis of the articular infinitive in the New Testament. If I could success-fully demonstrate the article's necessity as a function word in connection with the infinitive, then we would have no basis to regard the article as having its normal semantic force as a determiner. In Chapters 3 and 4, I showed examples of the articular infinitive in the New Testament in which the appearance of the article is grammatically obligatory—either to mark the case of the infinitive and/or to specify a syntactical function that can only be made explicit by the presence of the article. In Chapter 5, I tested this thesis by apparent exceptions that have been cited in the LXX. In all 23 of these 'exceptional' examples, I showed that these anomalous texts do not in fact undermine my thesis as I have argued it. Now it remains to give a sketch of the implications of my thesis.

2. *Implications*

The implications of my thesis come in two kinds: grammatical and exegeti-cal. That is, my thesis has valuable insights for both the study of New Testament Greek grammar and for the interpretation of specific New Testament texts. I have identified at least three areas of Greek grammar study that are effected by my conclusion, and I will address each one below. Then I will show how my conclusion informs and illuminates the exegesis of some selected texts from the New Testament.

a. *Implications for Hellenistic Greek Grammar*
(1) *The semantics of the Greek article*. It is fair to say that scholars of New Testament Greek have not devoted adequate attention to what we mean when we say something is 'definite'. The standard works on the grammar of the New Testament do not take into account the work in general linguistics on the concept of definiteness and how this concept relates to the conventions used in Greek to mark for definiteness. For instance, D.A. Carson has alerted Greek readers that it is a 'fallacy to suppose that because the Greek text has an article, the English translation must have one, or because the Greek text is anarthrous at some point, the English translation must follow suit'.[1] This observation is fair enough and would not be disputed by anyone with a modicum of knowledge of New Testament Greek. However, Carson's conclusion is unhelpfully vague:

> I suspect that some uses are determined more by 'feel' of the speaker or writer of the language than by unambiguous principles...the exegete must be careful regarding conclusions drawn from the mere presence or absence of an article. Apart from certain idioms, only context and the feel gained by experience in the Greek text will serve as adequate control.[2]

Carson is correct to point out the errors that commentators have made in interpreting the Greek article, but to suggest that something so amorphous as 'feel' to be a guide in interpretation is not helpful.

Carson's constructive suggestion is to conceive of the semantics of the article according to the chart in Table 14:[3]

Table 14. *Chart from Exegetical Fallacies*

	Use 1	Use 2
Articular	(a) definite	(c) generic
Anarthrous	(b) indefinite, i.e., qualitative	(d) non-generic (individual item)

Stanley Porter adopts this table as the basis for his analysis of the article, and formulates a principle for the interpretation of the Greek article: 'When the article is used, the substantive may refer to a particular item, or it may represent a category of items. When the article is not used, the substantive may refer to the non-particular or qualitative character of an item, or it may refer to an individual item'.[4]

---

1. Carson, *Exegetical Fallacies*, p. 79.
2. Carson, *Exegetical Fallacies*, pp. 79-80.
3. Carson, *Exegetical Fallacies*, p. 79.
4. Porter, *Idioms*, p. 104.

The problem with Carson and Porter's chart is that it does not reflect the full range of meaning that is possible with the Greek article. On the one hand, the chart does not make room for the article's frequent use as a pure function word.[5] As we have seen throughout the course of this study (especially in Chapter 2), there are many contexts in which the article appears with neither the 'definite' or the 'generic' meaning. I introduced a host of texts where the article's only value is that of marking the case or syntactical function of a given substantive. On the other hand, the chart does not accurately reflect the relationship between the semantic idea of definiteness and all the other specific semantic nuances of the definite article (e.g. anaphoric, well-known, etc.). According to the definition of 'determination' in Chapter 2, the only semantic value that a determiner has is that of marking for definiteness. Carson and Porter leave the impression that the article can either determine as definite or determine as generic. Such a conclusion is not an accurate reflection of the article's usage in Koine Greek. All of the semantic nuances of the article (e.g. generic, anaphora, well-known, etc.) are but subcategories of definiteness. So the first question that one brings to any articular substantive is whether or not the article bears its normal semantic load as a determiner—that is, marking as definite. The second question that one asks is what specific nuance of definiteness is being expressed (e.g. generic, anaphora, etc.). What I have argued in connection with the infinitive is true also of other kinds of substantives. When the article is grammatically obligatory, it often does not determine the substantive as definite.

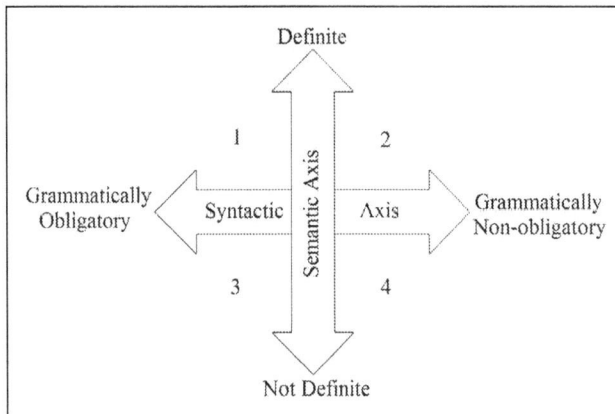

Figure 7. *The Article's Range of Meaning*

<hr>

5.   There are too many grammars that do not address the article's frequent appearance as a function word. Wallace's grammar is a happy exception to this trend (Wallace, *Greek Grammar*, pp. 238-43). Funk also includes a section on 'the article as a grammatical device [i.e. a function word]' (*A Beginning–Intermediate Grammar*, II, pp. 557-60).

The best way to outline the full range of meaning that an article can possibly have is to account for its potential value both as a determiner and as a syntactical marker. This range is summarized in Figure 7.

It should be noted, however, that even this chart is not perfect since it may suggest that the possible uses of the article are evenly distributed across the New Testament. In actuality, the use of the article in the New Testament tends to fall in quadrants 2 or 3, but not in quadrants 1 or 4.

(2) *Case semantics.* General linguistics has not been able to produce a consensus on the definition of *case.* Linguists of the Fillmore school still assert a disjunction between form and function in the definition of *case.* For the followers of Fillmore, *case* refers not to the inflectional variation in a noun, but to innate semantic roles that nouns fulfill in relation to a verbal idea. These semantic roles are not at all tied to the inflectional variation in a given noun. We have seen that Simon Wong is an example of a New Testament scholar who is trying to apply Fillmore's *case grammar* to the study of New Testament Greek.[6] The result has been the reopening of an issue that many New Testament scholars have regarded as closed—namely, whether case should be defined in terms of form or function.[7]

The approach to case in this book is one that assumes a link between morphology and semantics. Stanley Porter states the matter very clearly: 'Greek has an iconic relationship of grammatical and semantic case, so that the grammatical cases grammaticalize a single complex semantic notion'.[8] Thus, the best way to approach the interpretation of Greek case is to assume that morphological and grammatical structure dictates semantics.[9] The approach that many have taken to understanding the articular infinitive runs roughshod over this assumption. In this line of thinking, the interpretation of the articular infinitive becomes a matter that is quite distinct from an analysis of the case-meaning of the neuter article.[10] The proper mode for studying

6. See Wong, *Classification of Semantic Case-Relations,* and 'What Case is This Case?'

7. In Chapter 3 I noted that this is a debate that has already taken place among scholars of New Testament Greek, albeit within the framework of a whole other set of linguistic assumptions. At the heart of Robertson's eight-case system is the assumption that case should be defined as a matter of function, not morphological form. Today, the majority of New Testament scholars remain unconvinced by Robertson's arguments in favor of defining case in terms of grammatical function. Most New Testament scholars adopt a five-case system that is defined by form, not function.

8. Quoted from a personal e-mail correspondence with the author dated 13 April 2005.

9. Wallace, *Greek Grammar,* pp. 5-7.

10. In Chapter 3, we saw that it is not just the proponents of case grammar who allow for a disjunction between morphological form and function. This fact is perhaps most

Greek case involves an observation of the inflectional case, a recognition of the fundamental meaning (*Grundbedeutung*) of that inflectional case, and an analysis of how that 'ground meaning' is actualized in a given context. This is the approach adopted by J.P. Louw[11] and Stanley Porter[12] and seems to hold out the most promise for future studies of the Greek case system.

(3) *Prepositional phrases.* Because structure dictates semantics, both the case of the object and the meaning of the preposition must be accounted for in the interpretation of prepositional phrases. As I noted in Chapter 4, many grammarians already follow this procedure. For example, Robertson writes that the proper method for studying prepositional phrases is, 'to begin with the case-idea, add the meaning of the preposition itself, then consider the context. The result of this combination will be what one translates into English, for instance, but he translates the total idea, not the mere preposition'.[13] This procedure precludes, therefore, approaches that dissolve the case-meaning of the prepositional object into the semantics of the preposition itself. I thus disagree with Wallace's suggestion that, 'Whenever any of the oblique cases follows a preposition, you should examine the use of the *preposition*, rather than the case usage, to determine the possible nuances involved'.[14] I do not agree with Wallace that prepositions govern cases, nor do I agree that cases govern prepositions. Actually, prepositions combine with cases in order to clarify/specify the case-usage.

b. *Implications for Exegesis in the New Testament*
The main conclusion of this study is that the article is not a *definitizer* when used in connection with the infinitive. It appears as a function word in order to clarify the case-meaning of the substantive or to mark a relation that can only be made specific by the presence of the article. While I have already provided a brief survey of all the relevant texts in Chapters 3 and 4, space forbids setting forth the precise implications of my thesis for each articular

conspicuous in the suggestion that the genitive case has completely lost its semantic force in certain uses of the genitive articular infinitive. In these texts (Lk. 17.1; Acts 10.25; 27.1; 1 Cor. 16.4), grammarians have suggested that the genitive articular infinitive functions as the syntactical subject, even though the case is genitive. But I have shown that there is plausible way to interpret these infinitives without arbitrarily suppressing the force of the genitive case. 'A proper syntactical approach investigates all of the relevant morpho-syntactic structures and then draws conclusions about the semantics, rather than foisting a semantic meaning on such structures when only a small sampling has been examined' (Wallace, *Greek Grammar*, p. 6).

11. Louw, 'Linguistic Theory and the Greek Case System'.
12. Porter, 'The Case for Case Revisited', and *Idioms*.
13. Robertson, p. 568.
14. Wallace, *Greek Grammar*, p. 360.

infinitive in the New Testament. However, it will be useful for us to consider how my conclusion can influence the interpretation of selected texts that employ this construction. In many texts, the significance of the article in the articular infinitive can have a pivotal effect on one's understanding of the author's meaning. It is, of course, never the linchpin, but it is often crucial nonetheless. Consider the following texts.

(1) *Mark 9.10*. In Mk 9.10, we find the disciples discussing among themselves what Jesus meant by referring to 'resurrecting from the dead' (τὸ ἐκ νεκρῶν ἀναστῆναι) in v. 9 (ὅταν ὁ υἱὸς τοῦ ἀνθρώπου ἐκ νεκρῶν ἀναστῇ). Commentators disagree about what particular 'resurrection' the disciples are discussing in v. 10. Are the disciples giving careful consideration to Jesus' resurrection for which Jesus had just told them to wait in v. 9, or are they discussing the resurrection more generally? Craig Evans claims that the disciples were wondering very specifically about 'Jesus' death and resurrection'.[15] Ezra Gould agrees that they were discussing, 'not what the resurrection means in general, which they as orthodox Jews at this time would know well enough; but what it meant in the case of Jesus, involving, as it did, his death'.[16] Others have suggested that the disciples did not have the theological framework that would have allowed them to understand Jesus as one who would be resurrected himself. As Lane states so clearly, 'The place of Jesus' passion and death, together with his resurrection, was the unexpected and incomprehensible middle term between the present and the magnificent future assured by the transfiguration'.[17] On this reading, the disciples' discussion dealt broadly with the eschatological hope of the resurrection of the righteous and its connection to the coming Messianic kingdom, not with Jesus' resurrection in particular. According to this latter interpretation, at this point in Mark's narrative the disciples simply did not understand Jesus' reference to himself.

Robert Gundry argues that the article with the infinitive in v. 10 (τὸ ἐκ νεκρῶν ἀναστῆναι) comprises an anaphoric reference to Jesus' prediction of his own 'resurrection' in v. 9 (ὅταν ὁ υἱὸς τοῦ ἀνθρώπου ἐκ νεκρῶν ἀναστῇ). Thus the disciples were not discussing the resurrection in general, for 'rising from the dead would not be meaningless to first century Jews'.[18] Rather, they were talking about the Son of Man's resurrection in particular.

15. Evans, *Mark 8.27–16.20*, p. 42.

16. Ezra P. Gould, *A Critical and Exegetical Commentary on the Gospel according to St Mark* (ICC; Edinburgh: T. & T. Clark, 1975), p. 164.

17. William L. Lane, *The Gospel according to Mark* (NICNT; Grand Rapids: Eerdmans, 1974), p. 324.

18. Robert H. Gundry, *Mark: A Commentary on his Apology for the Cross* (Grand Rapids: Eerdmans, 1993), p. 463.

Gundry agrees with BDF in his assessment of the significance of the article in this particular text,[19] though he obviously uses this grammatical item to bolster a larger exegetical point. The disciples at this stage in the narrative comprehend to some degree Jesus' reference to his own passion. This conclusion is highly debatable, and we certainly should not rest too much weight on an anaphoric reading of the articular infinitive.

If the thesis I am proposing is correct, then the only reason for the article's appearance in this text is to distinguish the syntactical subject (τὸ... ἀναστῆναι) from the predicate nominative (τί). In this interpretation, the article does not mark the infinitive as definite (and thereby anaphoric), but it merely appears as a function word to distinguish the infinitive as the subject of its clause. This reading of the articular infinitive allows more of a theological disconnect between the resurrection that Jesus had in mind vs. the resurrection that the disciples began to discuss among themselves. In his comments on this text, N.T. Wright argues to this effect. The disciples would not have been able to comprehend a reference to Jesus' resurrection, but would have been wondering and debating about the resurrection of the dead at the end of the age. Wright contends that the disciples did not know about what would be:

> a significant Christian innovation: the idea that 'the resurrection' has split into two, with Jesus' resurrection coming forwards into the middle of history. Mark, clearly, intends his readers to recognize that they share with hindsight the knowledge that Jesus seemed to have in advance. The reader understands what was, for the disciples at the time, still a puzzle.[20]

Given that the disciples' expectations concerning the Son of Man were often at odds with what Jesus actually turned out to be, this reading of Mk 9.10 has the most to commend it.[21] The disciples' understanding of resurrection is still at odds with Jesus' teaching at this point in Mark's presentation. A non-anaphoric reading of the article makes this interpretation possible.

---

19. BDF §399(1). In BDF's estimation, Mk 9.10 is one of the clear and obvious anaphoric uses of the articular infinitive.

20. N.T. Wright, *The Resurrection of the Son of God* (Christian Origins and the Question of God, 3; London: SPCK, 2003), p. 415.

21. One might object that the article might still be understood as definite in the sense that Jewish belief in an eschatological resurrection of the righteous was 'well-known'. After all, even Wright acknowledges that the phrase τὸ ἐκ νεκρῶν ἀναστῆναι 'normally referred to the rising of all the righteous at the end of time' (Wright, *The Resurrection of the Son of God*, p. 415). Yet this general resurrection is referred to elsewhere without the alleged 'well-known' article (e.g. 2 Macc. 7.14; 12.44). So it is more likely that the article is compelled by grammatical considerations, not by an attempt to definitize the infinitive.

(2) *Acts 25.11*. It is widely known that παραιτέομαι has two meanings, either 'to ask/request' or 'to refuse/reject'.[22] What is not as widely acknowledged is the difference in meaning that occurs when παραιτέομαι is followed by an infinitive vs. when it is followed by an accusative object. When παραιτέομαι is followed by an anarthrous infinitive elsewhere in the New Testament, the meaning of the verb is always 'request',[23] and the infinitive is always intended as indirect discourse.[24] When παραιτέομαι is followed by an accusative object elsewhere in the New Testament, indirect discourse is not intended, and the sense of παραιτέομαι is always 'refuse' or 'reject'.[25] The presence of the article with the infinitive ἀποθανεῖν enables us to adjudicate between these two possible meanings of παραιτέομαι in Acts 25.11. The accusative neuter article τό marks ἀποθανεῖν as the direct object of παραιτέομαι and removes the possibility that the infinitive will be construed as indirect discourse. Without the article, παραιτέομαι might be misinterpreted as 'request'. Clearly, the correct interpretation is 'reject', and the presence of the article makes this meaning clear. C.K. Barrett arrives at the interpretation that I do here, but he has to appeal to extra-biblical sources to do so. Barrett misinterprets the article as anaphoric when he should have understood it as a structural marker that clarifies the function of the infinitive following the verb παραιτέομαι.[26]

(3) *Romans 13.8*. In Rom. 13.8, significant debate has centered upon the force of the articular infinitive in Paul's injunction, Μηδενὶ μηδὲν ὀφείλετε εἰ μὴ τὸ ἀλλήλους ἀγαπᾶν. BDF interprets the article as definite in connection with the infinitive ἀγαπᾶν, and therefore understands the article as an anaphoric hearkening back to the 'well-known command' of Jesus that is quoted in v. 9: 'Love your neighbor as yourself' (cf. Mk 12.31; Mt. 22.39; Jn 13.34; 15.12, 17).[27] This interpretation has garnered support in some significant commentaries over the years,[28] and unfortunately has added to the confusion over the interpretation of the main verb ὀφείλω and the conjunctive phrase εἰ μή.

22. LSJ, *s.v.* παραιτέομαι, pp. 1310-11; BDAG, *s.v.* παραιτέομαι, p. 764.
23. Lk. 23.23; Jn 4.9; Acts 3.14; 7.46; 13.28; Eph. 3.13; Heb. 12.19.
24. On the use of the infinitive after verbs of perception, see BDF §397(3); Wallace, *Greek Grammar*, p. 603.
25. 1 Tim. 4.7; 5.11; 2 Tim. 2.23; Tit. 3.10; Heb. 12.25.
26. Barrett, *Commentary on the Acts of the Apostles*, II, p. 1130.
27. BDF §399(1).
28. Not the least of which is C.E.B. Cranfield, *A Critical and Exegetical Commentary on the Epistle to the Romans*. II. *Commentary on Romans IX–XVI and Essays* (ICC; Edinburgh: T. & T. Clark, 1979), p. 674 n. 2.

Some have suggested that εἰ μή means 'but', while others argue for the translation, 'except'. The force of εἰ μή determines to some extent how one will interpret ὀφείλω as it applies to the second half of the verse. John Murray argues for the former meaning and favors a rendering like the following: 'Owe nothing to anyone; but [you ought] to love one another'.[29] In Murray's interpretation, ὀφείλω does not refer to a *debt owed* in the second half of the sentence (the verb has to be supplied in this elliptical construction), but to a *continuing moral obligation*. C.E.B. Cranfield argues that εἰ μή means 'except' and that ὀφείλω has the same sense when it is supplied in the second half of the clause as it does in its appearance in the first half of the clause. According to Cranfield, the 'but' interpretation

> involves supplying in the second half of a sentence a verb used in the first half, and supplying it not just in a different sense but also in a different mood; and, while the supplying of the same verb in a different sense would be quite feasible word-play…the combination of change of sense and change of mood, where the verb is not repeated, is surely so harsh as to be extremely improbable. Moreover, the presence of τό is a further difficulty in the way of this interpretation… If ὀφείλετε is to be understood in the indicative after εἰ μή, then the τό cannot very well be explained as anaphoric.[30]

Cranfield therefore favors a rendering like the following: 'Leave no debt outstanding to anyone, except the debt of love to one another'. Cranfield takes BDF's analysis for granted that the article is anaphoric, and on that basis argues for a particular interpretation of ὀφείλω. As I will demonstrate below, the neuter accusative article is related to the interpretation of ὀφείλω, but not in the way that Cranfield has it.

Douglas J. Moo has proposed another possible reason for the article's use in this text. He suggests that the article may be employed here simply as a substantivizer.[31] But this interpretation is based on an inappropriate analogy with v. 9, where Robertson and BDF indicate that the article appears to be introducing a series of quotations from the Decalogue:[32] τὸ γὰρ οὐ μοιχεύσεις, οὐ φονεύσεις, οὐ κλέψεις, οὐκ ἐπιθυμήσεις ('For this, "You shall not commit adultery, You shall not murder, You shall not steal, You shall not covet"'). But Robertson and BDF only interpret the article in this way in connection with v. 9, not with the infinitive phrase in v. 8. On this point, Robertson and BDF's omission of v. 8 is consistent with what I argued in

---

29. John Murray, *The Epistle to the Romans* (NICNT; 2 vols.; Grand Rapids: Eerdmans, 1965), II, p. 159.

30. Cranfield, *Romans*, II, p. 674 and n. 2.

31. Moo (*The Epistle to the Romans*, p. 812 n. 9) allows that the article might be anaphoric, while not ruling out the possibility that the article may simply be substantivizing the infinitive phrase.

32. Moo appeals directly to Robertson, p. 243; BDF §267(1).

Chapter 1 of this book. The infinitive is a substantive with or without the article.[33] Therefore the article is not needed in order for the infinitive phrase to be understood substantivally. Such is not the case with the articular phrase in v. 9. So Moo's explanation of the article's presence is not satisfactory either.

The neuter article appears in Rom. 13.8 neither as a *definitizer*[34] nor as a *substantivizer*. The article appears in order to clarify the meaning of ὀφεί-λετε. The verb ὀφείλω requires either a *complementary* infinitive or an accusative *object*.[35] When it is followed by a *complementary* infinitive in Paul's writing, the sense of ὀφείλω is always 'ought' or 'be obligated'.[36] When followed by an accusative *object*, the sense of ὀφείλω is always 'owe'.[37] Thus in Rom. 13.8, the article marks the infinitive as accusative object and shows that the infinitive is not complementary. This interpretation is further confirmed by the appearance of the ὀφείλω/ἀγαπᾶν pair in Eph. 5.28 where ἀγαπᾶν is anarthrous and thus *complementary*. The article in Rom. 13.8, therefore, does not hearken back to the 'well-known' command from Jesus. The article appears simply to mark the infinitive as the *direct object*, a function that is distinct from the *complementary* use.[38]

(4) *Philippians 2.6.*[39] BDF suggests that the articular infinitive has an anaphoric force in the hotly debated text in Phil. 2.6: ὃς ἐν μορφῇ θεοῦ ὑπάρχων οὐχ ἁρπαγμὸν ἡγήσατο τὸ εἶναι ἴσα θεῷ. According to this view, 'equality with God' should be interpreted in close association with 'form of God'. N.T. Wright has adopted the view contained in BDF, and his

33. Robertson, p. 1057.

34. As I noted already in Chapter 2, the 'well-known' use of the article is a subcategory of *definiteness*. I defined *definiteness* as follows: 'Marking [a noun phrase] as definite means to locate its referent(s) in a set of objects shared by the speaker and the hearer' (Heinz Vater, *Toward a Generative Dependency Grammar* [Trier: Linguistic Agency University at Trier, 1973], p. 122). In BDF's interpretation of the article in Rom. 13.8, the object is shared in the minds of the speaker and the hearer because it is 'well-known'.

35. BDAG, *s.v.* ὀφείλω, p. 743, confirms this twofold usage.

36. Rom. 15.1, 27; 1 Cor. 5.10; 7.36; 9.10; 11.7, 10; 12.11, 14; Eph. 5.28; 2 Thess. 1.3; 2.13.

37. Only Rom. 13.8 and Phlm. 18 in Paul. But compare with the following texts: Mt. 18.28, 30, 34; Lk. 7.41; 16.5, 7.

38. This is not to say that Paul would not have had access to this tradition from Jesus. It is just that the text of Rom 13.8 would be an atypical way for Paul to refer to such tradition when he means to quote it in a direct way (cf. 1 Cor. 11.23; 15.3; Gal. 1.9, 12).

39. I have written an article on the significance of the articular infinitive in this particular text; see my 'On the Articular Infinitive in Philippians 2.6: A Grammatical Note with Christological Implications', *TynBul* 55 (2004), pp. 253-74. Much of the material in this section appears in that article.

christological conclusions are based in part on an anaphoric reading of the articular infinitive: 'A further reason, not usually noticed, for taking τὸ εἶναι ἴσα θεῷ in close connection with ὃς ἐν μορφῇ θεοῦ ὑπάρχων is the regular usage of the articular infinitive (here, τὸ εἶναι) to refer "to something previously mentioned or otherwise well known"'.[40] A host of other commentators have picked up this interpretation and have incorporated it into their own analysis of this passage.[41]

Wright contends that '*the* being equal with God' (τὸ εἶναι ἴσα θεῷ) refers back to 'the form of God' (μορφῇ θεοῦ) mentioned in the first part of the verse. The exegetical result is that 'equality with God' is equal to or synonymous with the 'form of God'. These two phrases (τὸ εἶναι ἴσα θεῷ and μορφῇ θεοῦ) are but two ways of referring to one reality. The christological significance of this anaphoric reading of the article is fairly obvious. If these two phrases are connected semantically on the basis of an anaphoric reading of the articular infinitive, then we have to say that Christ had 'equality with God' in his pre-existent[42] unity with God. Since the two phrases refer to the same thing, then he must have possessed both because they are one.

Wright's interpretation has little grammatical basis because he has misunderstood the semantics of the article in the phrase τὸ εἶναι ἴσα θεῷ. The article does not appear as an anaphoric marker, but as a function word. And in this text, the article τό is a grammatical necessity in order for the double-accusative construction to make sense; the article marks the components of

40. Wright, 'ἁρπαγμός', p. 344.
41. E.g. Peter T. O'Brien, *The Epistle to the Philippians* (NIGTC; Grand Rapids: Eerdmans, 1991), p. 216; Gerald F. Hawthorne, *Philippians* (WBC, 43; Waco, TX: Word Books, 1983), p. 84; Gordan D. Fee, *Paul's Letter to the Philippians* (NICNT; Grand Rapids: Eerdmans, 1995), p. 207; Kenneth Grayston, *The Letters of Paul to the Philippians and the Thessalonians* (Cambridge Bible Commentary; Cambridge: Cambridge University Press, 1967), p. 27.
42. J.D.G. Dunn continues his opposition to seeing a pre-existent Christ in this text; see his *Christology in the Making: A New Testament Inquiry into the Origins of the Doctrine of the Incarnation* (Grand Rapids: Eerdmans, 2nd edn, 1989), pp. xix, 113-21, and 'Christ, Adam, and Preexistence', in Ralph P. Martin and Brian J. Dodd (eds.), *Where Christology Began* (Louisville, KY: Westminster/John Knox Press, 1998), pp. 74-83 (78-79). However, it is not necessary to argue against an Adam-Christology in order to maintain Christ's pre-existence (e.g. Charles Arthur Wanamaker, 'Philippians 2.6-11: Son of God or Adamic Christology?', *NTS* 33 [1987], pp. 179-93). Wright correctly points out that the presence of an Adam-Christology in Phil. 2.5-11 does not rule out the possibility of Christ's pre-existence; see his 'Adam in Pauline Christology', *SBLSP* 22 (1983), pp. 359-89. I am in general agreement with Markus Bockmuehl that μορφῇ θεοῦ 'refers in Phil. 2.6 to the visible divine beauty and appearance which Christ had in his pre-incarnate state, before taking on the visible form and appearance of a slave' (Markus Bockmuehl, '"The Form of God" [Phil 2.6]: Variations on a Theme of Jewish Mysticism', *JTS* 48 [1997], pp. 1-23 [4]).

the double accusative phrase. Sometimes there is the potential for confusion in distinguishing the accusative object from the accusative complement. For this reason, Daniel Wallace has set forth a set of rules that help to distinguish the accusative object from the accusative complement.[43] The object will either be a *pronoun* or a *proper name*, or it will have the *definite article*. In Phil. 2.6, the only way we can distinguish the accusative object from the accusative complement is by the definite article at the beginning of the infinitive. If the article were absent, the syntactical relation of the infinitive phrase to the rest of the sentence would be unclear. So the article does not show up here in order to link 'equality with God' to the 'form of God'. The definite article appears here to distinguish the object (τὸ εἶναι ἴσα θεῷ) from the complement (ἁρπαγμόν).

The exegetical result is that it is grammatically possible to regard 'form of God' and 'equality with God'' not as synonymous phrases, but as phrases with distinct meanings. In the absence of an explicit link between τὸ εἶναι ἴσα θεῷ and μορφῇ θεοῦ, it may very well be that the phrases refer to separate realities. This interpretation has profound implications if one assumes a *res rapienda* interpretation of the enigmatic term ἁρπαγμός.[44] Consider the following rendering of the verse: 'Although[45] Jesus existed in the form of God, he did not consider equality with God as something he should go after also'. In other words, although Jesus actually possessed an identical characteristic of his Father with respect to his deity (i.e. 'he existed in the form of God'), he did not want to grasp after this other thing that was not his— namely, 'equality with God'. So what is this 'equality with God' if it is not something that he already possessed? The adversative 'but' (ἀλλά) in v. 7 helps us to understand what 'equality with God' means. 'Equality with God' is something that would have prevented Jesus from his self-emptying, from his taking the form of a servant, from his becoming in the likeness of men. In his pre-existent Trinitarian fellowship with his Father, Jesus decided not to go after 'equality', but to go after *incarnation*.[46]

43. These rules correspond directly with the rules for distinguishing subject from predicate nominative (Wallace, 'Object-Complement Construction', pp. 103-105, and *Greek Grammar*, pp. 184-85). Wallace notes that Eugene Van Ness Goetchius first suggested the analogy between these two constructions (Goetchius, *The Language of the New Testament*, pp. 46, 142-44).

44. An interpretation that I argue for in my Master's thesis (Dennis Burk, 'The Meaning of *Harpagmos* in Philippians 2.6' [ThM thesis, Dallas Theological Seminary, 2000]).

45. I take the present participle ὑπάρχων as concessive. See BDAG, *s.v.* μορφή, p. 659.

46. In one respect, my interpretation falls into the category of a 'functional', as opposed to an 'ontological', reading of τὸ εἶναι ἴσα θεῷ, an interpretation Wright ascribes to Ralph P. Martin (Wright, 'ἁρπαγμός', p. 326 n. 20). In another respect, my

(5) *Hebrews 10.31.* This text of this verse reads as follows: φοβερὸν τὸ ἐμπεσεῖν εἰς χεῖρας θεοῦ ζῶντος. In his commentary on the Epistle to the Hebrews, Paul Ellingworth suggests that 'τό before the infinitive indicates either the judgment previously mentioned in vv. 26-30, or knowledge which the readers are assumed to have'.[47] Ellingworth, therefore, offers two interpretive options: (1) that this is an anaphoric use of the article, or (2) that this is the 'well-known' use of the article. In either case, he assumes that the article carries its normal force as a determiner, either referring back specifically to the preceding context or, more generally, to some 'well-known' idea that he shares in common with his readers.

Although Ellingworth is probably interpreting correctly the overall argument of this warning passage, he has nevertheless read too much into this use of the articular infinitive. It is not very likely that it would have been 'well-known' that 'falling into the hands of the living God' was a bad thing —a fact which Ellingworth himself concedes.[48] When similar terminology is used elsewhere in the Jewish Scriptures, it is 'more often conceived as the

reading differs markedly from Martin's 'functional' interpretation. Whereas Martin connects *equality with God* to *form of God*, I do not. Martin argues that by virtue of his unity with God, Jesus had access to a *function* of deity—namely, the *function* of lordship over the world. So, while Jesus pre-existed as deity, he did not attempt to take advantage of the prerogatives of deity. In his pre-existent state, Jesus possessed the *form of God* (*res rapta*), but he did not reach out and seize the rightful authority that flows from his status as deity (*res rapienda*); see Ralph P. Martin, *A Hymn of Christ: Philippians 2.5-11 in Recent Interpretation and in the Setting of Early Christian Worship* (Downers Grove, IL: InterVarsity Press, 1997), pp. 152-53. Martin's Preface to the 1983 edition confirms that this is his interpretation, 'The soteriological drama moves forward from the station the pre-existent one held as ἐν μορφῇ θεοῦ ὑπάρχων to His decision not to use such a platform as a means of snatching a prize (τὸ εἶναι ἴσα θεῷ), but chose rather to divest Himself of that advantage and take the μορφὴ δούλου as an act of voluntary humiliation (ἐταπείνωσεν ἑαυτόν)' (p. xxiii). My reading does not connect *form of God* to *equality with God* as Martin's does. In my view, Paul is not saying that Christ's *equality with God* derives from his being *in the form of God*. Jesus' refusal to grasp after *equality with God* is a function of his subordinate role as the second person of the Trinity. This reading resembles the theological conclusions of H.A.W. Meyer's commentary on this text (though he reached his conclusion through an exegesis different than my own): 'In this pre-existence the Son appears as *subordinate* to the Father, as He does throughout the entire New Testament, although this is not…at variance with the Trinitarian equality of essence in the Biblical sense. By the ἁρπαγμὸν ἡγεῖσθαι κ.τ.λ., if it had taken place, He would have wished to *relieve* Himself from his subordination' (H.A.W. Meyer, *Critical and Exegetical Handbook to the Epistles to the Philippians and Colossians* [trans. John C. Moore from the 4th German edn; rev. William P. Dickson; Edinburgh: T. & T. Clark, 1875], pp. 83-84).

47.   Ellingworth, *The Epistle to the Hebrews*, p. 543.

48.   Ellingworth writes, 'The Greek Bible nowhere else speaks so negatively of falling into the hands of the living God' (Ellingworth, *The Epistle to the Hebrews*, p. 543).

instrument of positive, especially protecting and saving, action'.[49] The most likely reason for the article in this text is to mark ἐμπεσεῖν as the subject of a new independent clause. Without the article, a number of syntactical ambiguities become possible. φοβερόν could be misinterpreted as the complement of the object τὸν λαὸν in v. 30.[50] Also, when κρίνω is followed by the anarthrous complementary infinitive, it often takes on the meaning 'decide' instead of 'judge'.[51] If the neuter article were absent, the infinitive might be mistaken as complementary following κρίνω, which would imply an awful conflation of vv. 30 and 31: 'The Lord has *decided* that his people should fall into the hands of the Living God'. Thus the article appears here because of grammatical necessity, not to indicate definiteness.

3. *Conclusion*

Ultimately, the goal of this book has been to take seriously our Lord's counsel that, 'Man shall not live by bread alone, but by every word that proceeds from the mouth of God' (Mt. 4.4). In this study, I have sought to hang on to every articular infinitive in the New Testament. I have endeavored to ask and answer the following question: What is the semantic and/ or syntactic value of the articular infinitive in New Testament Greek? We have found that the article primarily serves as a function word when used with the infinitive. When the article appears in conjunction with the infinitive, it expresses a grammatical/structural relation that may not otherwise be apparent. The article bears great structural meaning, but little, if any, lexical meaning. The article does not effect a semantic difference to the meaning of the infinitive with respect to definiteness. Therefore, it is not correct to say that the article can have the same significance with the verbal noun as it does with any other noun (e.g. anaphora, marker of definiteness, substantivizer, etc.). Nor is it correct to say that the article adds no meaning at all to the infinitive. On the contrary, the structural/syntactical significance of the article is prominent in the appearances of the articular infinitive throughout the New Testament.

49. Ellingworth, *The Epistle to the Hebrews*, p. 544. See, e.g., Ps. 30.6 (LXX) εἰς χεῖράς σου παραθήσομαι τὸ πνεῦμά μου ἐλυτρώσω με κύριε ὁ θεὸς τῆς ἀληθείας.
50. See Acts 13.46; 16.15; 26.8; Rom. 2.27, for examples of κρίνω followed by the object-complement construction.
51. Cf. Acts 3.13; 20.16; 21.25; 25.25; 27.1; 1 Cor. 2.2; 7.37; Tit. 3.12.

Appendix

TABLES OF ANARTHROUS AND ARTICULAR INFINITIVE USAGE

Table 15. *How the Articular Infinitive Grew in Use in the Classical Period*[1]

Heiny's Division of Texts	Date BCE	Author	Number of Examples of Art. Inf.	Type	Source
Homer, Hesiod, Pindar, Lyric Poets	8th century	Homer	1	Epicus	L-S, xxvii; BDAG, xlvi
	pre-6th century?	Hesiod	2	Epicus	L-S, xxvi; BDAG, xiv
	5th century	Pindar	9	Lyricus	L-S, xxxiii
		Lyric poets	9		
Dramatists and Herodotus	5th/4th centuries	Aeschylus	51	Tragicus	L-S, xvi
	5th century	Sophocles	97	Tragicus	L-S, xxxv
	5th century	Euripides	93	Tragicus	L-S, xxiv
	5th/4th	Aristophanes	65	Comicus	L-S, xix
	5th century	Herodotus	49	Historicus	L-S, xxvi
Thucydides, the Attic Orators, Plato, and Xenophon	5th century	Thucydides	298	Historicus	L-S, xxxvii
	5th century	Antiphon	26 (36)*	Orator	L-S, xviii
	5th/4th centuries	Andocides	18	Orator	L-S, xvii
	5th century	Lysias	36 (44)*	Orator	L-S, xxix
	5th/4th centuries	Isocrates	271 (305)*	Orator	L-S, xvii
	4th century	Isaeus	36	Orator	L-S, xvii
	4th century	Lycurgus	26	Orator	L-S, xviii
	384–322	Demosthenes	784 (1130)*	Orator	L-S, xxii
	4th century	Aeschines	61	Orator	L-S, xvi
	4th/3rd centuries	Dinarchus	33	Orator	L-S, xxii
	4th century	Hyperides	42	Orator	L-S, xxxvii
	5th/4th centuries	Plato	1680 (2023)*	Philosophus	L-S, xxxiii
	5th/4th centuries	Xenophon	1306 (1310)*	Historicus	L-S, xxxviii

1. This table is based on the statistics compiled by Birklein (*Entwicklungsgeschichte*, pp. 91-92), which were adapted later by Heiny, 'Articular Infinitive', pp. 10-11. The dates and types are from L-S and BDAG. Numbers in parentheses marked * represent inclusion of works considered spurious.

Table 16. Articular Infinitives Not Governed by a Preposition

	τό		τοῦ	τῷ	Totals
	Nominative	Accusative	Genitive	Dative	
Matthew	15.20; 20.23		2.13; 3.13; 11.1 (×2); 13.3; 21.32; 24.45		9
Mark	9.10; 10.40; 12.33 (×2)				4
Luke			1.9, 57, 73, 77, 79; 2.6, 21, 24, 27; 4.10, 42; 5.7; 8.5; 9.51; 10.19; 12.42; 17.1; 21.22; 22.6, 31; 24.16, 25, 29, 45		24
John					
Acts		25.11	3.2, 12; 5.31; 7.19; 9.15; 10.25, 47; 13.47; 14.9, 18; 15.20; 18.10; 20.3, 20 (×2), 27, 30; 21.12; 23.15, 20; 26.18 (×2); 27.1, 20		25
Romans	4.13; 7.18 (×2); 14.21 (×2)	13.8; 14.13	1.24; 6.6; 7.3; 8.12; 11.8 (×2), 10; 15.22, 23		16
1 Corinthians	7.26; 11.6 (×2)	14.39 (×2)	9.10; 10.13; 16.4		8
2 Corinthians	7.11; 8.11; 9.1	2.1; 8.10 (×2), 11; 10.2	1.8; 8.11	2.13	11
Galatians			3.10		1
Ephesians					
Philippians	1.21 (×2), 22, 24, 29 (×2)	2.6, 13 (×2); 4.10	3.10, 21		12
Colossians					
1 Thessalonians		4.6 (×2)			2
2 Thessalonians					
1 Timothy					

2 Timothy					
Titus					
Philemon					
Hebrews	10.31		5.12; 10.7, 9; 11.5		5
James			5.17		1
1 Peter			3.10; 4.17		2
2 Peter					
1 John					
2 John					
3 John					
Jude					
Revelation			12.7		1
Totals	24	16	80	1	121

Table 17. Articular Infinitives Governed by a Preposition

	Accusative				Genitive						Dative	Total
	εἰς τό	διὰ τό	μετὰ τό	πρὸς τό	πρὸ τοῦ	διὰ τοῦ	ἕως τοῦ	ἕνεκεν τοῦ	ἐκ τοῦ	ἀντί τοῦ	ἐν τῷ	
Matthew	20.19 (×3); 26.2; 27.31	13.5, 6; 24.12	26.32	5.28; 6.1; 13.30; 23.5; 26.12	6.8						13.4, 25; 27.12	18
Mark	14.55	4.5, 6; 5.4 (×3)	1.14; 14.28; 16.19	13.22							4.4; 6.48	12
Luke	5.17	2.4; 6.48; 8.6; 9.7; 11.8; 18.5; 19.11 (×2) 23.8	12.5; 22.20	18.1	2.21; 22.15						1.8, 21; 2.6, 27, 43; 3.21; 5.1 (×2), 12; 8.5, 40, 42; 9.18, 29, 33, 34, 36, 51; 10.38; 11.1, 27, 37; 12.15; 14.1; 17.11, 14; 18.35; 19.15; 24.4, 15 (×2), 30, 51	49
John		2.24			1.48; 13.19; 17.5							4
Acts	3.19; 7.19	4.2 (×2); 8.11; 12.20; 18.2, 3; 10.41; 15.13; 19.21; 20.1 27.4, 9; 28.18			23.15		8.40				2.1; 3.26; 4.30 (×2); 8.6 (×2); 9.3; 11.15; 19.1	28

Romans	1.11, 20; 3.26; 4.11 (×2), 16, 18; 6.12; 7.4, 5; 8.29; 11.11; 12.2, 3; 15.8, 13, 16										3.4; 15.13	19
1 Corinthians	8.10; 9.18; 10.6; 11.22 (×2), 33		11.25								11.21	8
2 Corinthians	1.4; 4.4; 7.3 (×2); 8.6			3.13				7.12	8.11			8
Galatians	3.17				2.12; 3.23						4.18	4
Ephesians	1.12, 18			6.11								3
Phillipians	1.10, 23 (×2)	1.7										4
1 Thessalonians	2.12, 16; 3.2 (×2), 3, 5, 10 (×2), 13; 4.9			2.9								11
2 Thessalonians	1.5; 2.2 (×2), 6, 10, 11; 3.9			3.8								8
Hebrews	2.17; 7.25; 8.3; 9.14, 28; 11.3; 12.10; 13.21	7.23, 24; 10.2	10.15, 26				2.15				2.8; 3.12, 15; 8.13	18
James	1.18, 19 (×2); 3.3	4.2								4.15		6
1 Peter	3.7; 4.2											2
Total	74	32	15	11	9	1	1	1	1	1	56	202

Table 18. Clauses That Have Anarthrous Infinitives as Subject

	Impersonal Verb	Passive Verb	Transitive Verb	Intransitive Verb	γίνομαι	εἰμί	Verbless	εἰμί with PA	Verbless with PA	εἰμί with PN	Verbless with PN
Matthew	12.2, 4, 10, 12; 14.4; 16.21 (×4); 18.33; 19.3, 10; 20.15; 22.17; 23.23 (×2); 24.6; 25.27; 26.35, 54; 27.6	13.11			18.13			3.15; 15.26 (×2); 17.4, 10; 18.8 (×2), 9 (×2); 19.24 (×2)	18.7		
Mark	2.26; 3.4 (×4); 6.18; 8.31 (×4); 9.11; 10.2; 12.14; 13.7, 10; 14.31		8.36 (×2)		2.15, 23			7.27 (×2); 9.5, 43 (×2), 45 (×3), 47; 10.24, 25 (×2)			
Luke	2.49; 4.43; 6.4, 9 (×4); 9.22 (×4); 11.42 (×2); 12.12; 13.14, 16, 33 (×2); 14.3; 15.32 (×2); 17.25 (×2); 18.1 (×2); 19.5; 20.22; 21.9; 22.7, 37; 24.7 (×3), 26 (×2), 44	8.10; 24.46 (×2), 47		1.3	3.21 (×2), 22 (×2); 6.1, 6 (×2), 12; 16.22 (×2)			2.26; 9.33; 16.17 (×2); 18.25 (×2)			
John	3.7, 14, 30 (×2); 4.4, 20, 24; 5.10; 9.4; 10.16; 12.34; 18.14, 31; 20.9										

Acts	1.16, 22; 2.29; 3.21; 4.12; 5.29; 9.6, 16; 14.22; 15.5 (×2); 16.21 (×2), 30; 17.3 (×2); 19.21; 20.35 (×2); 21.37; 22.22, 25; 23.11; 24.19 (×2); 25.10, 24; 26.9; 27.21, 24, 26	26.1	7.23; 15.22, 25, 28; 21.35; 25.27	4.5; 9.3, 32, 37, 43; 11.26 (×3); 14.1 (×2); 16.16; 19.1 (×2); 20.16; 21.1, 5; 22.6, 17, 18; 27.44; 28.8, 17	1.7	4.19; 6.2; 10.28 (×2); 13.46; 19.36 (×2); 20.16, 35 (×2)	26.14	25.16	
Romans	12.3				12.15 (×2)				5.12
1 Corinthians	8.2; 11.19; 15.25, 53 (×2)	14.34				7.9 (×2); 11.13; 14.35; 16.4	7.1; 9.15	5.12	
2 Corinthians	2.3; 5.10; 11.30; 12.1, 4								
Galatians				6.14			4.18		
Ephesians	6.20					5.12			
Philippians	4.4, 6					1.7	3.1		
Colossians	4.1 (×2)								
1 Thessalonians	3.7								
2 Thessalonians	3.2, 15								
1 Timothy							1.6		
2 Timothy	2.6, 24 (×2)								
Titus	1.7, 11								
Hebrews	2.1, 10; 9.26	4.6; 9.27		9.5			8.3; 11.6; 13.9		

James	3.10										
1 Peter	3.11								3.17		
2 Peter									2.21 (×2)		
Revelation	1.1; 4.1; 10.11; 11.5; 17.10; 20.3; 22.6	6.4; 7.2; 13.7 (×2), 14, 15; 16.8									
Total	154	16	2	7	36	2	2	46	13	1	1

Table 19. Clauses That Have Articular Infinitives as Subject

	Impersonal Verb	Passive Verb	Transitive Verb	Intransitive Verb	γίνομαι Verb	εἰμί	Verbless	εἰμί with PA	Verbless with PA	εἰμί with PN	Verbless with PN	Total
Matthew			15.20					20.23				2
Mark								10.40; 12.33 (×2)		9.10		4
Romans				7.18 (×2)					14.21 (×2)			4
1 Corinthians									7.26; 11.6 (×2)			3
2 Corinthians			7.11				8.11	9.1				3
Philippians		1.29 (×2)					1.22		1.24		1.21 (×2)	6
Hebrews									10.31			1
Total		2	2	2			2	5	7	1	2	23

Table 20. Use of Genitive Articular Infinitives in the New Testament

	Adverbial						Adnominal		Totals
	Verbs Taking Partitive Genitive Object	Compound Verbs Requiring a Genitive Object	Verbs Taking Genitive of Separation	Purpose	Result	Epexegetic, Explanatory	Limiting Nouns	Limiting Adjectives	
Matthew				2.13; 3.13; 11.1 (×2); 13.3; 21.32; 24.45					7
Luke	1.9		4.42; 24.16	1.73, 77, 79; 2.24, 27; 4.10; 5.7; 8.5; 9.51; 12.42; 22.31; 24.29, 45			1.57; 2.6, 21; 10.19; 21.22; 22.6	17.1; 24.25	24
Acts			14.18; 20.20 (×2), 27	3.2; 5.31; 7.19; 13.47; 15.20; 18.10; 20.30; 21.12; 23.20; 26.18 (×2)	3.12; 10.47	10.25; 27.1	9.15; 14.9; 20.3; 27.20	23.15	24
Romans			15.22	6.6; 11.10		7.3	1.24; 8.12; 11.8 (×2); 15.23		9
1 Corinthians							9.10; 10.13	16.4	3
2 Corinthians		1.8					8.11		2
Galatians						3.10			1
Philippians				3.10			3.21		2
Hebrews				10.7, 9; 11.5			5.12		4
James						5.17			1
1 Peter						3.10	4.17		2
Revelation						12.7			1
Totals	1	1	7	37	2	7	21	4	80

BIBLIOGRAPHY

Primary Works

Bible Companion 1.6.4; GRAMCORD Morphological Search Engine 2.4 cx. Copyright 1988–98 Loizeaux Brothers, Inc.

Esdrae liber I (ed. Robert Hanhart; *Septuaginta: Vetus Testamentum Graecum, auctoritate Academiae Scientiarum Gottingensis editum*, 8.1; Göttingen: Vandenhoeck & Ruprecht, 1974).

Esdrae liber II (ed. Robert Hanhart; *Septuaginta: Vetus Testamentum Graecum, auctoritate Academiae Scientiarum Gottingensis editum*, 8.2; Göttingen: Vandenhoeck & Ruprecht, 1993).

Genesis (ed. John William Wevers; *Septuaginta: Vetus Testamentaum Graecum, auctoritate Academiae Scientiarum Gottingensis editum*, I; Göttingen: Vandenhoeck & Ruprecht, 1974).

Iudith (ed. Robert Hanhart; *Septuaginta: Vetus Testamentaum Graecum, auctoritate Academiae Scientiarum Gottingensis editum*, 8.4; Göttingen: Vandenhoeck & Ruprecht, 1979).

Maccabaeorum liber I (ed. Werner Kappler; *Septuaginta: Vetus Testamentum Graecum, auctoritate Academiae Scientiarum Gottingensis editum*, 11.1; Göttingen: Vandenhoeck & Ruprecht, 1967).

The Old Testament in Greek according to the Septuagint (ed. Henry Barclay Swete; 3 vols.; Cambridge: Cambridge University Press, 1894).

Psalmi cum Odis (ed. A. Rahlfs; *Septuaginta: Vetus Testamentaum Graecum, auctoritate Academiae Scientiarum Gottingensis editum*, 10; Göttingen: Vandenhoeck & Ruprecht, 1931).

Sapientia Iesu Filii Sirach (ed. Joseph Ziegler; *Septuaginta: Vetus Testamentaum Graecum, auctoritate Academiae Scientiarum Gottingensis editum*, 12.2; Göttingen: Vandenhoeck & Ruprecht, 1980).

Sapientia Salomonis (ed. Joseph Ziegler; *Septuaginta: Vetus Testamentaum Graecum, auctoritate Academiae Scientiarum Gottingensis editum*, 12.1; Göttingen: Vandenhoeck & Ruprecht, 1980).

Septuaginta: id est Vetus Testamentum graece iuxta LXX interpretes (ed. Alfred Rahlfs; Stuttgart: Deutsche Bibelgesellschaft, 1935).

Tobit (ed. Robert Hanhart; *Septuaginta: Vetus Testamentaum Graecum, auctoritate Academiae Scientiarum Gottingensis editum*, 8.5; Göttingen: Vandenhoeck & Ruprecht, 1983).

Secondary Works

Aalto, Pentti, *Studien zur Geschichte des Infinitivs im Griechischen* (Helsinki: Suomalaisen Tiedeakatemian Toimituksia, 1953).

Allen, Hamilton Ford, *The Infinitive in Polybius Compared with the Infinitive in Biblical Greek* (Chicago: University of Chicago Press, 1907).

Barr, James, *The Semantics of Biblical Language* (Oxford: Oxford University Press, 1961; repr., Philadelphia: Trinity Press International, 1991).

Barrett, C.K., *A Critical and Exegetical Commentary on the Acts of the Apostles* (ICC; 2 vols.; Edinburgh: T. & T. Clark, 1994–98).

Beckwith, I.T., 'The Articular Infinitive with εἰς', *Journal of Biblical Literature* 15 (1896): 155-67.

Bierwisch, Manfred, *Modern Linguistics: Its Development, Methods and Problems* (Janua Linguarum; The Hague: Mouton, 1971).

Birklein, Franz, *Entwicklungsgeschichte des substantivierten Infinitivs* (Beiträge zur historischen Syntax der griechischen Sprache; Würzburg: A. Stuber, 1888).

Black, David Alan, 'Introduction', in Black, Barnwell, and Levinsohn (eds.), *Linguistics and New Testament Interpretation*, pp. 10-14.

—*Linguistics for Students of New Testament Greek: A Survey of Basic Concepts and Applications* (Grand Rapids: Baker Book House, 2nd edn, 1995).

Black, David Alan, Katharine Barnwell, and Stephen Levinsohn (eds.), *Linguistics and New Testament Interpretation: Essays on Discourse Analysis* (Nashville: Broadman, 1992).

Blake, Barry J., *Case* (ed. J. Bresnan, *et al.*; Cambridge Textbooks in Linguistics; Cambridge: Cambridge University Press, 1994).

Blass, F., and A. Debrunner, *A Greek Grammar of the New Testament and Other Early Christian Literature* (trans. and rev. Robert W. Funk; Chicago: University of Chicago Press, 1961).

Bloomfield, Leonard, *An Introduction to the Study of Language* (New York: Henry Holt, 1914).

—*Language* (New York: Henry Holt, 1933).

Bockmuehl, Markus, '"The Form of God" (Phil 2.6): Variations on a Theme of Jewish Mysticism', *JTS* 48 (1997), pp. 1-23.

Bodine, Walter R., 'How Linguists Study Syntax', in Walter R. Bodine (ed.), *Linguistics and Biblical Hebrew* (Winona Lake, IN: Eisenbrauns, 1992), pp. 89-107.

Bodmer, Frederick, *The Loom of Language* (ed. Lancelot Hogben; New York: W.W. Norton, 1944).

Boyer, James L., 'The Classification of Infinitives: A Statistical Study', *GTJ* 6 (1985), pp. 3-27.

—*Supplemental Manual of Information: Infinitive Verbs* (Winona Lake, IN: Boyer, 1986).

Brooks, James A., and Carlton L. Winbery, *Syntax of New Testament Greek* (Lanham, MD: University Press of America, 1979).

Bruce, F.F., *1 and 2 Thessalonians* (WBC, 45; Waco, TX: Word Books, 1982).

Brugmann, Karl, *Griechische Grammatik (Lautlehre, Stammbildungs- und Flexionslehre und Syntax)* (Handbuch der klassischen Altertums-Wissenschaft; Munich: C.H. Beck, 1900).

Burguière, Paul, *Histoire de l'infinitif en grec* (Etudes et commentaires, 33; Paris: C. Klincksieck, 1960).

Burk, Dennis (Denny), 'The Meaning of Harpagmos in Philippians 2.6' (ThM dissertation, Dallas Theological Seminary, 2000).

—'On the Articular Infinitive in Philippians 2.6: A Grammatical Note with Christological Implications', *TynBul* 55 (2004), pp. 253-74.

Burton, Ernest De Witt, *Syntax of the Moods and Tenses in New Testament Greek* (Grand Rapids: Kregel Publications, 3rd edn, 1900).

Bussmann, Hadumod, *Routledge Dictionary of Language and Linguistics* (trans. and ed. Gregory Trauth and Kerstin Kazzazi; London: Routledge, 1996; originally published as *Lexikon der Sprachwissenschaft* [Stuttgart: Kröner Verlag, 2nd edn, 1990]).

Carson, D.A., *Exegetical Fallacies* (Grand Rapids: Baker Book House, 2nd edn, 1996).

Chamberlain, William Douglas, *An Exegetical Grammar of the Greek New Testament* (New York: Macmillan, 1941).

Chaski, Carole Elisabeth, 'Syntactic Theories and Models of Syntactic: A Study of Greek Infinitival Complementation' (PhD dissertation, Brown University, 1988).

Chomsky, Noam, *Aspects of the Theory of Syntax* (Cambridge, MA: M.I.T. Press, 1965).

—*Current Issues in Linguistic Theory* (Janua Linguarum; The Hague: Mouton, 1964).

Cignelli, L., and G.C. Bottini, 'L'articolo nel greco biblico', *Studii biblici franciscani liber annus* 41 (1991), pp. 159-99.

Comrie, Bernard, 'Form and Function in Identifying Cases', in Plank (ed.), *Paradigms: The Economy of Inflection*, pp. 41-55.

—*Language Universals and Linguistic Typology: Syntax and Morphology* (Chicago: University of Chicago Press, 2nd edn, 1989).

Conybeare, F.C., and St George Stock, *Grammar of Septuagint Greek: With Selected Readings, Vocabularies, and Updated Indexes* (Boston: Ginn, 1905; repr., Peabody, MA: Hendrickson, 1995).

Conzelmann, Hans, *Acts of the Apostles: A Commentary on the Acts of the Apostles* (trans. James Limburg, A. Thomas Kraabel, and Donald H. Juel; ed. Eldon Jay Epp and Christopher R. Matthews; Hermeneia; Philadelphia: Fortress Press, 1987).

Cranfield, C.E.B., *A Critical and Exegetical Commentary on the Epistle to the Romans*. I. *Introduction and Commentary on Romans I–VIII* (ICC; Edinburgh: T. & T. Clark, 1975).

—*A Critical and Exegetical Commentary on the Epistle to the Romans*. II. *Commentary on Romans IX–XVI and Essays* (ICC; Edinburgh: T. & T. Clark, 1979).

Cripe, Matthew Allen, 'An Analysis of Infinitive Clauses Containing both Subject and Object in the Accusative Case in the Greek New Testament' (ThM thesis, Dallas Theological Seminary, 1992).

Crystal, David, *A Dictionary of Language* (Chicago: University of Chicago Press, 2nd edn, 2001).

—*Linguistics* (Harmondsworth: Penguin, 1971).

—*Linguistics, Language, and Religion* (Twentieth Century Encyclopedia of Catholicism; New York: Hawthorn Books, 1965).

Dalman, Gustaf, *The Words of Jesus Considered in the Light of Post-Biblical Jewish Writings and the Aramaic Language* (trans D.M. Kay; Edinburgh: T. & T. Clark, 1902).

Dana, H.E., and Julius R. Mantey, *A Manual Grammar of the Greek New Testament* (New York: Macmillan, 1927).

Davies, W.D., and Dale C. Allison, Jr, *A Critical and Exegetical Commentary on the Gospel according to Saint Matthew*. I. *Introduction and Commentary on Matthew I–VII* (ICC; Edinburgh: T. & T. Clark, 1988).

Dimitropoulos, Panagiotis, *Untersuchungen zum finalen Genetiv des substantivierten Infinitivs bei Thukydides* (Commentationes humanarum litterarum, 114; Helsinki: Societas scientiarum fennica, 1999).

Dunn, J.D.G., 'Christ, Adam, and Preexistence', in Ralph P. Martin and Brian J. Dodd (eds.), *Where Christology Began: Essays on Philippians 2* (Louisville, KY: Westminster/John Knox Press, 1998), pp. 74-83.

—*Christology in the Making: A New Testament Inquiry into the Origins of the Doctrine of the Incarnation* (Grand Rapids: Eerdmans, 2nd edn, 1989).

Eakin, Frank, 'The Greek Article in the First and Second Century Papyri', *American Journal of Philology* 37 (1916), pp. 333-40.

Ellingworth, Paul, *The Epistle to the Hebrews: A Commentary on the Greek Text* (NIGTC; Grand Rapids: Eerdmans, 1993).

Erickson, Richard J., 'Linguistics and Biblical Language: A Wide-Open Field', *JETS* 26 (1983), pp. 257-63.

Ernout, A., 'Infinitif grec et gérondif latin', *Revue de philologie, de littérature et d'histoire anciennes* 19 (1945), pp. 93-115.

Evans, Craig A., *Mark 8.27–16.20* (WBC, 34B; Nashville: Thomas Nelson, 2001).

Fee, Gordon D., *Paul's Letter to the Philippians* (NICNT; Grand Rapids: Eerdmans, 1995).

—'The Use of the Definite Article with Personal Names in the Gospel of John', *NTS* 17 (1970–71), pp. 168-83.

Fernández García, Aurelio J., *El infinitivo en el Dafnis y Cloe de Longo: estudio funcional* (Classical and Byzantine Monographs; Amsterdam: Adolf M. Hakkert, 1997).

Fillmore, Charles J., 'The Case for Case', in Emmon Bach and Robert T. Harms (eds.), *Universals in Linguistic Theory* (New York: Holt, Rinehart & Winston, 1968), pp. 1-88.

Forbes, P.B.R., 'Greek Pioneers in Philology and Grammar', *The Classical Review* 47 (1933), pp. 105-12.

Fox, Andrew Jordon, 'The Evolution of the Hebrew Infinitive, Form and Function: A Diachronic Study with Cross-Linguistic Implications (Biblical, Semitic, Afroasianic)' (PhD dissertation, University of California, 1984).

Funk, Robert W., *A Beginning–Intermediate Grammar of Hellenistic Greek* (Sources for Biblical Study; 3 vols.; Missoula, MT: Society of Biblical Literature, 2nd edn, 1973).

—'The Syntax of the Greek Article: Its Importance for Critical Pauline Problems' (PhD dissertation, Vanderbilt University, 1953).

Gaeng, Paul A., *Introduction to the Principles of Language* (New York: Harper & Row, 1971).

Gesenius, Wilhelm, *Gesenius' Hebrew Grammar* (ed. A.E. Cowley and E. Kautzsch; Oxford: Clarendon Press, 2nd Eng. edn, 1910).

Giannecchini, Giulio, *Il controllo infinitivo in greco antico* (Università degli Studi di Perugia; Naples: Edizioni scientifiche italiane, 1995).

Gildersleeve, Basil Lanneau, *Syntax of Classical Greek from Homer to Demosthenes* (2 vols.; New York: American Book Company, 1911).

Gleason, H.A., *An Introduction to Descriptive Linguistics* (New York: Henry Holt, 1955).

Goetchius, Eugene Van Ness, *The Language of the New Testament* (New York: Charles Scribner's Sons, 1965).

Goodwin, William W., *Syntax of the Moods and Tenses of the Greek Verb* (Boston and Cambridge: Sever, Francis & Co., 3rd edn, 1870).

Gould, Ezra P., *A Critical and Exegetical Commentary on the Gospel according to St Mark* (ICC; Edinburgh: T. & T. Clark, 1975).

Grant, Lawrence O., 'The History of ἐν τῷ with the Infinitive and its Bearing on Luke's Writings' (PhD dissertation, The Southern Baptist Theological Seminary, 1945).

Grayston, Kenneth, *The Letters of Paul to the Philippians and the Thessalonians* (Cambridge Bible Commentary; Cambridge: Cambridge University Press, 1967).

Grünenwald, L., *Der freie formelhafte Infinitiv der Limitation im Griechischen* (Beiträge zur historischen Syntax der griechischen Sprache; Würzburg: A. Stuber, 1888).

Gundry, Robert H., *Mark: A Commentary on his Apology for the Cross* (Grand Rapids: Eerdmans, 1993).

Hagner, Donald A., *Matthew 1–13* (WBC, 33A; Dallas: Word Books, 1993).

Hall, Robert A., Jr, *Introductory Linguistics* (Philadelphia: Chilton, 1964).

—*Leave Your Language Alone!* (Ithaca, NY: Linguistica, 1950).

Harris, Murray J., 'Prepositions and Theology in the Greek New Testament', in *NIDNTT*, III, pp. 1171-15.

Hawkins, John A., *Definiteness and Indefiniteness: A Study in Reference and Grammaticality Prediction* (London: Croom Helm; Atlantic Highlands, NJ: Humanities Press, 1978).

Hawthorne, Gerald F., *Philippians* (WBC, 43; Waco, TX: Word Books, 1983).

Hebold, Maximilian, *De infinitivi syntaxi Euripidea* (Halle: Fr. Lintz, 1881).

Heim, Irene, *The Semantics of Definite and Indefinite Noun Phrases* (Outstanding Dissertations in Linguistics; New York: Garland Publishing, 1988).

Heiny, Stephen Brooks, 'The Articular Infinitive in Thucydides' (PhD dissertation, Indiana University, 1973).

Higgins, Martin J., 'New Testament Result Clauses with Infinitive', *CBQ* 23 (1961), pp. 233-41.

Hockett, Charles F., *A Course in Modern Linguistics* (New York: Macmillan, 1958).

Hoehne, Adolphus, *De infinitivi apud graecos classicae aetatis poetas usu qui fertur pro imperativo* (Bratislava: Typis Grassi, Barthii et Soc. [W. Friedrich], 1867).

Hofius, Otfried, 'The Lord's Supper and the Lord's Supper Tradition: Reflections on 1 Corinthians 11.23b-25', in Ben F. Meyer (ed.), *One Loaf, One Cup: Ecumenical Studies of 1 Cor 11 and Other Eucharistic Texts. The Cambridge Conference on the Eucharist, August 1988* (New Gospel Studies, 6; Macon, GA: Mercer University Press, 1993), pp. 75-115.

Holland, Gary Brian, 'Problems of Word Order Change in Selected Indo-European Languages' (PhD dissertation, University of California, Berkeley, 1980).

Hui, Timothy K., 'Paul's Use of the Infinitive in 2 Corinthians' (ThM thesis, Dallas Theological Seminary, 1975).

Jannaris, Antonius N., *An Historical Greek Grammar Chiefly of the Attic Dialect as Written and Spoken from Classical Antiquity Down to the Present Time, Founded upon the Ancient Texts, Inscriptions, Papyri and Present Popular Greek* (London and New York: Macmillan, 1897; repr., Hildesheim: Georg Olms, 1987).

Kalén, Ture, *Selbständige Finalsätze und imperativische Infinitive im Griechischen* (Skrifter utgivna av K. Humanistiska Vetenskaps-Samfundet, I; Uppsala, 34.2; Uppsala: Almqvist & Wiksell, 1941).

Kempson, Ruth M., *Semantic Theory* (Cambridge Textbooks in Linguistics; Cambridge: Cambridge University Press, 1977).

Klund, Robert W., 'The Use of the Infinitive of Purpose in the New Testament' (ThM thesis, Dallas Theological Seminary, 1994).

Koseka-Toszewa, Violetta, with Georgi Gargov, *The Semantic Category of Definiteness/ Indefiniteness in Bulgarian and Polish* (Warsaw: Slawistyczny Ośrodek Wydawniczy, 1991).

Krämer, Helmut, 'Zur explikativen Redeweise im neutestamentlichen Griechisch', in Wolfgang Schrage (ed.), *Studien zum Text und zur Ethik des Neuen Testaments: Festschrift zum 80. Geburtstag von Heinrich Greeven* (Beiheft zur Zeitschrift für die neutestamentliche Wissenschaft und die Kunde der älteren Kirche; Berlin: W. de Grutyer, 1986), pp. 212-16.

Kuryłowicz, Jerzy, *The Inflectional Categories of Indo-European* (Indogermanische Bibliothek; Heidelberg: Carl Winter, 1964).

Kurzová, Helena, *Zur syntaktischen Struktur des griechischen Infinitiv und Nebensatz* (Tschechoslowakische Akademie der Wissenschaften; Amsterdam: Adolf M. Hakkert; Prague: Academia, 1968).

Lane, William L., *The Gospel according to Mark: The English Text with Introduction, Exposition and Notes* (NICNT; Grand Rapids: Eerdmans, 1974).

Levinsohn, Stephen H., *Discourse Features of New Testament Greek: A Coursebook on the Information Structure of New Testament Greek* (Dallas: SIL International, 2nd edn, 2000).

Lightfoot, J.B., *St Paul's Epistle to the Philippians* (repr., Peabody, MA: Hendrickson, 1993).

Locke, Earle Winfred, 'The Significance of the Tense of the Infinitive in the Gospel of John' (PhD dissertation, University of Chicago, 1938).

Longman, R.H., *General Linguistics: An Introductory Survey* (Longman Linguistics Library; New York: Longman, 3rd edn, 1980).

Louw, J.P., 'Linguistic Theory and the Greek Case System', *Acta Classica* 9 (1966), pp. 73-88.

Lovelady, Edgar J., 'Infinitive Clause Syntax in the Gospels' (ThM thesis, Grace Theological Seminary, 1976).

Martin, Ralph P., *A Hymn of Christ: Philippians 2.5-11 in Recent Interpretation and in the Setting of Early Christian Worship* (Downers Grove, IL: InterVarsity Press, 1997).

Mayser, Edwin, *Grammatik der griechischen Papyri aus der Ptolemäerzeit, mit Einschluss der gleichzeitigen Ostraka und der in Ägypten verfassten Inschriften.* II.1. *Satzlehre, analytischer Teil, erste Hälfte* (Berlin and Leipzig: W. de Gruyter, 1926).

McKay, K.L., 'Aspect in Imperatival Constructions in New Testament Greek,' *NovT* 27 (1985), pp. 201-26.

—*A New Syntax of the Verb in New Testament Greek: An Aspectual Approach* (SBG, 5; New York: Peter Lang, 1994).

Metzger, Bruce M., *A Textual Commentary on the Greek New Testament* (Stuttgart: Deutsche Bibelgesellschaft/German Bible Society, 2nd edn, 1994).

Meyer, H.A.W., *Critical and Exegetical Handbook to the Epistles to the Philippians and Colossians* (trans. John C. Moore; rev. William P. Dickson; Edinburgh: T. & T. Clark, 1875).

Middleton, Thomas Fanshaw, *The Doctrine of the Greek Article Applied to the Criticism and Illustration of the New Testament* (London: Gilbert & Rivington, new edn, 1833).

Moeller, Henry R., and Arnold Kramer, 'An Overlooked Structural Pattern in New Testament Greek', *NovT* 5 (1962), pp. 25-35.

Moo, Douglas J., *The Epistle to the Romans* (NICNT; Grand Rapids: Eerdmans, 1996).

—*The Letter of James* (PNTC; Grand Rapids: Eerdmans, 2000).

Morris, Leon, *The First and Second Epistles to the Thessalonians* (NICNT; Grand Rapids: Eerdmans, rev. edn, 1991).

Moule, C.F.D., *An Idiom Book of New Testament Greek* (Cambridge: Cambridge University Press, 2nd edn, 1959).

Moulton, James Hope, *A Grammar of New Testament Greek. I. Prolegomena* (Edinburgh: T. & T. Clark, 3rd edn, 1908).

—*A Grammar of New Testament Greek. II. Accidence and Word-Formation*, by Wilbert Francis Howard (Edinburgh: T. & T. Clark, 1929).

—*A Grammar of New Testament Greek. III. Syntax*, by Nigel Turner (Edinburgh: T. & T. Clark, 1963).

Murray, John, *The Epistle to the Romans* (NICNT; 2 vols.; Grand Rapids: Eerdmans, 1965).

Mutzbauer, Carl, *Das Wesen des griechischen Infinitivs und die Entwicklung seines Gebrauchs bei Homer: Ein Beitrag zur historischen Syntax der griechischen Sprache* (Bonn: F. Cohen, 1916).

O'Brien, P.T., *The Epistle to the Philippians* (NIGTC; Grand Rapids: Eerdmans, 1991).

O'Donnell, Matthew Brook, 'Designing and Compiling a Register-Balanced Corpus of Hellenistic Greek for the Purpose of Linguistic Description and Investigation', in Stanley E. Porter (ed.), *Diglossia and Other Topics in New Testament Linguistics* (JSNTSup, 193; Studies in New Testament Greek, 6; Sheffield: Sheffield Academic Press, 2000), pp. 255-87.

Ogden, Charles Jones, *De infinitivi finalis vel consecutivi constructione apud priscos poetas graecos* (New York: Columbia University Press, 1909).

Owings, Timothy, *A Cumulative Index to New Testament Greek Grammars* (Grand Rapids: Baker Book House, 1983).

Palmer, Michael W., *Levels of Constituent Structure in New Testament Greek* (SBG; New York: Peter Lang, 1995).

Pei, Mario, *Invitation to Linguistics: A Basic Introduction to the Science of Language* (Garden City, NY: Doubleday, 1965).

Plank, Frans (ed.), *Paradigms: The Economy of Inflection* (Empirical Approaches to Language Typology, 9; New York: Mouton de Gruyter, 1991).

Porter, Stanley E., 'The Basic Tools of Exegesis: A Bibliographical Essay', in *idem* (ed.), *Handbook to the Exegesis of the New Testament* (New Testament Tools and Studies; Leiden: E.J. Brill, 1997), pp. 23-31.

—'The Case for Case Revisited', *Jian Dao* 6 (1996), pp. 13-28.

—*Idioms of the Greek New Testament* (Biblical Languages: Greek, 2; Sheffield: JSOT Press, 1992).
—'A Modern Grammar of an Ancient Language: A Critique of the Schmidt Proposal', *Forum* NS 2 (1999), pp. 201-13.
—'Studying Ancient Languages from a Modern Linguistic Perspective: Essential Terms and Terminology', *Filologia Neotestamentaria* 2 (1989), pp. 147-72.
Porter, Stanley E., and Reed, J.T., 'Greek Grammar since BDF: A Retrospective and Prospective Analysis', *Filología Neotestamentaria* 4 (1991), pp. 143-64.
Radermacher, Ludwig, *Neutestamentliche Grammatik: Das Griechisch des Neuen Testaments im Zusammenhang mit der Volkssprache* (Handbuch zum Neuen Testament; Tübingen: J.C.B. Mohr, 1925).
Reed, Jeffrey T., 'The Infinitive with Two Subtantival Accusatives: An Ambiguous Construction?', *NovT* 33 (1991), pp. 1-27.
Rensburg, J.J. Janse van, 'A New Reference Grammar for the Greek New Testament: Exploratory Remarks on a Methodology', *Neotestamentica* 27 (1993), pp. 133-52.
Robins, R.H., *General Linguistics: An Introductory Survey* (Longman Linguistics Library; New York: Longman, 3rd edn, 1980).
Rosén, Haiim B., *Early Greek Grammar and Thought in Heraclitus: The Emergence of the Article* (Proceedings of the Israel Academy of Sciences and Humanities, 7, 2; Jerusalem: Israel Academy of Sciences and Humanities, 1988).
Russell, David Michael, 'Toward a Discourse Motivation for the Intrusive Infinitives in the Temporal Subclauses of Herodotean Reported Narratives' (PhD dissertation, University of Texas at Arlington, 2000).
Rydbeck, Lars, 'The Language of the New Testament', *TynBul* 49 (1998), pp. 361-68.
—'What Happened to New Testament Greek Grammar after Albert Debrunner?', *NTS* 21 (1975), pp. 424-27.
Sansone, David, 'Towards a New Doctrine of the Article in Greek: Some Observations on the Definite Article in Plato', *Classical Philology* 88 (1993), pp. 191-205.
Saussure, Ferdinand de, *Course in General Linguistics* (ed. Charles Bally and Albert Reidlinger; trans Wade Baskin; New York: Philosophical Library, 1959).
Schmidt, Daryl D., *Hellenistic Greek Grammar and Noam Chomsky: Nominalizing Transforms* (SBLDS, 62; Chico, CA: Scholars Press, 1981).
—'Preface', *Forum* NS 2 (1999), pp. 177-78.
—'Revising Blass–Debrunner–Funk', *Forum* NS 2 (1999), pp. 179-99.
—'The Study of Hellenistic Greek Grammar in the Light of Contemporary Linguistics', *Perspectives in Religious Studies* 11 (1984), pp. 27-38.
Schreiner, Thomas R., *Romans* (Baker Exegetical Commentary on the New Testament; Grand Rapids: Baker Book House, 1998).
Schwyzer, Eduard, and Albert Debrunner, *Griechische Grammatik auf der Grundlage von Karl Brugmanns Griechische Grammatik*. II. *Syntax und syntaktische Stilistik* (Handbuch der Altertumswissenschaft; Munich: C.H. Beck, 1950).
Silva, Moisés, *Biblical Words and their Meaning: An Introduction to Lexical Semantics* (Grand Rapids: Zondervan, rev. and expanded edn, 1994).
—*God, Language, and Scripture: Reading the Bible in the Light of General Linguistics* (Foundations of Contemporary Interpretation; Grand Rapids: Zondervan, 1990).
Stahl, J.M., *Kritisch-historische Syntax des griechischen Verbums der klassischen Zeit* (Indogermanische Bibliothek; Heidelberg: C. Winter, 1907).

Stein, Robert H., 'Our Reading of the Bible vs. the Original Audience's Hearing It', *JETS* 46 (2003), pp. 63-78.

Thackeray, Henry St John, *A Grammar of the Old Testament in Greek according to the Septuagint* (Cambridge: Cambridge University Press, 1909; repr., Hildesheim: Georg Olms, 1987).

Thiselton, Anthony C., *The First Epistle to the Corinthians: A Commentary on the Greek Text* (NIGTC; Grand Rapids: Eerdmans, 2000).

—'Semantics and New Testament Interpretation', in I. Howard Marshall (ed.) *New Testament Interpretation: Essays on Principles and Methods* (Exeter: Paternoster Press, 1977), pp. 75-104.

Thorley, John, 'Aktionsart in New Testament Greek: Infinitive and Imperative', *NovT* 31 (1989), pp. 290-315.

Turner, Max, 'Modern Linguistics and the New Testament', in Joel B. Green (ed.), *Hearing the New Testament: Strategies for Interpretation* (Grand Rapids: Eerdmans; Carlisle: Paternoster Press, 1995), pp. 146-74.

Turner, Nigel, *Grammatical Insights into the New Testament* (Edinburgh: T. & T. Clark, 1965).

Van der Auwera, Johan (ed.), *The Semantics of Determiners* (London: Croom Helm; Baltimore: University Park Press, 1980).

Vanséveren, Sylvie, *Prodige à voir: recherches comparatives sur l'origine casuelle de l'infinitif en grec ancien* (Bibliothèque des Cahiers de l'Institut de linguistique de Louvain; Louvain-la-Neuve: Peeters, 2000).

Vater, Heinz, 'Determination and Quantification', in Violetta Koseska-Toszewa and Danuta Rytel-Kuc (eds.), *Semantyka a konfrontacja językowa* (Warsaw: Slawistyczny Osrodek Wydawniczy, 1996), pp. 117-30.

—*Toward a Generative Dependency Grammar* (Trier: Linguistic Agency University at Trier, 1973).

—'Zur Abrenzung der Determinantien und Quantoren', in *idem* (ed.), *Zur Syntax der Determinantien*, p. 30.

Vater, Heinz (ed.), *Zur Syntax der Determinantien* (Studien zur deutschen Grammatik, 31; Tübingen: Gunter Narr Verlag, 1986).

Vaughan, Curtis, and Virtus E. Gideon, *A Greek Grammar of the New Testament: A Workbook Approach to Intermediate Grammar* (Nashville: Broadman, 1979).

Völker, F., *Syntax der griechischen Papyri: Der Artikel* (Münster: Druck der westfälischen Vereinsdruckerei, 1903).

Votaw, Clyde W., *The Use of the Infinitive in Biblical Greek* (Chicago: Clyde Votaw, 1896).

Wagner, Richard, *Der Gebrauch des imperativischen Infinitivs im Griechischen* (Wissenschaftliche Beilage zum Programm des grossherzoglichen Gymnasium Fridericianum zu Schwerin I. M. für des Schuljahr 1890/91; Leipzig: Hesse & Becker, 1891). Text-fiche.

Wallace, Daniel B., *Greek Grammar beyond the Basics: An Exegetical Syntax of the New Testament* (Grand Rapids: Zondervan, 1996).

Waltke, Bruce K., and M. O'Connor, *An Introduction to Biblical Hebrew Syntax* (Winona Lake, IN: Eisenbrauns, 1990).

Wanamaker, Charles A., *The Epistles to the Thessalonians: A Commentary on the Greek Text* (NIGTC; Grand Rapids: Eerdmans, 1990).

—'Philippians 2.6-11: Son of God or Adamic Christology?', *NTS* 33 (1987), pp. 179-93.

Winer, G.B., *A Treatise of the Grammar of New Testament Greek, Regarded as a Sure Basis for New Testament Exegesis* (trans. W.F. Moulton; Edinburgh: T. & T. Clark, 3rd edn, 9th Eng. edn, 1882).

Winstead, John H., 'The Greek Infinitive in Luke's Gospel' (PhD dissertation, The Southern Baptist Theological Seminary, 1930).

Wong, Simon S.M., *A Classification of Semantic Case-Relations in the Pauline Epistles* (SBG, 9; New York: Peter Lang, 1997).

—'What Case is This Case? An Application of Semantic Case in Biblical Exegesis', *Jian Dao* 1 (1994), pp. 49-73.

Wright, N.T., 'Adam in Pauline Christology', *SBLSP* 22 (1983), pp. 359-89.

—'ἁρπαγμός and the Meaning of Philippians 2.5-11', *JTS* ns 37 (1986), pp. 321-52.

—*The Climax of the Covenant: Christ and the Law in Pauline Theology* (Edinburgh: T. & T. Clark, 1991; Minneapolis: Fortress Press, 1992).

—*The Resurrection of the Son of God* (Christian Origins and the Question of God, 3; London: SPCK, 2003).

Young, Richard A., *Intermediate New Testament Greek: A Linguistic and Exegetical Approach* (Nashville: Broadman & Holman, 1994).

INDEXES

INDEX OF REFERENCES

Old Testament

Jeremiah (cont.)			Micah			Ecclesiasticus	
2.19	113		1.12	125		1.5	119, 123
4.22	113, 115		6.8	115		1.18	73
13.25	115					2.9	125
14.11	125		*1 Esdras*			7.13	125
15.11	125		1.54	117, 119-		9.13	115
21.10	125			21		11.12	125
24.5	125		2.23	114		11.22	73
24.6	125		4.51	117		13.25	125
39.39	125		6.6	117, 119,		38.27	119, 124,
46.16	125			120			126
47.5	115		6.27	117		39.27	125
			8.68	118		46.10	113
Ezekiel						46.12	73
13.3	71		*2 Esdras*			49.10	73
13.22	71		2.24	119		50.10	73
17.10	118		8.22	125			
17.24	71, 73		12.18	125		*1 Maccabees*	
18.23	113		15.19	125		3.58	115
21.11	115		22.24	124, 126		4.46	117
23.40	118					5.39	115
29.9	88		*Tobit*			9.45	115
33.11	113		2.10	117		10.19	115
34.7-9	88		6.16	118		10.30	118
36.3	88		8.1	113		10.73	115
			11.1	119, 120		11.11	118
Daniel			12.6	113		12.25	115
2.13	118					12.40	115
3.15	118		*Judith*			13.37	115
3.50	71		3.2	58		16.9	78, 119,
			3.3	58			123
Hosea			4.15	119, 124,			
8.9	73			125		*2 Maccabees*	
			12.16	115		1.14	118
Amos			12.18	113		2.28	113
3.3	71					2.32	113
3.4	71		*Wisdom of Solomon*			3.31	113
3.5	117		4.4	73		3.33	113
8.11	115		6.18-19	123		3.35	113
9.4	125		6.19	119		7.14	134
			8.19	65		12.16	58
Jonah			11.21	113		12.44	134
4.3	113		12.18	113			
4.8	118		15.3	113			

New Testament

Matthew (cont.)		26.17	41	2.2	24, 73
19.24	150	26.18	41	2.9	56
19.28	41	26.19	41	2.12	24, 73
20.8	89	26.25	41	2.15	150
20.15	150	25.27	150	2.23	150
20.19	24, 98, 99,	26.2	148	2.25	41
	148	26.12	148	2.26	41, 78,
20.23	24, 55, 56,	26.32	15, 24, 82,		150
	146, 153		98, 148	3.4	150
20.29	41	26.34	24	3.10	24, 73
20.30	41	26.35	150	3.17	41
20.31	41	26.36	41, 89	3.20	24, 73
21.1	41	26.44	34	3.22	41
21.5	41	26.49	41	4.1	24, 73
21.9	41	26.54	150	4.4	24, 94,
21.11	41, 78	26.69	39, 41		148
21.15	41	26.75	24	4.5	24, 98,
21.32	24, 61, 64,	27.1	24, 73		105, 148
	146, 154	27.3	41	4.6	24, 98,
22.17	150	27.6	150		105, 148
22.32	41	27.9	41	4.32	24, 73
22.36	89	27.12	24, 94,	4.37	24, 73
22.39	135		148	5.4	15, 24, 82,
22.42	41	27.14	24, 73		98, 105,
22.43	41	27.17	41		148
22.45	41	27.19	41	5.41	41
23.5	24, 98,	27.22	41	6.14	41
	107, 148	27.31	24, 98, 99,	6.18	150
23.7	41		148	6.24	41
23.8	41			6.45	41
23.16	41	27.33	41	6.48	24, 94, 96,
23.23	150	27.42	41		148
23.24	41	27.46	41	7.11	41
23.35	39, 41	27.56	41	7.23	35
23.37	41	27.57	41	8.22	41
24.6	150	27.59	41	7.27	150
24.12	24, 98,	27.61	41	8.31	81, 150
	105, 148	28.1	41	8.36	150
24.15	41, 78	28.5	41	9.5	41, 150
24.24	24, 73			9.9	133
24.37	41	*Mark*		9.10	12, 24, 55,
24.38	41, 86	1.2	85		56, 133,
24.45	24, 61, 64,	1.4	41		134, 146,
	146, 154	1.9	41, 78		153
26.2	24, 41, 98	1.14	24, 82, 98,	9.11	150
26.12	24, 35, 98,		148	9.26	24, 73
	107	1.27	24, 73	9.43	150
		1.45	24, 73		

Luke (cont.)					
3.28	41	8.5	24, 61, 64, 94, 95, 146, 148, 154	11.15	41, 42
3.29	41			11.18	41, 42
3.30	41			11.19	41, 42
3.31	41	8.6	24, 98, 105, 148	11.27	24, 94, 148
3.32	41			11.37	24, 94, 95, 148
3.33	41	8.10	150		
3.34	41	8.38	72	11.38	86
3.35	41	8.40	24, 94, 96, 148	11.42	150
3.36	41			11.51	41
3.37	41	8.42	24, 94, 148	12.1	24, 73
3.38	41			12.5	24, 98, 148
4.10	24, 61, 146, 154	9.7	24, 98, 105, 148	12.12	150
4.16	41, 80	9.10	41	12.15	24, 94, 96, 148
4.22	41	9.18	24, 94, 148		
4.25	41, 42			12.23	68
4.27	41, 42	9.22	150	12.42	24, 61, 64, 146, 154
4.29	24, 73	9.29	24, 94, 148		
4.42	24, 61, 64, 66, 146, 154	9.33	24, 94, 148, 150	13.3	146
		9.34	24, 94-96, 148	13.4	41, 42
				13.14	150
4.43	150	9.36	24, 94, 148	13.16	41, 150
5.1	24, 94, 148	9.38	72	13.28	41
		9.51	24, 61, 64, 94, 146, 148, 154	13.33	150
5.7	24, 61, 64, 73, 146, 154			13.34	41
				14.1	24, 94, 95, 148
5.12	24, 94, 148	9.52	24, 85	14.3	150
		10.1	85	15.17	70
5.17	24, 98, 100, 148	10.12	34	15.22	38, 39
5.23	56	10.13	41	15.32	150
6.1	150	10.19	24, 61, 67, 68, 146, 154	16.5	137
6.3	41			16.7	137
6.4	150			16.10	106
6.6	150			16.17	150
6.9	150	10.30	41	16.22	41, 150
6.12	150	10.35	24, 94	16.23	41
6.15	41	10.38	24, 94, 148	16.24	41
6.48	24, 98, 105, 148	10.39	41	16.25	41
		10.42	41	16.29	41
7.9	41, 42			16.30	41
7.11	41	11.1	24, 94, 148	17.1	24, 61-63, 68, 132, 146, 154
7.27	85				
7.41	137	11.8	24, 98, 105, 148	17.11	24, 94, 148
8.2	41				

John (cont.)		18.31	150	4.18	24, 71, 72
8.53	41, 68	18.39	41, 42	4.19	151
8.56	41	19.13	41	4.25	41
8.57	41	19.14	41	4.27	41
8.58	24, 41	19.17	41	4.30	24, 94, 96,
9.2	41	19.38	41		148
9.4	89, 150	20.9	150	4.36	41
9.7	41	20.16	41	5.15	24, 73
9.11	41	20.18	41	5.21	41
9.24	34, 35	21.2	41	5.23	85
10.8	85, 86			5.29	151
10.16	150	*Acts*		5.31	24, 41, 42,
11.2	41	1.3	24, 98,		61, 64,
11.8	41		148		146, 154
11.16	41	1.6	41, 42	5.34	41
11.19	41	1.14	41, 42	5.36	86
11.20	41	1.16	41, 151	5.37	39, 41
11.28	41	1.19	24, 41, 73	6.2	151
11.31	41	1.22	151	7.2	24, 41, 42
11.32	41	1.23	41	7.4	24, 41, 42,
11.45	41	2.1	24, 94,		86, 98,
11.54	41		148		148
11.55	41, 86	2.16	41	7.8	41
12.1	41, 86	2.20	24, 39, 40	7.9	41
12.3	41	2.25	41	7.10	41
12.13	41	2.29	41, 151	7.11	41
12.15	41	2.34	41	7.12	41
12.21	41, 78	2.36	41	7.13	41, 42
12.34	150	3.2	24, 61, 64,	7.14	41
13.1	41, 86		146, 154	7.15	41
13.19	24, 84, 86,	3.12	24, 61, 64,	7.16	41, 42
	87, 148		146, 154	7.17	41, 42
13.34	135	3.13	41, 57	7.18	41
14.13	85	3.14	72, 135	7.19	24, 61, 64,
14.27	39	3.19	24, 98, 99,		98, 146,
14.29	24		148		148, 154
15.12	135	3.21	151	7.21	41
15.17	135	3.24	41	7.23	41, 151
17.5	24, 84, 86,	3.25	41	7.29	41
	87, 148	3.26	24, 94, 96,	7.30	41
17.24	86		148	7.32	41
18.1	41	4.2	24, 98,	7.35	41
18.2	41		105, 148	7.37	41
18.5	41	4.5	151	7.38	41
18.14	41, 150	4.10	41	7.40	41, 42
18.28	41	4.12	151	7.42	41

INDEX OF AUTHORS

www.ingramcontent.com/pod-product-compliance
Lightning Source LLC
Chambersburg PA
CBHW070911100426
42814CB00003B/130